BRIAN D'ARCY

It has to be said ...

BRIAN D'ARCY

It has to be said

Copies available to order from: sliabhbanproductions1@gmail.com

ISBN: 978-1-9993549-1-6

A CIP record of this book is available from the British Library.

If the publishers have inadvertently overlooked any copyright holders,
we would be happy to make appropriate arrangements.

Photography:
Special thanks to Ray McManus and his team at Sportsfile,
Lunny Imaging, Ronan McGrade, Tommy McGowan, The Impartial Reporter,
Fermanagh Herald, Sunday World and
the many private photographers too numerous to mention.

Layout and design: Denise Campbell
Printing - binding: PB Print Solutions

This book is printed and bound in Ireland using
environmentally certified and sustainable pulp from managed forests

Dedication

For Hugh D'Arcy,
Ellen Corrigan and their son,
my brother, Gabriel D'Arcy.

May they be at Heaven's door to welcome me home.

Acknowledgements

It's risky to mention names, but I don't know of any other sincere way to say thanks to so many people who helped me throughout my life, but particularly in the preparation of this book. A special thanks to Brian and Trish Carthy. They encouraged me to write another volume reflecting on the latter years of my life.

Now, through their Sliabh Bán publishing company, the day has arrived. Thanks to all at Sliabh Bán for all your hard work.

I am grateful to those who helped me put the text together especially editor Fiona Biggs, who ensured the narrative unfolded in a meaningful and hopefully interesting way.

My thanks to the Sunday World who have retained me as a columnist for over 43 years and who supported this book at every stage. BBC Radio Ulster and BBC Radio2 in London have a special place in my life too.

I want to thank Declan Coyle for gently pushing me unto The Green Platform which helped me overcome my reticence. He, along with a cohort of fellow pilgrims who worshipped at The Graan, finally convinced me to write down what had to be said. It took a skillful combination of fear and guilt. He assured me that if I began writing, the book would write itself. He had a point.

Declan read and re-read the book during its different stages and as a theologian and Pastoral Counsellor guided me through some minefields – personal and theological.

Michael Dundon read the final proofs, generously sharing his experience and offering much appreciated advice.

Denise Campbell did a superb job with her design and layout of the book as well as many helpful suggestions about the contents. Of course Ray McManus, once again, almost succeeded in making a silk purse out of a sow's ear by means of his unequalled expertise in photography.

I am grateful to you for buying 'It Has to Be Said' because, as is the case with all of my books, every cent of my profits will be donated to help the poor at home and overseas. Homeless charities in Ireland will benefit most from this book. I will continue to donate the profits to where it is most needed and best used.

Sincere thanks to my Passionist Brothers for their understanding since I first entered on the 1st September 1962.

I know you will forgive me if my last word of thanks is to my family, particularly my late brother Gaby, his wife Maura, my sisters, Marie and her late husband Pat Brogan, Joan and husband Kevin Lunney, my nephews, nieces, grandnephews and grandnieces. Without their love, understanding and loyalty I would be a lost soul.

I have to express my deep gratitude to the multitude of people who have loved me and befriended me throughout my 50 years of priesthood. Only God knows the true number of that loyal community and when God knows, nothing else matters.

FOREWORD

For over a decade, different publishers have encouraged me to write another volume of my memoir. The first volume 'a Different journey' was successful, but has been out of print for ten years. Events in my life have taken many unusual turns in recent years and Irish society bears no resemblance to the Ireland of a decade ago.

The many different lives I've lived – priesthood, journalism, broadcasting, political mediation and entertainment - have given me a privileged place. My unique position means that some of the events I've lived through need to be amplified upon; an unreflected life is a wasted life.

I am fifty years an ordained priest this year; I am not getting any younger; most of my closest friends are dead so I can't have many years left on this earth. I cannot take life for granted; nor can I assume my memory will remain intact; now is the time to do whatever it is I have to do.

For that reason, memoir has more appeal than autobiography for me. I wanted the stories, and how they influenced me, to be the central core of the book. My story is not more important than yours; indeed my hope is that these reflections might encourage you to make the most of your experiences too.

Thomas Merton, the Trappist monk, fuelled the spiritual revolution of the 1960s, and is one of my heroes in life. He put words on my dilemma. "If you want to identify me, ask not where I live, or what I like to eat, or how I comb my hair. But ask me what I think I am living for; ask me what is keeping me from living fully for the thing I want to live for?" (Thomas Merton 1975).

And so here it is. The book is entitled 'It Has to Be Said' because there are too many vital issues not discussed in our society and in our churches. Having survived censure from on high and endured imposed secrecy for a lifetime, I am convinced that if it has to be said, now is the time to say it.

I've tried to present you with a readable book and one which is accessible to the loyal readers of the Sunday World as well as to the wonderful people who encouraged me to stay within the Church and in the priesthood throughout our awful recent history.

I want this book to encourage those interested in our Church to question constructively and purposefully from within. I mourn for the good people who needlessly walk away from the spiritual support which is rightly theirs through Baptism, when all they need to leave behind is a dysfunctional clericalism.

What I don't want is an angry book. And that is why I submitted the text to an independent editor first and then to a theologian/Pastoral Counsellor, as well as critical readings from numerous people whose opinions are trustworthy.

I have written about key events rather than plodding chronologically through the story of a life from the cradle to pretty close to the grave; I have written honestly about the struggle I have to stay a priest in a Church in crisis; I have written about the labored little journeys I have made, be they right or wrong, fully realising that because of my unique position, mine has been 'a Different journey'.

Each of us has to make our own choices in life. My journey cannot be yours. But perhaps what I share with you might encourage you to reflect on your own journey and to realise that no matter where it has taken you, your journey has been good. It's good because God welcomes every sincere traveller no matter how many diversions or side roads we've gone down. God understands and accepts our sincerity especially when Church and society reject us. That, 'It Has to Be Said,' is where true hope resides.

I have no doubt there will be different reactions to what I have written. I needed to truthfully communicate the lifelong personal effects of sexual abuse. I owed it to victims of abuse everywhere, especially those without a voice.

I also had to balance telling the truth with being unnecessarily graphic about the intimate details of abuse. I hope you will not be unduly disturbed by what I have put on paper. But if you are, be sensible enough to seek help and support. It is important to take care of yourself.

Lastly, I'm aware that some people could be hurt by what I've written. That was not my intention. Trust me when I tell you that my main purpose in revising the text repeatedly was to edit out what might be hurtful. Life is too short to waste on spitefulness.

As I sit in the departure lounge of life now I torture myself by seriously doubting if anything I did was worth writing about. That's up to you to decide now.

I keep going for many reasons some of which were summed up by Nelson Mandela when he said that what counts in life is not the mere fact that we have lived. It is what difference we have made to the lives of others that will determine the significance of our achievements.

INTRODUCTION

'Never pray in a room without windows' is a profound insight from the Talmud. We do not pray in a vacuum and we do not pray in order to escape the world. We pray best when we are grounded in the real world; we pray to become co-creators of the future; a future founded on hope; a future that is authentic.

John F. Kennedy said, 'We should not let our fears hold us back from pursuing our hopes.' I believe hope overcomes fear. I've given up on many dreams and visions in my life, but I've never given up on hope. Maya Angelou believed that hope and fear cannot occupy the same space at the same time. Whether we know it or not, we always invite one of them to stay; that choice determines how we live.

I've spent so many years thinking about whether I should write this book, that fear almost paralysed my thoughts and my priesthood. I realised I had to write it now or forget about it forever. I don't know if I've made the correct decision, but I've done it for the right reason. It's my way of holding on to hope; it's my way of crawling out from under the influence of a debilitating fear.

I wrote because I have a duty to my friends and to my very supportive family to record the facts about parts of my life that affected them. The long-running difficulties with the CDF in the Vatican and the ongoing effects of living with abuse were foremost in my mind.

I was tempted to surrender to cynicism which would be a wilful waste of the good life I've been gifted with.

In his best-selling book 'God's Politics', Jim Wallis writes that one of the obstacles to a living faith is the fundamental choice between cynicism and hope.

'First, let's be fair to the cynics,' he states. 'Cynicism is the place of retreat for the smart, critical, dissenting, and formerly idealistic people who are now trying to protect themselves. They are not naive ... They know what is going on, they might even have tried for a time to change it. But they didn't succeed ... So they retreated to cynicism as a refuge from commitment...'

In his view, cynicism is a form of protection against vulnerability; ultimately it protects one from having to commit positively to an unknown future. 'Cynicism ... protects you from seeming to be foolish to believe that things could and will change.'

I suspect that's the kind of cynicism that forces many of us in the Church to give up and walk away. That for me would be the ultimate denial of my faith in a caring God. I have a duty to speak out, to name what is harmful and to be prophetic enough to believe in a different, better future, and that is no more than taking God at His Word.

Wallis wrote that the people who view the world most realistically are the cynics and the saints. The only difference between them is the possibility of hope.

Hope is a choice not a feeling. Hope grows out of our most basic convictions about our possibilities and what the future holds. For me hope has to be rooted in faith. I have to choose hope, not as a naive wish, but as a decision, with my eyes wide open to the reality which often works against hope.

I realised eventually that if I am to prevent my own life from falling apart in anger and disappointment, I must personally admit that the world I grew up in is gone forever; that the moral values of society are not the same as the moral choices required by my faith; that cynicism will destroy me, and that hope tells me all will be well no matter how things turn out, as long as I live by my convictions.

Pope Francis inspires me when he hangs on to hope despite the back-stabbing that goes on in the Curia. However, his most serious challenge to believers and non-believers alike is his unambiguous call to protect the earth. We show we are people of hope by the way we cherish creation. The major sin of this era is to destroy the earth by wasteful living.

Recent elections across Europe were dominated by the Green agenda and that too filled me with hope. The commitment of young people everywhere to respecting the earth will, I believe, ensure Mother Nature survives.

Pope Francis gets it. He took the name Francis in honour of the patron saint of ecology, Francis of Assisi.

This generation finds it difficult to appreciate our traditional morality. Churches preach moral Do's and Don'ts to their youth in a language the young neither know nor understand.

For parents, morality begins and ends with sexual sins. This generation sees their parents driving earth-destroying diesel SUVs which they don't need, and they recognise that such irresponsibility is a much greater sin. It is not true to say youth have no morals; they just have different moral values. And again Pope Francis gets it.

'A Christian who doesn't safeguard creation is a Christian who ignores God's work – a work that was born out of God's love for us,' Francis told the people of the Philippines.

The Pope's description of the world today as 'an immense pile of filth' is both memorable and accurate. The central message in Laudato Si' is that we have received this earth as an inheritance from past generations and, more importantly, we have it on loan from future generations to whom we will have to return it. We have to treasure the earth 'as if it were a caress from God'.

Francis continually highlights some of the issues that plague our common home on this earth, namely pollution, which is entirely due to human bad behaviour, climate change, the unfair distribution of the world's essential resources, especially water, and human greed.

He hasn't won many friends in capitalist countries. He admits that although nature invites us to care for the world, we fail to do so because of selfishness and an empty fascination with material consumption. Care of our world is not just the moral duty of Christians but is part and parcel of the vocation given by God to all people.

Francis encourages each of us to examine how we live and to change what is destructive. A change of heart, a conversion actually, is demanded. To destroy creation, or even to risk not protecting, it is a serious sin.

Laudato Si' will be the highlight of this pope's reign. It is this hope-filled view of the world that will become the agenda for the reform of the Church.

That is why Pope Francis and the issues he raises give me so much hope. It's a different approach to religion and one that resonates with people today. Nothing will be achieved by imposing the Church of the past. We don't have a crisis of religion; we have a crisis of faith.

The famous basketball coach John Wooden had a remarkable trust in human nature. He outlined a different way of living to his young college stars. His coaching method was holistic in that he wanted to develop fulfilled human beings, not just successful athletes.

For Wooden 'Success is never final; failure is never fatal; it's courage that counts.' His oft-quoted remark that 'things turn out best for those who make the best of the way things turn out' has become a way of life for me. As a member of an institution which protected its reputation above all else, it takes courage, honesty and conviction to state difficult truths in season and out of season. But 'It has to be said'.

I was tempted to remain silent and to leave well enough alone; I'd said and written enough. I tried to convince myself to remain silent. It was a genuine option. I've had seventeen books published and I've written 1200 words fifty-two weeks of the year for forty-four years in The Sunday World. The Vatican said I was too negative about the Church. Colleagues told me to be more 'prudent' and less explicit – like most of them. There were good reasons for me to leave well enough alone.

However, it became clear to me that I was trapped inside my own small ego; I lived in perpetual fear, which deprived me of hope and joy. I wasn't true to myself and I was deceiving those who want me to go on speaking truth to power. Ultimately I was failing as a priest and as a human being. Abraham Lincoln told us that 'To sin by silence when they should protest makes cowards of men.' What's left unsaid, says it all.

I don't have all the answers. That's okay. Richard Rohr says that 'as long as you think you have to fix everything, control everything, explain everything, and understand everything, you will never be a peaceful person.'

But then how could I live with myself if I kept silence for the sake of a trouble-free life? That's not just cowardice, it's a denial of what a vocation is, and is unforgiveable. It's a rule of life for me that I do not let what I cannot do interfere with what I can do. I'm not a vital part of any major plan in the Church or in society. But it's my duty to distinguish between right and wrong in my own life and be a sign of hope for others endeavouring to do the same.

Wisdom is not so much about knowing what to do in the long term as knowing what to do next. I reflected long and hard about what to tackle in this book because I discovered from Thomas Merton's writings that God is always present to those who are present to themselves. I had to be sure I was at peace with myself. I have no right to pollute the atmosphere with anger and bitterness.

Thinking isn't enough, though. Reflection is not just a head activity. I had to push myself to move out of the 'head' and into action. Richard Rohr believes "We do not think ourselves into new ways of living; we live ourselves into new ways of thinking".

After reflecting for years, I knew I had to write my truth and accept the consequences. I wrote at every opportunity – on plane journeys, at airports, in the car parked at the side of the road, and at my desk late into the night. Mostly I wrote from ten at night until two in the morning. I knew the areas that would tear at my guts so I began with abuse. Perhaps it wasn't the right thing to do, as I discovered the more I wrote about personal abuse, the more upset I became. I deleted pages and pages only to rewrite them immediately.

I learned once again that when a child is sexually abused a whole life is destroyed. Despite having an otherwise happy childhood, there are many days now when I can't recall a worthwhile happy memory from childhood. To cope with the present I can't risk reliving the past. It's a constant struggle to live a balanced life.

Then it dawned on me that I was the one in need of hope. I also realised it is a very good place to start. So I did. The more difficult it was to write, the more I was determined to carry on relentlessly. I reminded myself never to put the key to my happiness in someone else's pocket. It was up to me to take control of my own story. I had to write it even if it destroyed my inner peace. There are stories that have to be acknowledged and feelings that have to be expressed to ensure that people get a proper insight into the evils of sexual abuse and its lifelong devastating effects.

I wrote enough for three books; I dumped at least half of it and then my publisher hired Fiona Biggs to edit what I had edited. I checked with trusted friends at every stage. I insisted that a qualified, knowledgeable, and wise counsellor read the final draft. It is important for me to know that I don't transmit unhealthy attitudes and practices. I have a duty to process my doubts and fears before publishing them because what I don't transform I transmit.

What finally convinced me to write this book was my transfer out of The Graan monastery in Enniskillen. During my time there, the Novena of Hope was a huge community event for the people of Fermanagh and surrounding counties. Thousands came to our rural church for a nine-day festival of prayer, music, fun and spirituality. It developed into a truly joyous event which lifted everyone at the end of winter. I insisted that most of the speakers had to be lay people, usually well-known and with a story of hope to share.

It was a genuine cross-community celebration and people of all religions and none appreciated that. Everyone agreed it was the kind of gathering that was needed to restore trust in religion and which they didn't often experience in their own churches. The congregation knew they were welcome exactly as they were and in a non-judgemental way. We had prayer, fellowship and genuine togetherness, which gave us a framework to express our joy as well as our doubts.

I was blessed that my friends in entertainment volunteered to perform their music on different nights. Hugo Duncan, Nathan Carter, Lisa McHugh, Philomena Begley, the late Gene Stuart, Michael English, Dominic and Barry Kirwan, Chris Logue, Ally and Marion, Paul Kellly, Matt McGranaghan, Eamonn McCann, Boxcar Brian, John Farry and dozens more too numerous to mention regularly reinforced our unity through music. The different talents of many generous people helped to build up the community.

Speakers from all over Ireland and England, many of whom had never spoken in Church before, shared their stories with our overflowing congregations.

The PSNI helped us with traffic; every night they turned away late arrivals. We had to be careful not to encourage dangerous overcrowding.

In my time we welcomed more than 150 speakers, men and women, from all religions and none, lay and religious. Every single one was unique because it was their own story of hope they shared. Hope came from the roots up; what appeared to be ordinary stories took on a sacred meaning; speakers were uplifted as they uplifted us.

The novena truly changed people's view of themselves; that's what hope in action does.

Off the top of my head I recall wonderful talks from Gay Byrne, Joe Duffy, Mary Kennedy, Henry Shefflin, Brian Cody, Johnny Murtagh, Jimmy Magee, Dame Nuala O'Loane, Brendan Graham (of 'You Raise Me Up' fame,) Joe Brolly, Mickey and Mark Harte as well as John McAreavey, Declan Coyle, Peter Quinn, Frances Black, Niall Quinn, Sean Boylan, Denis Bradley, Alan Mc Bride (shortly after his wife Sharon was murdered in the Shankill bombing) Dame May Blood, Brian Crowley MEP and 130 others who were without exception inspirational.

Those novenas were God's gift to us. I created a platform; God did the rest and the faithful encouraged me to keep going. They reminded me each year of what a powerful influence for good the Church can be when the Church truly is the People of God.

When I left Enniskillen, a group of dedicated lay people decided to take up the idea and to organise their own weekend of hope each New Year. They arrange lectures and discussions similar to the themes we had during the novenas. That was proof to me that when the laity are empowered the Holy Spirit takes over. The seed, once planted, grows where it will.

The Novenas of Hope opened my eyes to what happens when someone overcomes their hesitancy and puts God on the agenda. I had to share my thoughts, my doubts, my vision.
Those same people convinced me to gather my experiences into a book as a source of hope for struggling believers everywhere. I had no choice, they said, but to start writing to mark fifty years of priesthood.

This second volume of my memoir has imported a small number of chapters from the first one, 'a Different journey'. The first reason for this is that 'a Different journey' has been out of print for a decade or more.

The second reason is that the details of where I was born, my early education and my first years in religious life needed to be included again to provide a proper perspective. Obviously such details remain the same so it would be pointless to rewrite them.

However, the vast bulk of 'It Has to Be Said' is new. I hope you will find it interesting, informative, a little challenging and, most of all, entertaining.
I want us to face the future with some hope, and I want to give you courage to examine your relationship with religion and the Catholic Church in a mature adult way.

My prayer is that everyone recognises their own unique journey, and that by sharing some of my life with you, you will have the courage to be proud of your own life and your achievements.

I would like to set you on a path where you will make your own positive choices as a mature adult should. You will see how long it has taken me to be honest about my life and to live with some integrity.

I learned eventually to trust my own judgements. It is bringing me great inner peace. I encourage you to trust your own judgements, to be grateful for your faith, and to be generous in your gratitude for God's outstretched hand.

'It is always better to travel hopefully than to arrive.'

CHAPTER 1

THE TOWN OF THE FLAGSTONES

My family is an ordinary working-class family. We lived in the village of Bellanaleck (which means 'the town of the flagstones'), about five miles from Enniskillen in County Fermanagh. I lived there with my father, Hugh, my mother, Ellie, my sisters, Marie and Joan, and my only brother, Gaby, in a nice cosy little house. Our house was beside the road and everybody who walked up and down dropped in. Old people collecting their pensions would call to my mother on the way home, get a cup of tea, have a rest and head off home restored. That's my abiding image of my mother - always at home, always doing her best to help and to encourage. Everybody who visited trusted her. My mother chatted to them all and she was a kind of a confessor for them. She was a huge influence on me; my way of being a priest comes from her.

Because my father was football mad, our house at night had callers who talked football, local and national. It was a dull night if nobody came in. That's where I learned the art of storytelling and the art of listening. I can still remember stories and characters from that time. Although I didn't know it at the time, it was where I discovered how to recognise and tell a good story. These people were experts who could hold you enthralled from beginning to end. They had rehearsed it and they made sure you never forgot it. They were superb teachers, although most of them could barely read or write. Maybe that's why Bellanaleck has produced eight well-known writers and broadcasters – Cormac, Mickey and Seán MacConnell, Martin O'Brien, Marion and Jennifer Cathcart, Derek Thornton and me.

Even in those days, in the mid-1950s, literacy could not be taken for granted. My father could read and write, and he used his skills to fill in forms for his neighbours. After the Second World War, the government handed out free shoes to some children and bus passes to others, and meal vouchers too. You could get free supplies of orange juice and cod liver oil, to build up strong, healthy bodies. The orange juice was lovely but the cod liver oil was a sickening dose. My father filled in the application forms for half the country for these. There were always visitors and they were always welcome. To this day, I love to see people calling for the tea and a chat; it seems a truly Eucharistic thing to do.

My mother baked bread. She'd roll it out on the table and bake it on the open fire, in an oven hanging from the crook. She'd put a row of coals on the top of it so it baked from the top and the bottom. I can still smell that bread baking. We called it fadge bread and nothing ever tasted as good. While it was still hot we spread butter on it, watched it melt, and ate it as quickly as we could. We caught the chicken out in the field, wrung its neck, plucked it, cleaned it out and cooked it in the pot, in the same way, over the big open fire with the turf flaming round it.

We always had a big, roaring turf fire. We were never short, but we never had anything extra, either. It was a struggle to make sure there would be enough on Thursday to buy what we needed, so that, when the wages came on Friday, we'd be able to start again. Thrift was encouraged, nothing was wasted. But we were no different from any other family in the parish. Working-class people lived close to the breadline.

Being young and Catholic meant I was an altar server and played Gaelic football morning, noon and night. If there was a wake, or if somebody was sick, my mother made bread and brought it to them. It was the same for both Protestants and Catholics. Being a good neighbour wasn't sectarian. There was, however, a strict code when it came to religious practise. I remember going to the door of the Protestant church but never entering. It was the same when Protestants came to Catholic funerals. Even then I knew it was stupid.

Hard work was part of the example handed down by my father. He was up at seven, got on his bicycle and started work at eight in Enniskillen Railway Station. He finished at five, was home about a quarter to six, ate spuds and bacon and cabbage and then started another day's work, setting potatoes and getting as much as he could from five acres of bad land. The day finished at ten when he'd come inside and get more tea. That's when the visitors came in. It was that kind of house, that kind of life.

In my young days we got one day's holiday a year. We went to Bundoran. My father worked on the railway and we thought it was a wonderful privilege to get a free pass on a train from Enniskillen to Bundoran. We really thought we were special, a step above the ordinary. I used to get so excited about our day out that my family couldn't tell me beforehand. On two occasions, I got, literally, sick with excitement, and the whole family had to stay home. They learned not to tell me about the day out until they were ready to travel.

Suddenly, I'd get a shaking in the bed very early in the morning. 'Come on, you have to get up, we're going to Bundoran today.' We'd get the eight o'clock bus to Enniskillen and catch the nine o'clock train to Bundoran. Our meal was the sandwiches we brought. There was no such thing as going to cafés, and if you did, you brought your sandwiches with you and bought the tea.

I was nearly drowned in Bundoran on one of those days out. I went walking along the sea pool and slipped in. Nobody saw me, and when eventually they did, none of them could swim. Someone pulled me out and I spent the day wet and shivering. It scared my mother. Another day, my father had me on a boat in Lough Erne and I fell out of the boat. He pulled me back by the hair of the head and, after that, my mother would never let me go near water or swim again. She said, 'The third time you'll die.' And it meant that I was thirty-five years of age before I had the courage to go to a swimming pool. I'm still not comfortable in the water, though.

My father was an active officer in the local GAA club. He was a famous footballer who played for Fermanagh for nearly a decade. It's not for me to boast, but those who saw him play reckon he was as good a half-back as ever played for the county. He was a respected man and a capable man, even though he had to leave school early. His constant mantra was, whatever you do, get a better education than I did. The key at the time in the North was the Eleven-plus. I was going to a small, two-teacher school in rural Fermanagh with fewer than thirty pupils in it. In its entire history, nobody had ever passed the Eleven-plus. My father concluded that not every child in this area was stupid, so it had to be the system that was wrong.

I had an aunt in Omagh, my mother's sister, who had a boarding house there. Aunt Maggie came to visit us and obviously heard some cheeky backchat from me. I can still hear her describe me: 'That's an ould-fashioned brat there and if I had him I'd put manners on him.' That's how I attended the Christian Brothers' school in Omagh. I went down every Sunday evening with my little case. My father brought me five miles on the crossbar of the bike, as far as the train. I got on the train, at nine years of age, went thirty miles to Omagh, got off the train, walked about a mile to my aunt's house and helped with the dishes and got ready for school the next day. I hate Sunday nights to this day. Sunday nights are leaving nights for me.

My aunt was a nice woman who was good to me. She had boarders as well as her own family and the first thing I did when I got up every morning was to set the table for the boarders. She spent her day cooking for them. There was no molly-coddling, no room for emotion. You did the job you were expected to do and there were no excuses taken for not doing it. But Aunt Maggie was good to me and I would have got nowhere without her foresight and the dedication of her son Donal, who taught me.

In Omagh School they had a superb system of preparing for the Eleven-plus. Every Friday we did test papers under exam conditions. When the actual days of the Eleven-plus came round it was just routine. After two years in Omagh, even I was able to pass the exam. It meant I got a free grammar school education.

There is a kind of providence about growing up which, in an unknowing way, directs the rest of our lives. For me it began with being chosen to go to school in Omagh, the loneliness I endured during that time, the preparation for future life that it entailed; all this I can see now as God's providential care. Why was I the one that my aunt's eyes lit on that particular day? If my brother, Gaby, had been the one who answered her back, he might have been the one taken by her and he'd have made a better, safer priest than me. I'd say there's many a bishop who thinks my aunt made the wrong choice and it should have been left to God, not her. Yet we know it's God who makes the choices and it's not always the most obvious one he chooses.

I came back to Enniskillen and went to St Michael's College in 1957. I was the only one from our whole area in it. That's why there's a part of me that is always lost. When I went to Omagh, I was a country boy, not only moving to a town, but a town thirty miles away. I was struggling all the time, both in Omagh and in St Michael's in Enniskillen.

In St Michael's College, priests ran the school like a junior seminary. The Presentation Brothers founded St Michael's but moved out in 1957 when the priests took over. The reason the priests came was to encourage Fermanagh boys to become priests in Clogher Diocese.

As a teenager, I had no real notion of being a priest. I was a normal, reasonably good young fellow who did what I was told, served Mass and tried to live the way my parents taught me. I didn't consider I had a vocation because I didn't think I was good enough to be a priest. My family wasn't wealthy enough to pay for me. At that time, you had to be a boarder in a junior seminary for two years before they'd accept you in Maynooth.

I wasn't the most suitable one in our family to be a priest because I was always interested in music and sport. I always had a variety of interests. I was more like my father and more influenced by him. I was a footballer like him. At sixteen I had played in the county championships at all levels.

My interest in popular music goes back to my earliest days. In our wee house in Bellanaleck we always had a wireless. Television was totally unheard of in those days. It sounds as if I'm going back to 'old god's time', but it's actually only sixty years, a short enough period as history goes. The wireless was in the kitchen and had a grand shelf all to itself.

Before we got electricity, the wireless ran on what were called wet batteries. They were two glass containers that held some sort of acid. These wet batteries had a short lifespan and had to be brought to a supplier in Enniskillen, who recharged or refilled them and so kept us up to date with the news for another couple of weeks.

Wet batteries were used sparingly. The wireless was put on for the news each night. We all had to be as quiet as mice as my mother and father and whatever visitor happened to be passing our door all gathered as close to the wireless as they could.

Another big occasion was the broadcast of Gaelic games on a Sunday afternoon. If we weren't quiet we were put out to play. Usually five or six men came and parked their bicycles along the tightly clipped hedge on the side of the road. They then proceeded to kick every ball with Mícheál O'Hehir as he broadcast in his wonderfully exciting fashion from the mecca itself: Croke Park in Dublin. For me, O'Hehir has always been the voice of the GAA.

Later we got electricity into the house. There were few enough appliances that could run on electricity and that we could afford. There was a light in each room, which was a godsend; there was one electric fire with two bars which was used sparingly because it was too expensive, and a little two-ringed cooker which was more effective for heating water and boiling eggs early in the morning before the turf fire took off. And there was a wonderful Morphy-Richards radio. This meant the wet batteries were gone forever and we could listen to the radio night and day.

That was when I discovered Radio Luxembourg. It had a famous catch-phrase: '208 on the dial'. And that's when I began to discover the world of pop music, especially the great Elvis Presley. For me, back in the 1950s, Elvis on Radio Luxembourg was eternal happiness on earth.

From that moment I was hooked on music. The highlight of the week was the Top Twenty from eleven to twelve on a Sunday night. The problem was that I had to wait until twelve to find out what was number one. No self-respecting student could dare enter St Michael's College the next morning without having listened to the number one the night before. That was 'cool' back then. To get staying up until twelve o'clock on a Sunday night was always a fight. But secretly I think even my parents were interested in the pop charts, though they constantly criticised the 'jungle music' of Elvis, Cliff, Bill Haley and Billy Fury.

In St Michael's College it was the custom for priests to visit and give a really good talk about the work their congregation or order did. Then they'd give you a slip of paper asking if you were interested in their work. If you were interested they sent you material. I remember one priest who came and gave a great talk about his work in South America. It was an appealing and idealistic life. He was from the Legionaries of Christ. At the time I showed some interest so, one evening, about a month afterwards, this priest arrived at our house. He was probably Spanish and looked awfully clean with his white cuffs and gold cufflinks. He looked perfect.

My father and I were out in the field working when this strange priest came out to us. He stood at the edge of the field and beckoned my father to come to him; they talked secretly for ten minutes or more. He never spoke to me at all. I never knew until thirty years later what he said to my father. First, he asked how much my father earned, and when my father told him, he said, 'I don't think your family is rich enough for your son to join us. We're not interested.' A cousin in whom my father confided told me that long after my father died. My father never told me, but I discovered that he was deeply hurt by this insult. When he came back to me in the potato drill, all he said was, 'You won't be joining that crowd, anyway.'

The founder of The Legionaries of Christ, in the spring of 2006, was silenced by the Vatican for the alleged abuse of young boys, especially young students who entered his order.

Looking back, I understand now why my father didn't want me to be a priest. He always said we weren't rich enough. Early on he did his best to change my mind. It would be a very long time afterwards before I understood why.

My first meeting with a very quiet Passionist priest in a mystical church attached to The Graan in Enniskillen in 1960 was a different experience. It was a quiet Saturday evening and I had gone there to confession. The priest obviously took time to speak to his penitents. I didn't know who he was then, but I got to know him later. His name was Father Angelo. His family name was Boylan from County Monaghan and he had two nephews in the Passionist congregation.

Angelo was a quiet man and saintly in a detached sort of way. When he left the world he was quite happy not to rejoin it. At the end of confession he whispered through the wire mesh, 'Have you ever thought of becoming a priest?' I answered that I hadn't and that was really the truth. Actually, I hadn't thought about it seriously even at the time of The Legionaries of Christ; I was only vaguely interested then.

He continued to whisper through the grille. 'I think you should think about it. Could you come down to meet me tomorrow evening?' It sounded a bit rushed to me, and anyway I had a football match to play for Kinawley minors the next day. And I told him the truth – that I couldn't do it. But he did make an appointment for the following Saturday. I was really scared of it but felt I had to keep it.

I told him what my parents had said – namely, that I was too fond of music and football to be a priest. I subsequently learned that Angelo had no great love of football although he would have claimed a certain musical ability.

My mother didn't want me to be a priest either, though her opposition was for a different reason from my father's. Maybe she understood the loneliness of a priest's life. My father worked for the parish priest in his local area at one time, so maybe he knew what a priest's life was like too, and didn't want it for his son.

I mentioned my dilemma to a friend at school, Artie McCann, and he shocked me by admitting he had decided to join the Passionists. His uncle was a Passionist priest. We began our journey together then. The life appealed to me because I heard our neighbours talking about going to The Graan to get blessed or going to The Graan for confessions. The Graan always seemed to be a place that people thought highly of. It was a place where people weren't afraid of priests. Or, if you were in trouble, The Graan had a special place in people's lives. That image of priesthood attracted me.

My mother tried to persuade me not to go. She prayed every day and got the rest of the family to try to persuade me not to go because my interests were incompatible with what they thought a priest should be. She gave in on my last summer in school. I would have been fifteen, going on sixteen, and she said to me, 'If you come with me on a pilgrimage to Knock, we'll pray there. Then, after that, if you still want to go, I'll not stand in your way.'

The parish was running a bus to Knock. We said fifteen decades of the Rosary on the way, fifteen decades while we were there, another fifteen on the way home. I had as much praying that day as I ever needed. But it was a lovely place and I still go to Knock once or twice a year, just to top up my vocation, as it were. Because that's where it came from.

About two or three weeks later, my mother asked me, 'Do you still want to be a priest?' And I said, 'I think I have to give it a try.' That's when she agreed to let me go.

It seems providential that out of very ordinary circumstances and out of basic choices, a life journey begins. We have no idea where the little decisions we make today will eventually lead us.

The priests of the diocese didn't want me entering the Passionists because there was a hint of mistrusting religious life. I was told I was making a mistake by joining the Passionists. It would make more sense to be a diocesan priest. The president of St Michael's College, when I asked him for a reference, gave it to me but made his displeasure obvious. I didn't understand it at the time and still don't.

The parish priest, Father McIlroy, who lived two miles up the road beside the church in Arney, was very good to me. I'd been an altar boy and he knew me well. His advice was simple and reflective: 'It takes a good man to enter, Brian, but it takes a great man to leave if it's not made for him.' Sound advice.

The next thing was to buy a new black suit. I didn't want my family to be out too much money, so I worked. Peter McKevitt had a pub in Arney and he used to see me going to morning Mass. He'd probably heard I was thinking of going on to be a priest. One day he approached me: 'I wonder if you would paint our pub, Brian?' He worked it out that I would get two shillings an hour. And I worked it out that if I painted for ten hours I could make a pound a day. The suit cost £24 in Tully's. I got the money for it by working for Peter and also by helping out my cousins and getting the odd fiver here and there. So my family weren't out too much money when I joined. Passionists didn't ask for much money from their families. Once you made your profession, you were a Passionist after that and they took care of you.

On the night of 30 August 1962, I went to Bundoran to a dance as a kind of a last fling, myself and my brother and a few neighbours. I went to dances regularly before I entered and I still wanted to hang on to the music. It was a double attraction that night. The Melody Aces were the first band and Butch Moore and the Capitol Showband were the second, in the Astoria Ballroom in Bundoran.

There's a quaint story that gives you an indication of the times we lived in back then. I actually played football for a neighbouring club, Kinawley, at underage level, and they took me onto the senior panel as well. I played in the county senior championship semi-final in August when I came on as a sub, even though I was only seventeen years old. We won the match and got to the final. But I had entered the Passionist monastery at The Graan before the final took place and I never played in the county senior final. We didn't get letters, papers, visits from people or anything like that while we were in the novitiate. We simply entered a monastery and from day one you became a contemplative monk. One day I was a teenager running around Bellanaleck and the next I was a contemplative monk. I never knew who won the county final until Christmas morning, when we were allowed one letter from my family. That was when I first realised that Roslea, not Kinawley, had won the cup.

The day I entered was a really, really sad day. I spent the day crying and saying goodbye to people, places of interest and even the sad old donkey out in the field. The day before I entered I had a sense of it being the last day of my life. I remember going on a bicycle to Enniskillen, crying because I was leaving home at seventeen years of age. It was almost like a death in the family. That was the feeling around the house. My mother and my sisters were crying all day. Somebody had arranged to get a car to bring me to The Graan, which was unusual in itself. All my worldly possessions were in one little case.

The bleakness of The Graan was awful.

CHAPTER 2

PLAYING BY THE RULES

I entered the monastery at six o'clock on a Saturday evening, 1 September 1962. The doors closed behind me and that was it. Other postulants came on the same day from Ireland and Scotland. This group of strangers were preparing to launch out on the Passionists' way of life, for the very first time. Eight of us entered that day as clerics and many more as brothers. Seven out of that eight were ordained, which is unusual. The eighth one, Jim Dougall, went on to become an influential broadcaster with RTÉ and the BBC.

My abiding memory now of that evening is one of darkness. A strip of polished lino up the middle of corridors of pitch pine. Unpainted, unvarnished, virgin pitch pine in the rooms resulting in white, wooden floors washed and scrubbed and bare. Just noisy, cold wooden floors. There was a basic iron bedstead with a hair mattress on it. There were a few woollen blankets on a chair. There was a pillow, just one pillow. A makeshift wardrobe you didn't need because you'd nothing to put in it and, literally, an orange-box standing on its end beside your bed. A crucifix hung on the wall, nothing else. There were well-spaced-out, naked, 40-watt bulbs on long corridors without windows. Just enough light not to bump into things. I often think it was a parable of what I was doing in real life. Enough light to see where I was but no idea where I was going.

On the first night we went to bed at nine o'clock, but sleep never came. We were wakened early the next morning, just to remind us that the easy life was gone for good. We went to Mass, but not in the public church, because we were entering the first phase of withdrawal from the big bad world. I was now a postulant and, after a month, if I was still there, I'd be a novice. Everything, even the language, was unreal and ancient.

Right at the start, the novice master called us individually into his spartan office. I had to bring him everything I brought with me – watch, pen, clothes, books, gifts I had been given, money. Everything was taken and locked in the novice master's cell. I was then given a simple, black, ill-fitting habit to wear. Underneath we wore a rough, khaki army shirt and funny-looking trousers called 'billies'. They came to just below the knee and made me itchy all over. Our rooms were called cells, and that's why they were spartan. The message was loud and clear – we were going to prison for a year to test what we were made of. As usual, though, it was given a 'religious' name – the novitiate. After three days of softening up, reality hit me and I cried secretly for a week, wondering how I could get out of the place with even a little respectability.

Why didn't I leave? I don't know. Fear of going home was one reason; fear of being a failure was another. One of the reasons why my mother and father didn't want me to enter was the fear that I'd leave and be called a 'spoiled priest'.

After three days, the routine began. Novices went to bed at nine o'clock. We got up at two for an hour's prayer. At three we went back to bed and then we got up again at six. I knew before I entered what the routine would be and so too did my family. I learned later that my mother often woke at two and wept at the thought of me up praying at that ungodly hour. My sisters let me in on that little secret on the night out we had to celebrate my being thirty years ordained.

There was more prayer for an hour and a half until half seven, when we were allowed to go for breakfast of black coffee and dry bread, eaten standing up. That may have been fine for a seventeen-year-old in Italy, where the order was founded, but the Roman model didn't work here. It's why our graveyards are full of thirty-year-old priests and brothers who died of TB because of lack of proper food and a too-rigorous lifestyle that put the emphasis on an unreal asceticism ahead of healthy, mature living. In 1962 we lived the lax version of Passionist life, yet it was a draconian regime. Why didn't we revolt against it? Because every second of the day was accounted for, so there was no time to think.

After a month we were clothed, which meant we got our own habit and sandals. I also got a new name. It was the rule at that time. The world was bad and I was leaving my 'old self' (and that was the phrase, 'old self') behind. I took on this new self, which was symbolised by the new name. From that day forward I was called by a different name, Desmond Mary. Desmond after a friend I knew, Dessie Corrigan, who went to be a priest in the Society of African Missions. And since there is no St Desmond, they attached Mary to it. After the Second Vatican Council we were allowed to go back to our baptismal names and I once again became Brian D'Arcy, even though one of my nephews was called Desmond, after me.

Thinking and individualism were discouraged. The institution was always right. If you couldn't fit into it, you hadn't a vocation. Vocation killed your own unique spirit and you had to become whatever the institution wanted you to be. It was cloning before its time.

The whole regime was designed to produce a compliant monk who would do what he was told. For example, we weren't allowed to speak to other people, even fellow novices, except for very short periods during the day. We couldn't read anything other than rules and regulations and some spiritual books, chosen to reinforce the system.

There wasn't much formal education involved, except perhaps in spiritual practices: how to meditate, be silent and repeat endless rosaries. We memorised the monk's alphabet, which had quotes like, 'I am a worm and no man'. It was about killing your self-esteem, even though most of us hadn't much of it to kill. To this day I'm often crippled by my own unworthiness. I have to constantly struggle with self-image.

Every night I had to confess my faults publicly, as had the other novices. I carried a black cross through the refectory and knelt before the rector, the novice master and the whole community. Faults like 'I broke silence', 'I didn't mortify my eyes', 'I looked at the paper I was using to clean the sanctuary lamp', 'I broke a plate at wash-up' were confessed. We then got a penance. It could be a prayer, or for something considered serious it could be to eat your supper off the floor. It could be to prostrate yourself in the corridor while all the community walked past and prayed for you. All of those were regular penances. I lived in fear of doing things the wrong way or being caught breaking any of those innumerable and often senseless rules.

One day I was given a great big ball of twine and given instructions on how to make scourges of tightly knitted cord. Each of us had five whips about four inches long of this tightly knitted twine with a rope handle long enough to make sure you could beat your backside. After night prayers, three times a week, we went to our rooms and whipped ourselves on the bum for as long as it took to say five Our Fathers, five Hail Marys and five Glorias. I'm ashamed to admit now that I did this for years. When we questioned it, we were told, 'You should count yourself lucky. Ten years ago we did it in common.' What? 'We did it in common. We went into the community chapel and everyone took down their pants and whipped themselves publicly.' To do it in the privacy of your cell was an advance. Even then it felt sick. Obviously they got sense and stopped the common flagellations in the 1950s. Our self-flagellation lasted all through the 1960s, but most of us knew it was such a sick practise that we gave it up as students. I stopped it when I was close to ordination. Others took it more seriously, and I could hear them whacking and whipping with gusto as I walked through the corridors at night.

Self-flagellation was supposed to be a reminder that Christ was scourged at the pillar. In fact, though, we believed the body was bad and had to be beaten into submission.

I'm not saying that the men who enforced this system were bad men. I've lived with many men whose lives were ruined, partly by the system and partly by their own choice. Many blamed the system for their own lack of maturity, but it was a form of training that enabled dysfunctional people to mask their shortcomings in the worst aspects of religion.

My novice master, though, was a good man, a nice man and a friend until the day he died. He was very encouraging, strict, fair and ascetic, and we knew that he himself was attempting to be holy. He wasn't a sadist. He believed in what he was carrying through. Some of the men who were novice masters before him were sadists and they left their mark on the men they put through their hands.

There's a story about a novice from Mayo whose family had money. When he entered, he was better dressed than the other novices. His dressing gown and shirts were of a fine quality. The novice master at the time, a sadistic tyrant of a man, opened the window on the top floor of The Graan and threw the clothes out the monastery window with the famous dictum, 'You're not bringing the dross of the world into the purity of the monastery.' That says it all – a sadist mentality in an arrogant man convinced that the world was bad and the monastery was somehow 'purer'.

The practices were meant to test us during that initial year. There was a reasonable aspect to it. If one could survive that first year of virtual imprisonment then there was a good chance you might survive the rest of student life. But it was a test of endurance rather than a test of a vocation. There was hardly any spirituality taught and most of the practices were designed to encourage blind obedience rather than an interior life of genuine holiness.

Most input came from what were called conferences. These were of two kinds – general and individual. At general conferences the master of novices gave talks on the vows of poverty, chastity, obedience and spreading devotion to the Passion, which is the fourth vow specific to our congregation.

All I knew about the vow of chastity at that time was that I could never have sex. That was as much as I knew, and as much as I was taught. The result was that life focused on a negative – make sure that you don't put yourself in danger of breaking your vow of chastity. Even having a 'bad' thought at night caused me crippling scruples. So you were forced to suppress and repress all your sexual inclinations at an early stage.

Chastity was the big one. At that time it was the moral law of the Church that when it came to matters of sex there was no 'parvity of matter'. In other words, if you stole two pounds it would not be serious enough to be a mortal sin because parvity of matter applied. Yet a bad thought was a mortal sin and as damning as rape. It was such an unhealthy view of sex. In theory it was believed that sex was good, but in practise it was always sinful and bad.

Not as much emphasis was put on the vow of poverty. Why I don't know. The vow of obedience was important for control, and it became the greatest criterion of what God's will was for me. If my superior asked me to take on some task, then I accepted that it was what God wanted me to do, even though I felt ill-equipped to carry it through.

As Passionists we are committed to preach the Passion of Christ. But nobody quite knew what this devotion to the Passion meant. How were you to spread devotion to the Passion? The rest of my life has been an attempt to make the Passion, Death and Resurrection of Christ relevant to my own life and to inspire those called to share his Passion through suffering.

It was pointed out that there were two ways of keeping our vows. The first was the letter of the law and the second, which was much more important, was the spirit of the vow or the virtue each of the vows taught. That was good and is still helpful to this day.

Individual conferences were almost like confession. Not being the perfect novice, I was quickly alerted by the master as to where I was going wrong.

I want to emphasise again that the novice master at the time, Father Bernard, was a good and kind man and I have nothing but the highest respect for him. What he taught us was outdated but he was handing on what had been taught to him. He was not a man of the world and devoted himself to the spiritual life. That was both a help and a hindrance. It was easy to take correction from him because I knew he was a decent, honest and holy man himself. But I also knew that the life that was so important to him never existed in reality.

Every three months we had to get through a chapter meeting. The community held a meeting to discuss each of us individually. We could have been sent home at any of those, if the community thought us unsuitable. They were a problem because it meant that you behaved externally in a perfect way so as to please the people who could vote against you in the chapter. I tried my best to live as good a life as I could. I found it extremely difficult. What made it even more difficult was that it never made sense to me. It revealed a part of me that I didn't like, namely that I was willing to put up with things so that I could be professed and ordained. I was doing it to get through the system rather than out of conviction. Some would call that hypocrisy and I wouldn't argue with that.

One of the practices that went on in the novitiate throughout my time entailed novices being ordered to do obviously stupid things to test our blind obedience. My inclination was not to do them, but not to do them was regarded as disobedience and therefore a fault for which you could be sent home. It meant that as novices we frequently did things we knew were stupid, but we did them because we were afraid we'd be thrown out. That's what you call blind obedience and it's also the perfect example of brainwashing at its most cynical.

A number of episodes come to mind. One of them happened in January 1963. Those who have long memories will know that we had a really serious fall of snow. We lived in cruelly cold cells on the top corridor of The Graan monastery. It was not pleasant to walk around in sandalled feet in deep snow.

Matters came to a head one Sunday early in January, when the snow was a foot deep. It was the custom, after Sunday evening devotions, that we would be allowed to play football. But because this was a dark time of year we were given the opportunity of playing football immediately after lunch and before the devotions. The novice master was away and the vice-master asked us in the sacristy if any of us would like to go out snowballing. Remember, most of us were seventeen at the time and would do anything to get out of the house. So most of us volunteered to go snowballing. I'd never done it in my life.

When it was agreed that most of the novices wanted to go snowballing, the vice-master told us to change for football. We were to put on one light jersey, one pair of togs, one pair of socks and football boots. Like fools we did it. We came to the back door of the monastery and were then ordered by the vice-master to go snowballing in our football gear. We were absolutely frozen and shivering as darkness fell.

One of the novices, unfamiliar with the geography of the garden, fell and broke his nose. But the rest of us had to stay out in the snow for two hours. We got in after two hours because others in the community were horrified to see young novices out shivering in the snow when there was absolutely no need for it. It was cruel and senseless.

Then there is the notorious case of a novice master telling a novice from a farming background to plant cabbages upside down. He knew it was wrong but did it out of blind obedience. Humiliations like that destroyed good young men.

As a result of the snowballing incident, some of the novices, including me, got a severe flu. With me it got so bad that I was brought for an X-ray for suspected TB. There was a shadow on the lung and it meant my future as a Passionist was in doubt. In those days a serious illness was enough for one to be sent home and many good men were sent home from the novitiate because of contracting TB. I survived but still can't donate blood and have an increasingly weak chest.

In the novitiate, we had no contact with our family. But on 1 June 1963 my family left me a birthday present at The Graan. It was the big hit record at the time, very appropriately called 'Bachelor Boy', by Cliff Richard. The novice master was disgusted. He never told me the record had been left in but brought it to the priests' recreation room. There one of the professed brothers, Brother Aloysius, breaking every rule in the book, called me aside and told me about my family's gift.

The next Thursday afternoon, when I was doing manual work in the garden, Brother Aloysius suggested that I should get the job of weeding around the front door of the monastery. When I was well placed down on my knees pulling weeds from the flower beds, he opened the window of the recreation room and played me Cliff's version of 'Bachelor Boy'. I thought it was a fantastic record and couldn't wait to get out of the novitiate four months later to hear it again. That was as close as I got to my family's present for my eighteenth birthday.

On another occasion I had a toothache and needed to be brought to the dentist in Enniskillen. It was one of the most humbling experiences of my life. I was well known in Enniskillen before I entered, mainly through football. I had to walk through the town dressed as a clerical student with a hat, black suit, white collar and black coat. The master held me by the hand, like a child, as we walked through the town. If there had been handcuffs I might have been given them. As we walked up the town we went to a hardware shop in the centre of the town, Dickie's, to buy a hammer.

My father by then was a bus driver, and as he drove the bus through Enniskillen, he saw me walking up the street hand in hand with the 'minder'. That was the first sighting Hugh D'Arcy had of his son since I left home the previous September. This was now summer of 1963. He got so excited that he drove the bus into the depot and rushed up to see if he could talk to me.

The meeting took place in the door of Dickie's shop. The priest had me by the hand walking out of the shop. My father walked into the shop. We met in the doorway. I was not allowed to speak to him or even look at him. The priest said, 'Isn't your son looking well, Mr D'Arcy?' and he chucked me by the hand in case I would touch, speak to or look at my own father. I glanced back as I was being pulled up the street and I saw my father with tears in his eyes, looking aghast as I disappeared around a corner.

Throughout our first year of novitiate there were regular meetings to assess if we could continue to 'first profession'. These were called chapters. The eleventh-month chapter, the month before profession, was the most important one. We lived in fear of that because members of the professed community, who didn't know us, voted on our future. How could they know us since we weren't allowed to speak to the professed members of the community? Yet they were observing us all the time. Monastic Big Brother before its time. It was an effective way to make us malleable, and it was designed by the institution to break our will. Conform because you are being watched. We were conforming, not because we wanted to but because if we didn't we wouldn't be professed or ordained. The fact that many of us came through this with a reasonable degree of integrity is a miracle in itself.

I was professed as a Passionist on 29 September 1963. Our profession ceremony itself was quite elaborate but it was a cruel ceremony for our families. In 1963 I was eighteen and a very unworldly, naive eighteen at that. I was asked to commit myself for life to poverty, chastity and obedience and to promote devotion to the Passion. It was emphasised we were taking vows before God, a frightening proposal at eighteen years of age, and maybe an impossible one.

The whole liturgy was built around the Passion. The Passion was read; death was a major theme and, at one part of it, I carried a cross on my shoulder as I paraded round the church. At eighteen years of age, we dressed in a full-length black habit, wore sandals that we made ourselves, rosary beads and a black-and-white plastic sign in the shape of a heart with the words 'The Passion of Jesus Christ' written on it. This is the distinguishing sign worn by Passionists. We processed solemnly around the packed church, carrying a cross each and with a crown of thorns on our heads. Real thorns, not driven in, but sitting on top of our heads, uncomfortably.

I remember looking at my mother's face as I walked nervously around the church. She just couldn't understand why this son of hers was doing this. Then I took the cross off and lay down flat on a terrazzo floor. All seven of us lay in a line on the cold floor. A big, black pall, a cloth for hanging over a coffin, a huge pall that covered the entire sanctuary, was spread over us to signify our death. All seven of us lay under this while the Passion was read out. When I got up I glanced at my family and by now my mother was crying.

That memory stays with me to this day. And it haunts me now more than it did then, because my mother understood what I was doing and I didn't. It didn't make sense to her that the son she reared had to die to be good. What was wrong with her rearing? And where did I get my vocation anyway?

I saw my mother at the profession celebration later that day and I saw her alive only once after that.

CHAPTER 3

THE ARGUS CATALOGUE

After profession I moved from The Graan to Mount Argus in Dublin. Our class was lucky to be sent to UCD, even though I didn't particularly want to go because I didn't feel bright enough. It was the best thing that ever happened to me, proving again that what we want is not always what's good for us. I would have been a very different character had I not gone to university. The concept of university, of broadening the mind, of listening, of challenging, of debating, did eventually outweigh the stifling scholastic philosophy of the time.

A priest, Dr Horgan, was Professor of Scholastic Philosophy in UCD. For him there was a right answer and a wrong answer for every question, which is a contradiction in itself. There was no room for lateral thinking or for living with the pursuit of truth. As (what was termed) 'an occasional student from the North', I did a pass course, not honours.

One day I met Professor Horgan on the corridor. He was a friendly man. There were hundreds of clerics, all dressed like little priests, cycling up and down to university. As a professed Passionist with vows I wore a Roman collar, black hat and suit at university. Trying to hold your hat on while negotiating a bicycle over tramlines is a rare skill in itself. You should try it some day. Hold your hat on with your left hand, turn your bike with your right and try to jump the front wheel out of the track before you fall under a car.

Even though we looked the same, Dr Horgan knew most of us by name. I told Dr Horgan that I had a difficulty with empiricism and the theory of knowledge. I had read 'O'Neill's book' and still didn't understand it, proving I was well and truly brainwashed already. He said, 'Now, Mr D'Arcy, you tell me what you know.' He took the time and the patience to listen. I tried to pick my words well and to explain my difficulties to this dignified old professor. When I was finished he said, 'Ho, ho, ho, Mr D'Arcy, you should be doing honours.' I felt about six feet tall at least. 'You talk very well about it, but I doubt if you know what you're talking about.' That's how to raise somebody up and put them down all in one sentence. It also says a lot about what he thought of honours students.

There was one lecturer in UCD who was entirely different. Fergal O'Connor, a Dominican priest, was the greatest influence for good on me in university, without a shadow of a doubt. I went to his class even when I wasn't taking exams and so did many others. I learned about politics, how to think freely and how to be different and have integrity.

He used to be on The Late Late Show often. He said this 'revolutionary' thing that hit all the front pages in the 1960s. He said that every married couple should have a sofa instead of armchairs in their living room, so that they could enjoy a good cuddle at night. Imagine a priest saying that there should be sex in marriage or that it should be enjoyable! And that was Fergal. He was crippled with arthritis yet lived a long life. He was a wonderful thinker and a great influence on my formative years. He explored the goodness of the human mind way back in the 1960s when it was unheard of. He influenced generations of politicians and thinkers who were at UCD in his time.

Another great influence was John Jordan, Professor of English, who had an acerbic wit but developed wonderful critical faculties.

The older I get the more I appreciate Fergal O'Connor's gifts and I even wrote to him to tell him so in the mid-1990s. I'd love to have gone to see him but couldn't get the courage to do it. When he died I offered Mass for him because this man sowed a seed of hope and never knew it bore fruit.

Even though we were at university, our superiors believed we needed extra training to be good and servile Passionists. They arranged evening classes in Mount Argus. One of these evening classes was in passiology – the science of studying the Passion of Christ. There was an English Passionist, Edmond Rankin, teaching us about new theories of the Passion. When did it happen? Did Jesus hang on a cross? Was he nailed or was he tied? It was good but not wildly exciting. We were in class in Mount Argus on a dull November evening when one of the priests knocked at the classroom door, to tell us, 'President Kennedy has been shot.' Father Edmond replied, 'Oh really? Now, let's get back to the discussing why Good Friday actually fell on Holy Thursday.' That was the interest he had in President Kennedy being shot. The class continued as if nothing ever happened.

President Kennedy being shot was totally irrelevant. It's another example of how he had been conditioned to think that the world doesn't matter and shouldn't matter. President Kennedy was shot but our wee world went on regardless. Our training was uninfluenced by the real world. There were answers to questions and you'd better know the answers. In many respects, that's what's happening in our Church today. Rome comes up with an array of wonderful answers to questions nobody's asking. We can still live in an ecclesiastical world as if it is the only world. President Kennedy is dead. Oh, really?

I met President Eamon de Valera once when I was a student. I had to look after him when he visited Our Lady's Hospice. At the Nationalist meetings around Fermanagh, where I come from, the phrase 'Up Dev' was a mantra. I didn't know much about politics then, but I met Dev, had a great chat with him and was really impressed by his patience and interest. I wish I could remember what we talked about, but I do remember he talked to me as if I were an old man. He advised, 'Don't waste your time fighting over insignificant things.' I don't remember the exact words but that was the import. He was saying it's prudent to know which fights are worth fighting and leave the rest aside. Let stuff go. The skill is in recognising what is worth fighting for.

When I went to Mount Argus the same strictures applied to listening to the radio and reading papers. There was no TV, of course. As a great concession we got to listen to the radio for an hour a week on a Wednesday. We could tune into Hospital Requests. That's when I first heard Terry Wogan, Mike Murphy, Joe Linnane and Treasa Davidson, as they played the hits of the time and read out lists of sick people in hospitals all over Ireland.

One of those hits was a song called 'There's a Hole in the Bucket', sung by the heroic civil rights singer Harry Belafonte. One Wednesday Treasa had obviously mistimed her script. A story song should never be faded halfway through – or at all. But all rules take second place when it comes to news bulletins. The 1.30 news loomed closer as Harry was no more than warming up. Treasa had to do the unthinkable – fade the record and introduce the news. And that is how one of the most famous links in Radio Éireann's history was made. 'And now as we come to the news at 1.30, I'm afraid we have to leave Harry Belafonte with his hole in the bucket.'

So maybe Hospital Requests wasn't as safe as our superiors thought.

When I was a student in Mount Argus, I rarely did anything that was seriously wrong. I was too timid and too scared. But I did once do something utterly mad. I sneaked out of the monastery the night the Beatles came to Dublin.

When I entered The Graan, I had never heard of the Beatles. But when I finished the novitiate and came to Mount Argus, the Beatles had arrived. I loved the pathetically small amount of their music I heard. So when I saw they were coming to Dublin I wanted to see them. The problem was I had no money and would never have been allowed to go out to such a worldly event and me out of the novitiate.

That's when the rebel in me took over. On the night they came to town I went to night prayers as usual and when everyone was safely in their cells I went to the recreation room and opened the big window on the ground floor. Then I got on my bicycle and made my way to Abbey Street in the centre of the city. I hardly knew where Abbey Street was, but the noise and crowds led me there.

It was sheer madness. I bobbed and weaved my way to where the crowds were. I have no idea how close I was to the Adelphi but I could hear the noise of a distant band and the screaming of out-of-control young women. I can't say I saw the Beatles play live, but I did my best to hear them.

After an hour I began to realise what I had done and I broke into a cold sweat as I imagined the superior looking for me, or the window having been locked. So off I went and got my bicycle and retreated sheepishly back up Clanbrassil

Street, along by Mount Jerome and round the back of Mount Argus. The window was open and in I got, promising never to do another wrong act in my life.

Over the next few days I was a nervous wreck, afraid to go to confession and unable to go to Communion until I confessed and did penance. Eventually I went to an old priest who was blind. Luckily for me, he'd never heard of the Beatles and wondered how looking at crawly insects could possibly be a sin. I got my absolution.

I never told any student what I did until I was ordained. I still feel slightly guilty even today.

However, I knew that night in Abbey Street that the world in which I was reared was gone forever and would never be the same again. To see young people my own age acting so differently and so freely disturbed me beyond words. Elvis, who was my hero before I entered, did his bit to change the world, but the Beatles took us to another world. For good or evil, the 1960s were the bridge between the old, safe world and the new, exciting world of free expression.

As students, we never got home but we did get letters. I got a letter from my mother and she hinted that she wasn't feeling well.

I asked permission to go to visit my mother on an Easter Monday. The student who entered with me, Artie McCann, said the two of us would go home that morning as we had to do it in one day. We could not get out of the monastery for even one night. We got on bicycles at Mount Argus on Easter Monday 1965 at three in the morning and we cycled from Mount Argus out to Blanchardstown. We left the bicycles at the Greyhound Bar. Dressed in our Roman collars and hats, there we were at four in the morning, two clerics thumbing on the road to Navan. The first car that came along was a Garda squad car. They were wondering what these mad clergymen were doing on the road at an unearthly hour. They thought we were drunk, or worse. We explained to them that we were going to Enniskillen and they drove out of their way to take us to Kells in the squad car. We got out and started thumbing again, and some guy in a green mini-car gave us a lift. When we got to Cavan, Artie McCann's brother borrowed a car and brought us home.

My mother was a big, strong, healthy, plump, even fat, woman. But when I saw her this time, she was a wee thin woman and obviously sick. The rest of the family whispered, 'She won't go to a doctor, maybe you could persuade her.' I had suddenly got powers because I had a Roman collar.

She had great devotion to Father Charles of Mount Argus (of whom much more later), because of what I wrote to her. I also sent her prayer leaflets. She told me, 'Well, if you say a novena to Father Charles, I'll make up my mind at the end of it.' Here was the same woman who had brought me to Knock to help me to make up my mind, now wanting me to pray for her to make up her mind. At the end of my novena, she went to the doctor and, of course, it was too late.

The next time I saw her was on the night before she died in hospital. I never got over the shock that she was so close to death. At seven o'clock in the morning we got word that Mammy had died. It was Ascension Thursday, 27 May 1965. If my mother had lived they were going to amputate her leg. She didn't want that and, luckily for her, she died before the amputation took place. Ever since that, Father Charles has had a really special place in my life.

When I came back to Dublin, I took it badly. I was in my second year at university. I was sent to the doctor because I was quite traumatised by it. The doctor advised me to start smoking, believe it or not. His own wife had died suddenly shortly before, leaving a young family behind her. The two of us shared our grief. He said that once as he walked in Stephen's Green, a lovely thought occurred to him. 'The other day, it just struck me that the one thing I wanted for her was that she would be happy and I contented myself that now she's happier than I could ever make her.' It was a nice phrase that stuck with me and gave me consolation at the time. He advised: 'You should ask your mother to help you and she will.' And I do to this day. I really am convinced that, had my mother not died, I would not have been a priest. And if I'm any good as a priest it's because of her influence from a better place.

What really kept me sane during these trying years was music. I was an innocent abroad when I sneaked out to see the Beatles. But later as a student I always cycled to the centre of Dublin on our free half day on Thursday to meet and talk with the showband musicians. This time there was nothing underhand. I had permission to meet with them as long as I got back for the night prayer.

I knew some of the showband musicians because I went to school with them – people like the Plattermen, the Polkadots and the Skyrockets. All the bands used to stay in the same Dublin hotel. Barry's Hotel was the in place at one time. The Belvedere Hotel later became our haunt. If you knew one band, eventually you got to know them all.

One day as a penniless student I was passing a free Thursday afternoon walking up and down O'Connell Street in Dublin, dressed in Roman collar, black suit, hat, fáinne and pioneer pin, hoping to meet someone who would invite me for a cup of tea or even an ice cream.

Outside the famous Gresham Hotel, I met Eddie Masterson and two friends. Eddie Masterson was the most famous solicitor in Ireland at the time. He lived in a single room in Barry's Hotel in Denmark Street, Dublin, for seventeen years. His office was the inside pocket of a heavy grey coat. He usually wore shirts that were once white but were now stained with tea and cigarette ash. He always had a cigarette hanging off his lower lip.

Eddie knew everybody, particularly those in showbands and in sport. He fixed break-ups in bands and wrote hits on the back of Sweet Afton cigarette packets about the current events of the day. When the great Jim Reeves died, Ireland went into mourning and Eddie, spotting the potential, wrote the first of his many tributes. It was cleverly put together and eventually Larry Cunningham and the Mighty Avons recorded it. Larry was a Jim Reeves soundalike and the song went into the British pop charts, the first showband record to do so.

Eddie was a legend. The two men with him outside the Gresham were Jimmy Molloy from Longford and one Albert Reynolds. He and his brother, Jim, owned a chain of ballrooms all around Ireland.

The big music magazine at the time was New Spotlight, a predominantly pop-oriented publication. Albert wanted to set up his own magazine and Jimmy Molloy was to be the editor and printer.

That's when Eddie introduced me to his friends.

'There's a guy who'll write for you,' Eddie said to Albert. 'He knows the scene and he'll write for nothing.'

I protested that I wasn't supposed to listen to radios or read papers, never mind write for them.

'You don't have to tell anybody. Be like the footballing priests and use someone else's name. What's your father's name?'

The next month two articles by 'Hughie' were published in The Dancing Gazette.

And that's how my career in journalism began – as simply and as accidentally as that. I wrote every month for the best part of four years under an assumed name, because I would have been sent home if I had been discovered writing without permission. I had entered the seminary in 1962 and this was 1965, the same year my mother died – that's how I remember it. Everyone in the bands knew who Hughie was, but my superiors knew nothing of it. Just before I was ordained, I had to come clean and tell my superiors about my nefarious writings for fear my ordination would be invalid. To my surprise they said very little and saw no obstacle to ordination.

My family bought me a small transistor radio. Even though it was against all the rules I had it in my room and used it sparingly to keep up to date with the music scene. The other students knew I had it and often came to me to listen to music or sporting events. Often in life we have to break the mould in a quiet, unrevolutionary way. As the spiritual writer Richard Rohr wrote, 'We don't think ourselves into new ways of living, we live ourselves into new ways of thinking.' That was the principle behind so many of the reforms in religious life, authenticated by the Second Vatican Council.

The Second Vatican Council went on all through my training. It was about radically rethinking our attitude to the world. The world is not bad. The world is good and the world is redeemed. The world can teach the Church and the community many things, just as the Church can teach the world something. They're not enemies. They should work hand in hand.

Pope John XXIII died in old age yet he died before the council ended. Pope Paul VI came after him and trusted the council, but got caught up in his encyclical Humanae Vitae. That was before my ordination. For my examinations I was learning theology in Latin for the oral examination. Throughout my student days I was living in two different worlds. To be ordained I knew I had to conform to the pre-conciliar Church, but I also knew I had to be conversant with the teachings of the council if I was to be a relevant priest. I knew I had to change to meet the needs of the world rather than the other way around.

One other classmate thought exactly as I did and we both spent our time reading up on the council so that we'd have something to offer after ordination. We learned what we needed to learn for our examination and studied what we needed to study for our future in our own time. I spent all my student days doing that.

It was essential for examinations to learn off the 'right answer', that is, the answer they needed. It was the opposite of being taught to think. If you asked a question in class that was remotely awkward, you were told "mysterium est." It's a mystery. You weren't supposed to question mysteries. It was a cultic way of training. Most people settled quietly into the system so that they could be ordained. You had to play the game but some of us knew it was only a game.

Religious weren't part of that hierarchical career structure and it gave us a little more freedom. Many of those who went to Maynooth admit that it was a stifling place to be, especially for those who wanted more than membership to a clerical club. Religious had their own taboos that had to be observed and, in Dublin anyway, we had to satisfy the diocesan authority by sitting their exams as well as our own. It was hard to escape the party line. As a result, many of those with get-up-and-go, got up and went.

On the morning of my ordination, 20 December 1969, I was surprised to find that a number of people from showbands came to the ceremony in St Michael's College in Enniskillen. I was surprised because most of them would have been working the night before and made a great effort to be there on a slippery winter's morning for nine o'clock.

I was ordained in St Michael's College because I owed much to them. 1969 was the beginning of change in many areas of the Catholic Church. One of those changes meant that candidates for ordination had a choice, within limits, of where they could be ordained. Previously, vast numbers were herded together in places that suited the ordaining bishop.

I chose St Michael's College to try to be some sort of healing between the Passionists and the diocese of Clogher. There had been, in the early days, bad feeling between the two, but Bishop Eugene O'Callaghan worked hard at mending bridges.

Bishop O'Callaghan was known for many things. One of them was that he had no time for showbands or dancing. During his time it was a mortal sin for a person in the diocese of Clogher to go to a dance that didn't end at midnight. So, in a way, it was ironic that so many of the bands came to an ordination service conducted by Bishop O'Callaghan.

As it turned out, I was the last priest he ordained. He retired very shortly after that. It has been said on many occasions, only half jokingly, that when he realised what he had done, it's no wonder he retired.

I'm the only priest to have been ordained in the college.

There was a quiet reception afterwards in Derrylin. The music and craic were good and Brian Coll kept us entertained all evening long. Only a limited number attended the ordination because the college chapel was small, and anyway I didn't want to put my family to any more expense.

One of the people who attended was Eddie Masterson. As you can see, he keeps popping up in the most unusual places. Because he was a solicitor he was asked to make a speech on behalf of my friends in show business. He was sitting beside the bishop. The bishop, unconcerned, listened to what Eddie was saying. After all, he had been introduced as a solicitor. That was impressive. Eddie got up in his grey suit and sparkling new white shirt for the occasion, but the ever-present cigarette hung off his bottom lip. As his opening text, spoken slowly as any good parish priest would, he had a quotation of sorts from Scripture. He said ponderously, 'What does it profit a man if he gain the whole world and never hears Big Tom sing "Gentle Mother"?' The bishop looked aghast. Most people didn't get the joke. And the twenty of us who did went under the table, partly with embarrassment and partly in admiration at the genius of the man. He got away with it.

CHAPTER 4

ALBERT REYNOLDS

When the first volume of my memoir, 'a Different journey', was published in 2006, we had a memorable Irish launch in the City West Hotel in Dublin. Brian Carthy ensured that everyone from the world of show business, sport and communications turned up. My family and friends made a night of it and arrived down from Enniskillen.

It turned out to be one of those special nights never to be repeated. The speeches seemed more like a premature canonisation than a book launch.

Peter Quinn, former President of Cumann Lúthchleas Gael, a neighbour and lifelong friend of mine, the incomparable Jimmy Magee and Brian Carthy all spoke kindly about what they knew of me. I spoke, for once briefly, and the formal launch was by former Taoiseach Albert Reynolds. Great football legends such as Mickey Harte, Joe Kernan, Donie O'Sullivan, Frankie Byrne and Dermot O'Brien spent the night smiling into fan's cameras.

From the entertainment scene genuine friends, such as Jim Aiken, Mike Murphy, Joe Dolan, Big Tom McBride, Tony Loughman and dozens more, were kind enough to make the long journey to City West and ensured that that part of my life was adequately represented.

I'm sad to say that within a short few years many of those friends were dead and gone. Their deaths continue to fill me with loneliness.

When Albert Reynolds made his speech, many of us noticed that he wasn't his usual bright and breezy self. His talk was comprehensive and well received. For the first time he revealed the inside story of the peace talks which led to the first ceasefire. He was kind enough to mention that I was steadfast in encouraging him to work for peace in the North. Naturally he let everyone know that he was responsible for bringing me into journalism in the 1960s.

I noticed his wife Kathleen was unusually anxious during his speech. She sat at the back of the platform beside their friend Joe Dolan. He told me afterwards that Kathleen kept urging Albert to get on with the launch.

What I didn't realise was that Albert was by now in the early stages of dementia. The family already knew the signs were very much there. In those circumstances it was particularly generous of Albert and the Reynolds family to agree to do the launch. I'm forever grateful to them.

Albert didn't make too many public appearances after that. I was deeply moved that he spoke sincerely as he launched 'a Different journey' for us.

A few short years later and I was the nervous one, and extremely sad too, as I prepared to officiate and preach at his funeral.

The morning of the funeral of my lifelong friend was particularly fraught for me. It was an official state funeral and was broadcast live on national television. Dignitaries of state and Church were present. It was held in Donnybrook Roman Catholic Church (beside RTÉ), the parish in which the Reynolds family now live.

At the height of the showband craze the Reynolds brothers were quick to build a dozen or more huge halls around Ireland. Albert and Jim were largely responsible for taking dancing out of the hands of the clergy when they built these bigger and better ballrooms, ensuring the outdated parish halls could not compete.

They unwittingly created centres where young people were free to dance, meet, and socialise as never before. The arrival of the motor car and electricity helped create a new Ireland and gave employment to tens of thousands of young men and women.

It was only when the showband industry began to wane in the 1970s that Albert entered politics. He never forgot his roots, though, and maintained his band connections for the rest of his life.

For the last few years of his life, Albert was lost in the mists of dementia. It was sad to watch, yet his family, particularly his wife Kathleen, cared for him at home with heroic devotion.

At his funeral, people from the worlds of business, sport, entertainment and politics all came to pay tribute to a man who became a genuine legend.

As well as being a state funeral it was also very much a family funeral. Kathleen, all the children and the beloved grandchildren wanted to remember not just a former politician but also a loving husband, father and grandfather.

Because I knew the Reynolds family since the 1960s and had known Albert long before he went into politics, the family wanted me to be the main celebrant at his funeral mass.

Presiding on the altar was the Archbishop of Dublin, Diarmuid Martin. There were many other priests on the altar and in the congregation. Some expected the Papal Nuncio, who was present, to preside. He chose to sit in the body of the church with the Diplomatic Corps. The media speculated that he sat in the pews rather than preside on the altar because I was the celebrant. It might not look good for his career if a priest, who was out of favour with the Vatican, was concelebrating Mass with the Papal Nuncio. I don't know if this is true or not. A few of the papers let it be known and I didn't see a denial. To be honest it's irrelevant; I couldn't have cared less – and I'm sure neither did he.

Chief among the political dignitaries was the former Prime Minister of Britain, Sir John Major. The Reynolds family was particularly happy that Sir John was present. I knew from them that he had flown over to visit Albert shortly before his death. It was a generous, decent and moving thing for John Major to have done. He and Albert were close friends as ministers for finance in their respective cabinets. They maintained that friendship when both became leaders of their countries. That friendship became the foundation on which the peace process progressed.

John Major was totally relaxed when he entered Donnybrook church. He spoke with Paddy Cole and Red Hurley, both of whom were providing the music for the family. Sir John seemed surprised that there would be such a range of music at a church funeral. He went straight up to them for a chat and really enjoyed both the spiritual and the jazz numbers.

I thought it best to welcome him privately as soon as he sat in his pew. I shook hands with him and told him we all very much appreciated his coming to the funeral. It was a kind and decent way to show how genuine their friendship really was. I assured him it meant the world to Kathleen, the family and to all of us, to have him present.

Sir John looked at me, smiled very sincerely and replied: 'Sure where else would I be on a day like today?'

At the beginning of Mass I welcomed him publicly and repeated the phrase Sir John had spoken to me. The entire congregation reacted instantly with warm enthusiastic applause.

Sir John really enjoyed the funeral in a good sense. He thought it was joyful, down to earth and respectful. 'I recognised the man you were burying,' he quipped. He told me at the meal afterwards that he would never get such a good funeral himself unless he either became an Irishman or joined the Catholic Church. 'I'm afraid we English Anglicans don't do funerals the way the Irish do,' he laughed.

Over the weekend of the funeral I had very little time to prepare the homily. After offering two masses on Sunday morning, I had a window of about an hour to get the script together. RTÉ Television wanted a copy of it at four o'clock on Sunday to insert into their folder and presumably to check out the contents. I made sure to consult the family first and they were happy. 'Sure who knew Dad better than you for over fifty years,' they assured me.

Personally, I always believed Albert never got the credit he deserved as Taoiseach. He was unfortunate in that many 'events' came together to work against him. I wanted to put the record straight as gently as I could.

Albert Reynolds was always interested in what happened in Northern Ireland. I told the congregation that long before he became Taoiseach, Albert was involved in show business and maintained many contacts with both Protestants and Catholics during the heyday of the showband era. Anyone associated with showbands had to be practical. They appealed to fans across the divide. The musicians taught him how to listen to people, to get along with all sorts, and how to communicate with what they called 'the ordinary punter'.

Albert knew exactly who his friends were. Before he became Taoiseach, I carried letters from him to people in the North. Quietly and anonymously I also delivered letters from the North to Albert. I have my own ideas who wrote and who received those letters, but I have no proof. Anyway, I didn't need to know the details. It was enough for me to be a trusted postman, helping in a quiet way to build contacts between those who genuinely wanted peace.

On the day he was elected Taoiseach I offered prayers in the Reynolds house. It was a small gathering of family and close friends. Before I started out on the long journey home to the North, Albert took me aside and promised: 'Brian, I know how important the North of Ireland is to you. Believe me, I promise you one thing; I will do my best to bring peace to your beloved North now that I'm Taoiseach.'

During his time as Taoiseach and indeed afterwards, if there was any important political decision to be made which could have unseen implications for the North, Albert always gave me a ring. That was his style – he checked things. Of course he knew he had to make up his own mind, and I'm sure there were others he consulted with too because he was sensitive to the subtle differences that others, south of the border, might not advert to. Albert knew his strengths and his weaknesses.

It's well known that it was Albert who persuaded me to write for his music magazine in the mid-1960s. I was a student and not allowed to read the papers, never mind to write for them. Albert could always find a way around obstacles. I wrote the articles for his magazine yet, at his suggestion, they appeared under my father's name. It was his encouragement which started me off writing over fifty years ago. Albert had a special place in my life because he helped me to nurture a gift I didn't even know I had.

On many occasions during his life Albert spoke about the futility of war. He knew that peace cannot be achieved by talking only to your friends; you must talk to your enemies as well. He often summed up his philosophy by asking, 'Who's afraid of peace?' He took personal and political risks to achieve peace. We owe an enormous debt to Albert Reynolds, John Major, John Hume, Gerry Adams, Alec Reed and others. They were the real risk-takers in the cause of peace.

'If you have words, there is always the chance you'll find a way,' wrote Seamus Heaney. Seamus went on to suggest what those words might be:

So hope for a great sea change, on the far side of revenge
Believe that further shore is reachable from here
Believe in miracles.

Albert believed in words and miracles. More importantly, he had the courage to risk everything for peace because nothing of real value is achieved by playing safe. He was also fully aware there were no votes to be gained by bringing peace to the North but it had to be done anyway.

I asked the congregation at his funeral Mass to think how many people are still alive and healthy today because of the risks taken by Albert and those who supported him.

First and foremost Albert was a family man. He told me and others that the best decision he ever made in his life was to marry Kathleen. They both had a simple faith and prayed daily for peace. He had a prayer for peace printed on a card which he handed out to those he met whom he thought might want to pray for peace in our country. Like St Ignatius of Loyola, he believed we should pray as if everything depended on God but work as if everything depended on us.

At the end of the funeral Mass each one of the Reynolds children spoke beautifully and emotionally, highlighting the qualities they found in their parents' love for each other. Andrea remembered coming into the family home quietly one night shortly before Albert died. She checked the room to see if he was sleeping peacefully. But she found both Kathleen and Albert lying on the bed praying the Rosary together. Andrea believed it would be a lasting picture of what undying love looks like.

In the sacristy after Mass Archbishop Martin told me how impressed he was by the funeral liturgy and especially so by the personal tributes given by the children. He confessed that he thought such prayerful families were a thing of the past.

'I was delighted to see such an influential family speaking out in public with such high ideals,' he said.

Chapter 5

BIG TOM

Another friend was showband legend Big Tom, who sadly left us in April 2018, a few weeks after his beloved wife Rose died.

Big Tom McBride came from Oram, near Castleblaney, where he lived to the day he died and where he is buried in a corner, near the entrance, of that country graveyard. Picture it in your mind. If his friend Johnny McCauley were still alive, he'd write a massive country hit with those details alone. Big Tom sang songs like that for a lifetime.

No matter how far he travelled, Oram was his home. That is probably the most important thing you can say about him. He knew where he came from and was content in his own place.

He was one of the most loved entertainers in Ireland and Britain for more than fifty years. In his heyday he packed 4,500 people into the Royal Ballroom in Castlebar on St Stephen's night. He held the record for the biggest crowd ever in the Galtymore Ballroom in Cricklewood. Nobody knows precisely how many were there, but it was more than 7,000 emigrant dancers.

Big Tom didn't have fans, he had lifelong friends.

It is over fifty years since I did my first interview with the living legend. I was a clerical student preparing for the priesthood and 'secretly' writing for The Dancing News in Longford. The biggest band in the country even then was Big Tom and The Mainliners.

But Tom was notoriously shy and dreaded doing interviews. His manager, the late John McCormack from Rockorry in County Monaghan, thought that he might talk to me. So he drove him up to the monastery I then lived in, Cloonamahon in County Sligo. I sneaked both of them up to my room, switched on a tape recorder, asked Tom basic questions as gently as I could, and recorded John McCormack's answers, for it was he who answered the questions.

When I asked Tom if he agreed, all he ever answered was, 'Aye, surely, that's the truth.' Through the years we often laughed at that first meeting. Tom loved retelling it, partly because it was true, and even more because he owed so much in those early days to John McCormack.

I have adored the man ever since and we remained good friends throughout our lives.

When I published an earlier memoir everybody in show business turned out to a mighty launch at the City West Hotel outside Dublin. I was hesitant to ask Tom and Rose for various reasons – mainly because I didn't want to invade their privacy. However, the publisher, Brian Carthy, rightly thought we couldn't have a launch without Tom. So he asked him. Tom said: 'When it's for Father Brian, we'll be there.' To my great delight they were.

Tom was a gentleman, and after Joe Dolan died, he was the greatest living icon of the showband era. But you couldn't tell Tom that. You would embarrass the life out of him.

All his life Tom remained a genuinely humble man who preferred farming, hunting, fishing and shooting to the bright lights of show business. When Big Tom and The Mainliners went back on the road in 2008 for a limited tour, they were a huge attraction everywhere they played. They made regular short, hugely successful tours for a decade.

Tom once told me that if he hadn't got a break in show business he would probably have continued building hay sheds. For that is what he was doing when he took to singing part time with the Finncarn Céilí Band in Monaghan. In the beginning they played strictly céilí for local GAA clubs.

In the early days there were four of them in the band and, as Tom once told me, 'We got a fiver a night. A pound each and a pound for the car.'

'I remember one night we played in the Congo,' recalled Tom. 'There was a war in the Central African country called the Congo at the time and there must have been trouble at a few dances in a certain Monaghan village, which I won't name. That's why they called the village the Congo. So it's true to say we started up in the Congo,' Tom laughed.

'We played a presentation dance there and we had to play céilí music until the presentation was made. And then we started to play a few waltzes and hits of the time. That is how we edged our way into becoming a real showband.'

Eventually they formed a full showband and, like many other bands, they began playing for what they could get in any hall that would take them. At that time Tom was in the band but he wasn't the lead singer. Ginger Morgan was the front man. Things changed when John McCormack spotted them and became their manager. He worked tirelessly for the band and without him they would never have made it.

Their name, The Mighty Mainliners, even now conjures up seedy scenes of drug addicts injecting fixes into their arms. The truth is more mundane; 'When I worked on the island of Jersey,' Tom explained, 'There was a country band I went to see as often as I could. They were called The Mainliners. When we started our band I borrowed their name!'

John McCormack convinced them to make a record. As Tom remembers it, 'A lock of country boys went up to the Eamonn Andrews studios in Dublin. There was a producer there and a few professional musicians. They didn't take much notice of us, and we didn't take much notice of them.'

But Ginger Morgan, being the lead singer, wrote 'Thinking of You' as the A-Side. That in itself was innovative because not many bands wrote their own songs. It stands up today as a good song.

The B-Side was Tom singing 'Gentle Mother'. Tom first heard 'Gentle Mother' in England. The twins Des and Ollie Finnegan knew part of the song. Tom learned it from them but they knew only one verse. They wrote home to their sister who knew the whole song and she supplied them with the complete lyrics.

The band's big break came when they appeared on television with Paul Russell on The Showband Show on what was then called Teilifís Éireann, now RTÉ.

'It was John McCormack who got us on the show. I don't think I have ever been as nervous in my life as I was that night. I could hear my own knees knocking! We were delighted to be on the show because two of the biggest bands at the time, Joe Dolan, and Larry Cunningham and the Mighty Avons were on the same show. That meant there was a huge crowd looking in. We were lucky it was 'Gentle Mother' that everyone wanted to hear.'

That paragraph brings tears to my eyes now. I preached at the funerals of Larry and Joe, attended Tom's funeral and celebrated the beautiful memorial mass for Tom, organised by his showband family. The heroes of the time are gone to a better place. They brought so much pleasure to our lives and left us so many happy memories. Time is moving on for me too and there won't be many more funerals for me to preach at.

The Mainliners achieved legendary status towards the end of the 1960s and Tom McBride remained one of the best loved entertainers Ireland has ever produced.

The showband era was often criticised for its lack of originality, but Big Tom and The Mainliners had hit after hit with original material. The man who wrote most of those hits was Johnny McCauley, a Derry man living in England. The most enduring hit of Tom's career was Johnny's song 'Four Country Roads', though at the end, a more recent hit, 'Going Out the Same Way you Came In', comes close.

All his life Tom had a fear of flying, to put it mildly. He was once on a plane when the engine went on fire after take-off. Tom still shakes when he remembers how they had to take off and, after what seemed an eternity, began to circle to try to land again with the engine still on fire. He looked out the window and saw fire brigades and ambulances all lined up.

'I thought I was going to die and I promised myself that if I got down to God's green earth safely, I would never fly again. Whatever the pilot did the fire went out and we did land safely. I hate flying. I have been on a plane since but it is never a comfortable experience.'

There is a famous story of Tom recording an album in Nashville. It is hilarious. He and Johnny McCauley set off from London and took a train to Southampton. There they boarded the QE2, and after six days arrived in New York. They had three big suitcases each. They spent a couple of days in New York and then took a Greyhound Bus to Nashville. They dragged the cases everywhere they went and, as Tom remembered, 'Greyhound Buses are not comfortable.'

Twenty-three hours later they got off the bus in Nashville, jaded and swearing never to do it again. They spent two weeks there recording what are probably the best recordings of Tom's career, but it was one of the few albums that didn't sell. People preferred the home-grown Tom singing quiet songs about life and love, backed by the fantastic dancing beat which The Mainliners showband always had. The Nashville sound was for others.

Eventually The Mainliners broke up and Tom left to form The Travellers Showband. Both bands continued to enjoy success but there was something magical about the original Mainliners. When they came back together the magic beat was still there.

That is why everyone was delighted when the original band got back together. Henry McMahon and his brother Seamus, now sadly departed from us too, Ginger Morgan, Ronnie Duffy, John Beattie and Cyril McKevitt were older and wiser. But then so were the fans who came to see them. Cyril McKevitt was the first to die suddenly after coming from morning Mass.

Nothing stays as it was, yet when Big Tom crooned 'Smoke Along The Track', 'Old Love Letters', 'Ashes of Love', and 'The Pain of Loving You', the dancers, in their minds, were back in a five-pole marquee reliving their lost youth. Music transports us to a world that lives eternally in our memory.

And what a memory we have of Big Tom and The Mighty Mainliners.

CHAPTER 6

BLUEBELL ISLAND - Gerry Ryan's Mass

Fermanagh is my special little piece of heaven. I want to live there; I want to die there; I want to be buried there. One incident in particular heightened my awareness of the incredible beauty I once took for granted.

Morah Ryan asked me to offer her late husband Gerry's first anniversary Mass for the immediate family and close friends. It was a difficult year. I was bitterly disappointed to learn that Gerry, a lifelong friend, dabbled in illicit drug-taking. It became public knowledge not long after his untimely death.

His family was subjected to huge media pressure; his sudden death left many unanswered questions. For his fans, his friends, his work colleagues and, most of all for Morah and the children, the year ended, as it began, in sadness and controversy.

I needed words of comfort and hope for such a sensitive time but nothing helpful came easily.

On the evening before the Mass, friends in Enniskillen suggested that the beautiful island of Inish Davar, known as Bluebell Island, on Lough Erne would be worth a visit. It was the end of April, the bluebells were in full bloom and might not last much longer. Against my better judgement, I headed down the lough to the island with Pat Lunny.

When we arrived the island of about twenty acres was completely carpeted in bluebells. Yet, as I walked through the paths it was not the bluebells but the blossoms on the blackthorn trees which impressed me even more. The pink-and-white blossoms stood out against the setting sun on a breezy, balmy evening.

As I stood still listening to the silence, I became aware of one special tree, which was leafless and naked. The last time I was on the island, that particular tree was perfectly dressed in full foliage. I remembered listening to a little bird with a wonderful singing voice perched on the top branch, making marvellous music from the hidden recesses of the layers of leaves.

This evening, though, the tree was a lifeless skeleton, obviously frozen to death during the harsh winter. Still, the little bird went on whistling his song of triumph from the very top of the now dead tree. The other trees were alive and blossoming, yet the lone bird chanted from the top of the dead tree. God can use even dead things to affirm life. It was a haunting, peaceful, life-giving moment in time

When the time was right I moved on to admire the bluebells. I sauntered through the paths, admiring this magic carpet of bluebells covering the entire island.

Under a tree I noticed a lone albino or white bluebell. It was a bluebell in every respect except colour. It had its own unique beauty. It told me we can be different and still be beautiful; different but still part of the team.

There were other white flowers, perhaps even weeds, pushing up through the bluebells. In a few days the bluebells might still be there, but won't be noticeable because the white flowers will smother them. But that evening it was just perfect, a tinge of white under a carpet of blue.

As the light faded I made my way to the water's edge to watch the setting sun. It wasn't a blood-red sun. It was a genuinely sun-coloured sun. This evening it was a perfect super-sized sphere. I stood at the water's edge in silence as the sinking sun rested on the peaceful waters of Lough Erne. In a matter of minutes the sun went to sleep in its watery bed.

We agreed it was a rare, precious moment not to be missed and probably never to be experienced again. Life goes on. Thousands of years before Christ, that same sun sank into that same lake, and, apart from the changed vegetation on the island, not much else was different. A thousand years is like a day in God's time.

As we walked back through the bluebells the falling darkness highlighted the pure blue of the bells and camouflaged the intrusive white weeds. When the sun went to bed the bluebells took on a fluorescent hue.

Nature teaches us that God's creation has no problem with death because it always blossoms into new life. Now I had a story for Gerry Ryan's Mass.

We humans, too, are transient creatures on this earth. The trees that I admired gave hope to other struggling human beings fifty, sixty, maybe a hundred years ago. They will probably do the same for people fifty years from now.

At Mass for Gerry Ryan next morning, I began by agreeing with Morah, the children and the friends present that it had been a tough, sad, awful year for everyone. Yet they should take hope. They had survived the worst of it. At one time they were too frightened even to think about a future. But because they worked together, encouraged and listened to one another, they survived.

I then shared the story of the island, the bird, the dead tree, the beautifully groomed trees, the bluebells, the weeds and the setting sun. The images proved life-giving and comforting to them too.

Afterwards in the family home, Gerry's friends remembered only the story of the island. Bono and his wife Ali were fascinated by the singing bird on the dead tree. We shared dreams, theories and visions. We found hope in death.

As I left for home Bono joked: 'When you write another volume of your memoirs you have the perfect title for it. Call it: The Tree Was Dead, But the Bird Still Sang.'

On the way home the images became a metaphor for my own efforts at life. Why do we continue to look for the living among the dead? I don't know, but the bird's song was hauntingly life-giving even though his pulpit was a dead tree.

At Sunday Mass I told the congregation again about our Bluebell Island right beside us. Only a few had heard of it; only a handful had visited it.

One of those listening was a six-year-old child. She went home and, without her parents' knowledge, she drew a straight line of perfect bluebells on a white sheet of paper. Then she drew an orange sun setting behind them. To the left was a matchstick man (me I presume). To the right was a tree with a bird singing on a branch. The tree was covered in green foliage. When her mother asked her why, the six-year-old replied: 'I just couldn't bring myself to draw a dead tree.'

Out of the mouths of babes …

CHAPTER 7

CARDINAL MARTINI - Afraid to Speak the Truth?

If Cardinal Mario Martini of Milan had not contracted Parkinson's disease he would have been the first Jesuit to be elected pope.

That's important to me especially when I think about how his life turned out. I had great hopes that he would bring the Catholic Church into the twenty-first century. I looked up to him during the times when hope melted into despair.

Martini was the leading churchman in Italy for three decades. A highly respected scholar, he gained a double doctorate in scriptural studies.

He was a brilliant communicator who was fluent in eight languages. Despite the difficult years under Pope John Paul II, he appeared to live out the vision of the Second Vatican Council. He believed the Church should be a compassionate refuge of sinners. This, he insisted, is the gift of the Holy Spirit. It is also the council's outstanding legacy.

The Roman Curia, though, rolled back on the Second Vatican Council, ushering in a legalistic Church with little regard for the people of God in their struggles to live in the modern world.

Martini was first and foremost a pastor, yet he was, doctrinally, as orthodox as they come during his years as Cardinal Archbishop of Milan.

He died on 31 August 2012. More than a quarter of a million people filed past his open coffin. He had the equivalent of a state funeral, which was televised around the world. Twenty thousand grateful believers, young and old, attended the funeral Mass. He was by any standards a giant of the Church.

However, when he died, he caused shock waves throughout the Church because he left behind a critical document, which he personally approved, to be published after his death.

Personally, I was shocked and saddened to learn that one of the most influential Church leaders in Europe expressly requested that his last interview should not be published until after his death. He feared that he would have been silenced during his last days had he published his thoughts when he was still living.

It beggars belief that such a senior churchman was paralysed by fear – so much so that he wouldn't allow his true thoughts about the state of the Church be known in his lifetime. If his reflections had been revolutionary, we might understand his fears. On the contrary, his insights are shared by the vast majority of ordinary Catholics then and now.

The dying cardinal wanted the world to know that in his opinion, 'the Church is 200 years out of date'. Too many are too easily silenced by fear. Yet, he went on, we should be courageous because faith is the foundation of the Church. Faith should give us the courage and the confidence to overcome fear.' In his case, however, his fear of the Vatican bureaucracy was greater than his courage.

'The Church is tired in Europe and America. Our culture has aged, our churches are empty, our religious houses are empty and the bureaucracy of the Church increases; our rituals and our clothes are pompous ... We stand like the rich young man who went away sad when Jesus called him to make him a disciple.'

The dying cardinal revealed his frustrations in an interview with a fellow Jesuit, Georg Sporschill. The interview was 'a kind of spiritual testament' and was read and approved by Cardinal Martini some weeks before his death.

Cardinal Martini died in 2012 at the age of eighty-five after a long illness. He was everyone's favourite to replace John Paul II. Despite his obvious afflictions as a result of Parkinson's disease, he received a large number of votes at the conclave which elected Benedict XVI, before Martini withdrew his name.

The cardinal's last interview became a source of encouragement for those of us who long for renewal in the Church. 'The Church must admit its mistakes and begin a radical change, starting from the pope and the bishops. The paedophilia scandals oblige us to take a journey of transformation,' he told the daily paper he wrote for, Corriere della Sera.

I find it most disturbing that a cardinal, who was a revered Scripture scholar and amongst the most respected spiritual leaders in the world, felt he could not express his vision of the Church of the future freely for fear of being silenced by Vatican officials, most likely the CDF.

Without being egotistical about it, these were the kind of proposals I and others were suggesting and which did lead to censuring and silencing. Martini was correct; he would have been censured. That's what's wrong with the civil service of the Church. They seem not only to be out of touch, but they are all-powerful too.

It was not just a few outspoken Irish priests who were judged to be 'a danger to the faithful'. Anyone, even the most respected cardinal in the world, who proposes a compassionate vision of church, will be silenced. How can that be tolerated? It helps me to understand why there is simply so much sinister opposition to the man who actually did become the first Jesuit to be elected pope, Francis himself.

Martini proposed a threefold plan. Firstly, there must be conversion, which should 'follow a path of radical change … we must ask ourselves if people any longer listen to the advice of the Church on sexual matters.'

Secondly, we must immerse ourselves in the Word of God. 'The Second Vatican Council returned the Bible to Catholics. Only the person who perceives in his heart this Word can be part of Church renewal ... .'

Thirdly, the sacraments are essential for healing and spiritual growth. 'The sacraments are not instruments of discipline but a help for people on their journey and in the weaknesses of life ... are we carrying the sacraments to the people who need new strength?'

Agreeing that the Church supports the indissolubility of marriage, he went on to pose the question of what happens to a woman with children whose marriage breaks down and who meets a man who loves her and takes care of the children?

'If the parents are outside the Church, or do not feel the support of the Church, the Church will lose the next generation. Before receiving Communion we pray, "Lord I am not worthy". We know we are not worthy. Love is grace. Love is gift. The question of whether the divorced can take Communion should be turned around.'

Those are the considered last words of a dying cardinal who should have been pope and who loved our Church. Cardinal Martini was respected and loved by his people. He understood their needs and spoke for them.

Why then was he so afraid of 'the bureaucrats'? What has happened to the Second Vatican Council's beautiful, all embracing, 'People of God'? Where is Pope John XXIII's vision of respectful dialogue? What has become of our Church?

What is clear is that priests and people together must be more resolved than ever to speak the truth with clarity and in charity, whatever the consequences.

I, and others like me, must take courage from Cardinal Martini's final, despairing plea for a renewed and relevant Church. We owe it not only to the good cardinal, but even more so to the Church we love.

CHAPTER 8

DON'T SHOOT THE MESSENGER

People have the right to have their personal secrets and failures treated with respect. In fact, they are sacred. Because I'm a priest, confidentiality is even more important. I am not just referring to confessional secrets. As most people know, I must be prepared to die rather than reveal a penitent's confession.

I also have to be scrupulous about confidential information shared outside the confessional. The personal lives of showbiz friends, the crippling doubts of prominent politicians, as well as the mistakes of the famous and influential, will go to the grave with me.

Even in everyday life, a priest who boasts or has a loose tongue should never be trusted. One of the invaluable contributions priests and religious make to the community is our availability to listen to family and personal traumas, in the sure and certain knowledge they will never be talked about inappropriately. It's the main reason why I don't drink alcohol. I could never live with myself if I thought I might have even inadvertently revealed a single secret a person trusted me with. I like to be in control of my senses at all times.

That sense of confidentiality was one of the reasons I was often asked to mediate in business disputes, and, on at least four occasions, kidnappings. As far as the general public is concerned, they vaguely remember two of those cases. Those are the only two I can talk about here; the other two never became public and, as far as I am concerned, never will.

The first time my role became public was when a gravedigger in Mount Jerome cemetery in Dublin was kidnapped. Even in the late 1970s and early

1980s it was obvious that particular areas of Dublin were training grounds for future criminals.

The Kimmage/Crumlin area of the parish I looked after had some of the best people I ever worked with. But in one small corner of the district there were a couple of families who did their best to hold the entire area to ransom. I had a constant battle with them because their tactic was to move into the flatland area, take over the flats and drive all the good families out of them. That's precisely what was happening when I came to the parish. Day after day I would make contact with good families and day after day they would ask me to write letters to the Corporation to try to get them new houses in a better area. They didn't want their children to be contaminated by the criminal element.

Part of my job was to make friends with the criminals. They had their own code of honour and if I was to influence them at all, I had to at least get to know them. Almost instantly I realised that many of them were serving an apprenticeship to a bigger and better life in crime. Starting at the very bottom rung, young boys and girls of eleven and upwards began by robbing old ladies' handbags and breaking into their houses when they were out.

I began by arranging a meeting with the politicians and Gardaí of the area. I needed their help to break this cycle of crime.

When the youngsters had served their apprenticeship of petty crime, they moved up to more serious activities like robbing milkmen and shop owners. Right at the top were their older brothers, who used guns for the big stuff.

Within a six-month period I noticed that as the older criminals were caught and sent to jail, those below moved up a rung on the ladder and took their place. When those young men went to jail, it was like completing their university degree in crime. They came out skilled in all the tricks of the trade, which meant they moved up in the criminal world to become involved in the growing, city- wide drug trade.

Subsequently some of the leading criminals in Dublin came from that area and a few of them were well connected with Martin Cahill, the General. Those were the circumstances in which we had to try to build a community. The politicians understood the problem but it was difficult to get overworked

Gardaí interested. Security and the North were their priority.

By the time I was asked to intervene in a kidnapping I knew the local scene thoroughly.

The events surrounding the kidnapping have been well documented elsewhere but have largely been forgotten about. It was connected to the infamous robbery of O'Connor's jewellery factory in Harold's Cross in Dublin.

At the time I was not privy to all the details and didn't want to know them. On that occasion an amalgam of criminals and illegal groups came together to carry out the robbery. Millions of pounds worth of jewellery was stolen. For its time it was a daring escapade. The problem was that nobody knew where the loot went afterwards and for years much of it remained unaccounted for.

It appears that when the various criminal groups who carried out the robbery fell out among themselves one of the people alleged to have been involved in the robbery had a brother who was a gravedigger in Mount Jerome Cemetery. Mount Jerome is an ancient burial place with many mysterious and ornamental vaults. The rumour was that the goods taken in the O'Connor robbery were buried in one of the vaults. Which one? That was the question. They decided to kidnap the gravedigger they wrongly suspected of hiding the gold.

He had been missing for days when his family called a press conference pleading for information about the missing man. This particular family lived outside our parish but were well known to me. Usually I was the one they loved to hate. But they also knew that I could be trusted. So they asked me to allow my name go forward as the person the kidnappers would contact if they knew where their son was. I gave my word that I would do my best as long as it was within the law. They accepted that, too.

Over the next few days there were many phone calls to me claiming sightings of the missing man. I diligently passed each one of them onto the authorities. Most of them were just deliberate decoys. The gangs went on with their own peculiar form of civil war, including a shoot-out in the Phoenix Park. Each night, some of them called, allegedly to brief me on where the missing man might be.

Towards the end of the week there was an urgent message for me to take a call at the front door of the monastery. On the other end of the phone an anxious and distorted voice shouted a brief message at me: 'Your f**king friend is on the side of the road at the ballroom outside Limerick.' The phone was slammed down before I could ask a question. I knew from my showband experience that he must have been near the Jetland, so I phoned the Gardaí to tell them, not knowing whether he was dead or alive.

I went straight to the family to tell them to expect some news about their brother soon. While I was there news came through that indeed he had been found on the side of the road outside Limerick, alive but very distressed. The family gave me more credit than I deserved and their associates made a solemn promise to me that they would never rob cars in Mount Argus again, out of gratitude. There was honour among thieves in those days.

The next kidnapping that I was publicly involved in was much more high profile.

By the mid-1980s kidnapping the newly rich was providing an instant income for members of criminal and illegal groups. One of the most notorious was Dessie O'Hare from Armagh. By this time he had passed through the ranks of the Provisionals and the INLA and was a maverick criminal with a reputation for great cruelty.

He was released from jail in 2006 having served a mere twenty years of a forty-year jail sentence which was handed down to him for kidnapping and mutilating the Dublin dentist John O'Grady in 1987.

It's only appropriate to say now that I agreed with John O'Grady and the Darragh Family never to be too precise about the details of the kidnapping negotiations or the extraordinarily lucky release of John O'Grady. This is for two reasons. First, if the full story were ever to be told, John O'Grady was the only one who had the right to tell it. Sadly John is now dead.

Second, the less detail given, the better, because it might put wrong ideas into other criminals' heads.

John O'Grady should not have been kidnapped at all. The man O'Hare and his gang were looking for was Professor Austin Darragh, now also departed from this world.

At the time he was a high-profile businessman and medical doctor. He had bought Sir Patrick Dun's hospital and estimates of his wealth, in many millions, appeared in the papers. That's the first lesson to learn. The higher the estimates of your wealth, the more vulnerable you become. Austin Darragh was well known in sporting circles too. He was a commentator and rugby analyst in the early days of Radio Éireann. His son, Paul, who died far too young in 2005, was a hugely successful horseman as a member of the Irish Show Jumping Team.

The Darraghs once lived in a beautiful house in Foxrock, a wealthy suburb of Dublin, but in 1985 they moved from Foxrock to a new location on the Hill of Tara. Their daughter and son-in-law, John O'Grady, moved into their old house in Foxrock. So when O'Hare plotted to kidnap Austin he got the most basic fact wrong. He kidnapped the wrong man.

I was friendly with Austin Darragh through broadcasting, and when John O'Grady was kidnapped in the most horrific circumstances, I contacted the family to tell them I would help in any way possible.

As the days went by and the police closed in on the gang with their kidnap victim, O'Hare and his men became more and more volatile. They sent notes demanding a ransom of £1.5 million (the equivalent of €5 million today) for the release of John O'Grady. They left the notes in churches under statues – but tragically they got their saints mixed up. Valuable time was lost looking for ransom notes under the wrong statues in the wrong churches. O'Hare thought the Darragh family were ignoring his notes. In fact they never got them because of the gang's wrong directions.

However, on Wednesday, 4 November 1987 I got a call to attend an urgent meeting in Dr Darragh's office. When I went there it was obvious that it was now a race to find John O'Grady alive.

In one of the notes that was found eventually, O'Hare had enclosed two half fingers, one from each of John's hands. Later we discovered that the criminals chopped off the top half of both John's little fingers. They put a towel in his mouth, put a foot on his hand and with a hammer and chisel hacked off both little fingers at the middle knuckle. John, with his medical experience, knew that he could bleed to death. To cauterise his fingers and stop the bleeding, he was given a knife. He heated it on the bar of an electric fire and applied the hot knife to the stumps of his fingers to stop the bleeding. Even now, thinking about it sends shivers down my spine.

O'Hare then enclosed the severed tops of the fingers in the ransom note with the threat that if the money was not paid over by noon on 5 November, he would continue to chop off more of John's limbs.

O'Hare phoned the Gardaí to tell them what he had done and what he intended to do. 'I just sent word to my men to chop off his fingers ... I'll ring you later and tell you where to pick these fingers up, and the photographs and the note. It's just cost him two of his fingers. Now I'm going to chop him up in bits and pieces and send fresh lumps of him every f**king day if I don't get the money fast.'

This was the news that greeted me at the meeting. The family wanted to pay the money to ensure they got John back alive. By now they had been able to negotiate with the Bank of Ireland to get the money in the form requested – used sterling currency in £20 and £10 denominations. The money was to be brought to the Bank of Ireland in Dublin that evening. The family asked if I would bring the money to O'Hare and if possible negotiate the release of John O'Grady on Thursday, 5 November.

It was made clear to me that it would be a very dangerous operation, and indeed I was told by more than one Garda to be aware that I might not come out of it alive. Austin Darragh gave me an hour to think about it. I told him I didn't need an hour; I would do it provided the Gardaí knew what I was doing and that they would not accompany me or come near me during the negotiations. I wanted to do everything in a trustworthy way. They could carry out their investigations afterwards, but if they wanted me to help negotiate John's freedom, then I wanted to do it on my own. I felt it was the only chance of success I had. John O'Grady had a wife and young children. They needed him. I was a celibate bachelor with no dependants. This is one of the few times I found celibacy to be an advantage.

The principles were agreed. It was to be a top-secret operation and I was sent home to rest until the next morning. I told them I wouldn't be able to rest, as I had to go to Omagh that night. A senior Garda there went apoplectic. Wherever I was going, I certainly was not going to the North of Ireland through Monaghan – the heart of O'Hare's territory. I told him I had to.

At the time, I was begging around Ireland, practically on a nightly basis, to raise money to restore Mount Argus Monastery and Church. People were helping me to raise the money by running little functions. On 4 November 1987, Kathy Coll, the daughter of the legendary country singer Brian Coll, was holding her twenty-first birthday party in the GAA Centre in Omagh. She was inviting as many of her friends as she could and charging them £4 each, with the money going to Mount Argus. I told the Gardaí I had to be there. If I didn't go I would be letting the family down, but also people would be wondering what I was up to. The safest thing was to go.

So, at five o'clock that evening I headed for Omagh in the company of the Coggins family, who were friends of mine and of Brian Coll's. I couldn't tell them what was supposed to happen the next day.

As it turned out it was one of the worst nights of my life. There was a pea-soup fog. I hoped it would clear by the time we were coming home. But when the function was over and I was about to head back to Dublin, the fog was worse than ever. And so we started for home at midnight, saying many a Rosary along the way. The fog never relented and we arrived back at Mount Argus at four in the morning. I was due to be collected at half past five to be brought down to the Bank of Ireland to collect the ransom money.

I lay in bed for half an hour and then offered Mass in the little oratory that was the former bedroom of the then Father Charles of Mount Argus – now of course a canonised saint. In that room I said what I was convinced would be my last Mass. I decided not to dwell on it but just do what I had to and leave the rest to God. And so, early in the morning, a Garda car brought me to the Bank of Ireland.

There I had the first inkling of what £1.5 million looked like. There were seven suitcases full of money chained to the floor of an adapted estate car. I was escorted out to the Naas Road to beat the traffic and sent on my way with what was then the best mobile phone available. It was in a small suitcase on the seat beside me. They didn't know what range it would have. It died at the Green Isle Hotel, half a mile down the Naas road. And that was me on my own.

All the way down to Cork in the car I listened to stories about Eamonn Andrews. That was the day after his death and the two are indelibly linked in my mind. Eamonn was a man I knew very well and in fact I had been on a plane with him a couple of weeks previously to London. A chauffeur-driven car awaited him and he kindly took me with him into London. He often came to Mount Argus and I knew him well from the entertainment industry. So I was doubly sad.

A little way down the road I realised just how impossible the journey was going to be. I had thought of everything except how to go to the toilet. I was dying to go to the toilet but couldn't. Can you imagine leaving £1.5 million unguarded on the side of the road to go into a toilet? Can you imagine even stopping along the road anywhere? I visualised people jumping out of the hedge to hijack me – and the money!

Eventually, after passing through all those familiar towns on poor roads I arrived in Cork with an aching bladder. I followed the instructions I was given by the Gardaí. I was advised to fill the car with petrol because, most likely, when I arrived at the rendezvous, the Silver Springs Hotel, I would be asked to drive somewhere else. The plan was to keep me driving around the country until darkness fell. Then, it was assumed, I would be stopped on a quiet road somewhere and the money would be taken from me, if I was lucky. If things went wrong something worse would befall me.

When I pulled into the petrol station I was supposed to be anonymous. But the owner of the station came out to me and greeted me with the words, 'Are you on the way to meet O'Hare with the ransom?' I was stunned. Apparently somebody had leaked the story to The Irish Independent. They had it on its front page that I was on my way to hand over the money. I had every right to be anxious on the way to Cork.

At the petrol station everything went wrong. I couldn't get the petrol cap off the tank. I was in a state of panic because I was now ten minutes late to meet O'Hare. Visions of John O'Grady being shot because I couldn't get the cap off a petrol tank were etched on my mind. I had a small relic of Father Charles of Mount Argus with me to keep me safe and I quietly blessed the petrol cap with the relic, praying for guidance. Instantly the cap came off and I got my car filled with petrol.

Being ten minutes late proved to be a blessing in disguise. As I tuned into RTÉ Radio a newsflash came on The Mike Murphy Show that John O'Grady had been found in a house in Cabra, alive.

For a second I panicked. What was I to do with the money? In the instructions I was given, I was told not to go on a solo run. It was always best to keep to the plan. That's what I did. When I got to the Silver Springs, two groups of Gardaí were close to firing at each other. The Cork/Dublin rivalry was there in the Gardaí too and they didn't recognise each other from opposite sides of the car park. Eventually I shouted at them to put their guns down and they did. I went in to await a phone call, but I knew it would never come now. Instead I went to the toilet and had the sweetest pee of my life!

At this point the Gardaí left me stranded in Cork with £1.5 million. Someone advised me to drive back to Dublin. I wasn't going to do that and run the risk of it being taken from me. So I drove to a Garda station and handed them the keys of the car. Dr Darragh was on the phone to tell me to get the money to the bank as quickly as possible. Obviously with interest rates as they were in 1987, it was clocking up by the second. But the bank wouldn't take it from me either. Eventually I got somebody to take charge of the money by abandoning the car and the money at a Garda station; I went to Cork airport and flew up to Dublin.

This is probably the only funny incident in the whole event. The late Brendan Grace was a good friend of mine. His late mother, Chrissie, was also a friend of mine and I looked after her during her last weeks in Our Lady's Hospice in Harold's Cross. She said to Brendan she wanted me to conduct her funeral in Mount Argus.

Before heading off to Cork I had to phone Brendan and say I wouldn't be able to do the funeral; that he would understand why not the next day. He was none too pleased. Now that I was back in Dublin on time, I made sure to fulfil my promise and was there to receive her remains into Mount Argus.

It seemed that every television station in the world had cameras waiting for me all around Mount Argus car park to find out if I'd handed over the money. One sneaky reporter, a religious correspondent with one of the national dailies, thought he would get the inside track. As I was about to sprinkle holy water on the remains of the late Mrs Grace he literally door-stepped me from behind a pillar in the church porch. He appeared right in front of me. 'We know each other a long time, Brian,' he said, 'and I know you're busy, but tell me how much money was handed over to O'Hare?'

On the only occasion I can remember being deliberately rude, I put the funeral book across my face and said to him, 'Would you ever f**k off,' and continued, 'eternal rest grant unto her, O Lord, and may perpetual light shine upon her.'

Unfortunately for me, one of the other reporters heard this and news went around town like wildfire. It was taken in the right spirit, I'm glad to say, by everyone except the recipient, and I wasn't too worried about him anyway. He never spoke to me again.

After the funeral I got into the car and drove to Lisnaskea, County Fermanagh, where a local group had a function in the Ortine Hotel. I had handed over £1.5 million pounds that day and now went to Lisnaskea to collect £250 to help replace the roof on Mount Argus Church. The world is ill-divided.

John O'Grady's rescue in Cabra was a total accident. Sadly, one of the Gardaí on the case, Martin O'Connor, was seriously wounded in the shoot-out. Thankfully, he survived and for many years afterwards, every November 5th, John O'Grady, Martin O'Connor and I had lunch to celebrate the gift of life. But for the grace of God all three of us would have been dead.

O'Hare went on the run and for a couple of weeks was one of the most wanted criminals ever in Ireland. He was wanted for questioning in connection with at least twenty-seven killings (some say it's thirty-three), not to mention robberies and crimes on both sides of the border.

He was on the run for three weeks before he was stopped at an army checkpoint near Urlingford, County Kilkenny. There was a shoot-out. A soldier was wounded, as was O'Hare. The man with O'Hare, Martin Bryan, was shot dead. The Gardaí told me it was the third time an accomplice died while O'Hare survived.

I got another call, this time from the prison authorities, asking me to visit O'Hare's wife and inform her that her husband had been shot. I duly did so, prayed with her and consoled her as best I could. That was the last time I had any direct dealings with the O'Hares.

O'Hare was sentenced to forty years in prison but served only half of it when he was freed under the terms of the Good Friday Agreement.

For almost five years after the shoot-out I was constantly reminded of my role, not only by the papers but also by the fact that some of O'Hare's gang thought I had tried to double-cross them. Nothing could have been further from the truth but mischievous statements by an opposition politician could have given that impression.

The result was that every couple of months, especially if I was in the border regions, a mysterious Toyota Hiace van would pull alongside me, usually in the dark of night. It would neither pass me nor pull in behind me. It would just drive alongside me. The first few times it was absolutely scary. Usually, a few days later, some shady character would appear out of nowhere and walk beside me in a Dublin street or outside Mount Argus to remind me I was still on their hit list.

My car was once completely wrecked outside Mount Argus. On another occasion the two front wheels of my car had the bolts loosened on them. Luckily the Gardaí had warned me always to check the car. I was heading out to do an early morning broadcast on 2FM and I still shudder at what might have happened had I not checked the wheels. Who did it? Who knows? But the local Gardaí were convinced it was O'Hare's friends. Thankfully, as time went by they left me alone.

There is, however, one bizarre incident which indicates the strange mentality of those involved in serious crime as well as some strange customs in the Catholic Church.

As part of the beatification process of the then Father Charles of Mount Argus, (now Saint Charles) a delegation from the Vatican visited Mount Argus Church. They came to exhume the remains of Father Charles, which were in a sealed coffin inside a lead container and preserved at a shrine inside the church. The Vatican officials were joined by representatives from Dublin Archdiocese and the Passionists. As rector, I had to oversee the practical details of digging up and filling in. They took some bones with them to Rome to place in the authentic First Class Relics later.

It was a busy day as everything was carried out in secret. Photographers were allowed in when the process was complete.

By coincidence, my car had been vandalised and wrecked outside the front door of the monastery on the night before. Normally I might have kept it secret, but the photographers didn't miss the opportunity.

The result was that The Evening Herald had a story about the wrecked car. At that time the notorious criminal Martin Cahill, known as the General, was waging a campaign against the Gardaí. He was wrecking their private cars parked outside their homes.

The Herald put two and two together and, since Mount Argus was the official church for the Gardaí, concluded my car was vandalised as part of the same campaign. They headlined the story 'General wrecks Fr Brian's car'.

I was fairly sure that it was O'Hare's supporters and not the General who had vandalised it. Because I was busy at the exhumation, I was completely unaware of the Herald story.

When all was finished in the church, the receptionist called me to say that what she called 'two very sinister looking men' had come to the front door asking for me. She put them in a waiting room. As soon as I entered the room I recognised the General and an accomplice. Greetings were exchanged.

Martin Cahill spoke first. He was shocked that I would think he or his friends would touch my car. They knew me for years and even though we had our rows, if they needed spiritual help I also did what I could for them and for their families. He rattled off all the times they had called on me.

'We'd never touch your car. I thought you'd know that,' he said with a disappointing groan.

At that, he took out a huge wad of notes, removed an elastic band and peeled off hundreds of pounds. 'Take that and get your car fixed,' he demanded.

I could see the headline in the paper the next evening; 'General donates new car to Fr Brian'. I had to think quickly. I asked Martin and his friend to look me in the eye and tell me honestly if they had wrecked my car. They both denied any involvement and swore vengeance on anyone who would do such a thing.

'Then, if you didn't do it, why are you giving me money to replace it?' I asked. 'Offering me money is making me suspicious that you must have been involved. If you didn't do it I won't take your money.'

Cahill got the point and put his money back in his pocket, much to my relief. We chatted about other things for a while. Cahill said he often came to the shrine of Father Charles to ask for help. We shook hands and they left, pointing out the two Gardaí who were shadowing them everywhere they went.

'I feel safe when they're with me,' the General told me.

I felt safe when they'd all left. I paid for the car myself, knowing that O'Hare's gang were unlikely to do so.

At that time of the kidnapping I was so busy I didn't stop to reflect, but it had a devastating effect on me two years later when I eventually found time to think about it as I had to move from Mount Argus to Enniskillen.

That's another sad story. Three days after the journey to Cork, a bomb exploded at a Sunday morning Remembrance service in Enniskillen. The bomb was placed in a former school – a school I had attended thirty years previously. Both traumatic events coming together had a major impact on my life. As I say it was two years before I got time to process the hurt, the shock and the trauma. I was in Chicago on a refresher course.

I was on my own away from all the attention and the rush. I began to have vivid dreams of what could have happened. It was of course delayed shock as well as exhaustion. I found myself full of uncharacteristic anger. Then one night I realised why. I had been in a dangerous situation, which I know could have cost me my life. In my mind I had faced death more realistically than I imagined. In a way I was feeling guilty because I was alive – when I should have been grateful. But what bothered me most was that none of my brethren asked me how I felt about it. I know none of them intended this, but in my loneliness I interpreted their silence as indifference as to whether I lived or died! It wasn't really what they felt, just how it was perceived by me.

As Martin Luther King Jr said: 'At the end of the day, it is not the words of your enemies that you remember; it's the silence of your friends.'
John O'Grady never liked to speak about the kidnap or the mutilation of his hands. He made a good recovery and practised dentistry until his retirement. He was dentist to the Irish rugby team for years. He liked to live a quiet life but he was certainly traumatised, as any normal human being would after meeting such vicious criminals.

Martin O'Connor, the injured Garda, had to retire from the force. His colleague Henry Spring suffered a debilitating stroke in the wake of the kidnapping.

In 2012, to mark the Silver Jubilee of our escapade, Martin O'Connor, John O'Grady and I had dinner together. It was the first time we told the full story of our experiences to one another. I found it harrowing but helpful. John was unaware of the anguish we carried and we were horrified at what John had had to endure. We had each suffered in relative silence for a quarter of a century.

Later that evening we visited the other Garda involved, Henry Spring in his home and we thanked God and circumstances to have lived reasonably fulfilled lives despite a close encounter with evil incarnate.

At John's funeral a few years ago the few remaining participants sat quietly in different corners of the Church. We looked around and wondered if Dessie O'Hare would turn up.

He did, of course, turn up in a different, more familiar situation in 2015. According to reports he was part of a gang who held another family hostage on the outskirts of Dublin.

As a result, after thirteen years of freedom, during which he lived with his wife in a gated luxury property near Newtownhamilton in his native Armagh, he appeared in court towards the end of 2018.

Eventually he pleaded guilty to the charge and was sentenced by the Special Criminal Court to seven years in jail. That's where he is today.

CHAPTER 9

PAIN AND FORGIVENESS

'I bear no ill-will. I bear no grudge. Dirty sort of talk is not going to bring her back to life.' Those words changed Gordon Wilson from a God-fearing Methodist shopkeeper in Enniskillen into an international hero for the cause of peace. They were not cheap words because they cost him dearly, especially within his own community, something that pained him deeply.

I heard news of the awful bomb in Enniskillen, my home town, through a Sunday morning phone call from my brother. It was a few days after I'd been involved in the John O'Grady/Dessie O'Hare kidnapping, so I was at a low point anyway. Then this.

The bomb was planted in what was formerly a school, one which I'd attended as a boy, in a yard where I kicked football, threw snowballs, played cards, sneaked a cigarette and admired the girls going to Mount Lourdes convent school on the hill. It was a deliberate attack aimed at decent people remembering their dead, dead who themselves gave their lives in the cause of peace in the First World War. Could anything be more evil?

I had a picture of Gordon Wilson in my mind. As a boy, walking through Enniskillen to and from the bus, I passed his shop. Often a tall, thin man stood outside. I didn't know him then – in those days we didn't talk much to older people and certainly not to one from 'the other side'. He seemed a pleasant man, though, and, for a teenager, impressions endure.

When he gave the interview to BBC Radio Ulster, he had no intention of becoming a hero, or becoming a worldwide voice for peace. He was what he was – a sincere Christian, a grieving father, and a decent man.

It wasn't just Gordon himself; it was also the strength of his entire family, especially his wife. Joan's resilience has never been fully appreciated. She is a deeply spiritual and supportive woman. Gordon was at pains to point this out repeatedly in every conversation and in every interview I ever did with him.

I was lucky, on occasions, to visit Gordon and Joan in their home when I came back to Enniskillen a few years later. Indeed, he often came to see me in The Graan for a chat. It was always an uplifting experience, a real blessing.

The talk was never of violence and death but rather of the power of God's word to heal. I never came away from meeting the Wilsons without feeling refreshed in a deeply spiritual way. Joan was and is a rock of faith. She had to endure even more tragedy when Gordon died.

As a couple they steadfastly believed in God's care, even though it hadn't been easy for them to recognise His presence.

We know about Marie's terrible death in the Enniskillen bomb in 1987. We also remember that tragedy struck again when her brother, Peter, was killed in a car accident. On that morning I was in South Africa and could only speak to the family on the phone. When Gordon himself died so suddenly and so quietly, he left a huge vacuum in all our lives.

Many memories of Gordon come back to me. One that remains vivid takes me back to the BBC studios in Enniskillen. I was doing an extended forty-five-minute interview with Gordon for my series 'Be My Guest'. As always, he was inspiring, in a quiet, common-sense sort of way. The interview was due for transmission a week later.

When we finished, Gordon called me aside. He asked for prayers, sincere prayers, as he was about to meet leading members of the Provisional IRA later in the afternoon. He also apologised, and this is the measure of the man, that he wasn't able to speak about it on the tape, and therefore made the interview out of date before it was transmitted.

After their meeting I met Gordon and I rarely saw him so dejected. Not only had he taken a huge risk by talking to the same organisation that had murdered his lovely daughter, but he also risked losing many of his lifelong friends who were not so forgiving as he was. Worse still, when he met the IRA, Gordon felt they demeaned him and dismissed him without the courtesy of a decent discussion. It broke his spirit. He was devastated.

All I could say to him was that perhaps they were bluffing and that his arguments got through to them more effectively than they were prepared to admit. I was clutching at straws but I knew from experience that was how they worked.

Some years later when the IRA ceasefire was eventually called, I reminded Gordon that God often brings new life from dark moments. He understood then that his dialogue with the Provisionals was more fruitful then he realised.

He loved Enniskillen, though he was born in County Leitrim. In bad times he did think of leaving his adopted town on more than one occasion because of bigotry. He told me in one of his last interviews that he thought of moving to Scotland, but couldn't contemplate life away from Fermanagh.

Gordon was a wise and politically alert man. He was a thinking man, not just a reactive, emotional man. Sometimes he pondered too long before he acted. His gut reaction was often lost as he pondered the possible interpretations of every word said and every deed done.

Probably the bravest thing he ever did was to take a seat in the Irish Senate. That made him vulnerable to cheap, personal attacks from the hard-line Unionists.

At Gordon's funeral the whole world mourned him, but apparently many of those in the Unionist Party did not. That is to their eternal shame. The paucity of official Unionist representation at his funeral was a scandal. Such a good man deserved better treatment from his own people.

I learned a crucial lesson about forgiveness from Gordon. One day in a peaceful conversation I asked him if he ever regretted his message of forgiveness on the night of Marie's murder. This is what he confided to me. He said that every night before sleeping he prayed to God to be able to forgive her killers again in the morning. Forgiveness was not a once-off decision but an ongoing daily decision that depended on God's grace and his acceptance of that grace. It was worth knowing Gordon for that insight alone.

Gordon Wilson, a Protestant from Leitrim, was catapulted by violence into the glare of publicity and he became a symbol of redemptive suffering. That's what made him an ordinary hero. He was no saint because, by his own admission, he was anxious, impatient, conservative and reluctant to change. Yet those are the saints I love, saints who have to struggle. No one can deny that the Wilsons struggled, but their struggles were not in vain.

Enniskillen and Omagh, two towns where I went to school, became synonymous with the evil of violence. Both bombings were so awful that they made decent people work even harder for peace. A crucial combination in bringing peace closer was the coming together of Hume, Adams, Reynolds and Major. For his part, Albert Reynolds would claim that President Bill Clinton was just as important as the others were.

I always liked Bill Clinton. I met him for the first time when he came to Belfast to encourage the peace process on a December day in the late 1990s. I'd known that Clinton was both brilliant and affable from talking to Albert Reynolds.

Albert recognised at once that Bill Clinton was really sincere in trying to bring peace to the North of Ireland. The President, like Albert, was willing to take risks, and Clinton more than once went against his political advisors, because he trusted Albert, to talk to Sinn Féin, who in turn could deliver the Provisionals. President Clinton ensured that the right people got to America to call off the dogs of war, even though it displeased the British government. He did it anyway, in the interests of peace.

For a politician who had tenuous connections with Ireland, he gave peace here a worldwide profile as well as top priority in his own schedule.

Clinton was a charismatic politician, as I witnessed at first hand when he came to Enniskillen to open the Clinton Centre. The centre is built on the site of the school where the Cenotaph bomb killed so many innocent people, including Marie Wilson, in 1987. It was named after Bill Clinton because of his part in the peace process. He visited it twice and I met him on both occasions. He impressed me each time. On his first visit he had work to do to win over his audience.

It was plain many of them didn't like him. They didn't want to condone his lifestyle outside of politics. When he entered the room many were silently hostile to him. He went to the podium and spoke eloquently without notes for twenty minutes. He surprised us all by admitting he'd made many mistakes as president but one in particular haunted him. He hadn't intervened in Rwanda to prevent the murder of hundreds of thousands of innocent people there. He admitted that as president he could have and should have intervened. It was an error of judgement which filled him with remorse. He was prepared to admit his mistake. He promised he and Hillary would work with Rwandans in the cause of peace and reconciliation.

They had just been to Rwanda to attend a groundbreaking conference at which both Hutus and Tutsis were present. They sat around in a large circle. Bill sat opposite Hillary. Of all the people in the circle there was only one person who was not disfigured, apart from the Clintons. Most of them were missing limbs, had badly scarred faces, no ears – all physically mutilated. He admitted he'd been shocked by the seriousness of their mutilation. All of them told their story of what happened. Each of them was determined it should never be allowed to happen again.

There was one extraordinarily good-looking woman in the circle. It puzzled observers that she seemed to have no disfigurement. When it came her turn to speak, everyone wondered why she was there at all. It transpired that she, her husband and their children were attacked by people who had lived in their village all their lives. They slashed her husband and children until they were dead. Then they slashed her back until they thought she was dead.

After the attackers left, she came to and saw the mutilated bodies of her entire family beside her. She was so angry with God because she was alive. She couldn't understand how God could be so cruel to leave her alive when she was so badly mutilated and when her entire family was dead.

She was brought to hospital and spent months recovering from her ordeal. Not surprisingly, she suffered a nervous breakdown. During her recuperation she concluded that God must have saved her for a reason.

She believed that the reason she was saved was because God wanted her to tell her story to anyone who would listen, to ensure that such murders would never happen again. The woman with no visible injuries then revealed her back, mutilated beyond belief. Clinton promised he would tell her story wherever he went.

The audience in Enniskillen was beginning to warm to him now. There were tears in his eyes as he told the story.

Despite his reputation, Clinton was a leader I would trust more than George W Bush or any President who followed him. He left a positive mark in Northern Ireland; I had to reassess my views about him; he was the most impressive communicator I ever met.

CHAPTER 10

FIFTY YEARS OF THE JIMMY MAGEE ALL-STARS

Support for worthy causes has always been a part of the Irish psyche. For fifty years the Jimmy Magee All-Stars were Ireland's most enduring band of brothers raising millions for charity. I was a member of the All-Stars since 1972 – a few years after I was ordained a priest – and remained with them for forty-three years. The experience made me the priest I am. Mixing with them and with the people they helped taught me about life, about people, about generosity and above all, genuine humility.

There were no stars in the All-Stars. I am forever grateful to those friends who kept me in touch with the real world. Every summer, we travelled the length and breadth of Ireland; we played a fun football match with some local celebrities, and then put on an All-Star concert organised in aid of a local charity. We had fun; they made money.

The Jimmy Magee All-Stars were drawn from well-known footballers, famous singers and not-so-famous performers from the world of entertainment; anyone in the public eye willing to make a fool of themselves on the football field was welcome. Every single penny earned went directly to the charity. None of us took any expenses. In all those fifty years we never handled money nor did we wish to.

We were well enough known and appreciated to be officially honoured by two presidents of Ireland, Mary McAleese and Michael D. Higgins. President Higgins invited the remnants of the All-Stars to a reception at Áras an Uachtaráin. We were all delighted, but none more so than Jimmy Magee himself, who had been the reason we stuck together for fifty years. 'They said it wouldn't last a week and they were right; it's lasted fifty years,' Jimmy was fond of saying.

Jimmy Magee, in 1966, organised a group of radio and television All-Stars along with the best known Irish showbands, including Brendan Bowyer, Larry Cunningham, Dickie Rock, Brendan Shine, Joe Dolan, Doc Carroll, Butch Moore, Declan Nerney, Philomena Begley, Frank McCaffrey, Gene Stuart, Ronan Collins and everybody who was anybody in the Irish entertainment world.

Their very first meeting, organised by the late Connie Lynch, was held on 6 June 1966 in Ballyjamesduff in County Cavan. The meeting was followed by a cabaret in the local St Joseph's Hall. The idea was to bring sporting legends from all sports together to play a Gaelic football match.

We were blessed that the biggest names in soccer and rugby, boxing legends and football and hurling heroes, all gladly turned up week after week. In the 1960s there was a ban in place in the official GAA rule book which meant that only GAA players could take part in GAA matches. But the Jimmy Magee All-Stars brought everybody together to support good causes. It was the only sporting event that was able to do that until the ban was rescinded. The Jimmy Magee All-Stars were sporting ecumenists in those days.

When we met we played mainly local sporting heroes who came out of retirement for the night. The Galway three-in-a-row team, the Kerry four-in-a-row team and, indeed, that Offaly team that stopped them being a five-in-a-row team, supplied many wonderful players for the Jimmy Magee All-Stars, including Seamus Darby, the man who scored the goal that broke Kerry hearts as they failed to make it five in a row.

Dublin legends Sean Doherty, Paddy Cullen, Gay O'Driscoll and Jimmy Keaveney; Galway stars Johnny Hughes, Mattie McDonagh, and Tommy Gilmore, as well as Jack O'Shea and Mick O'Connell from Kerry, not forgetting Paddy McCormack, Brendan Lowry (Shane Lowry's father) and Greg Hughes from Offaly. Among the other legends, soccer star Mick Leech and Meath great Frankie Byrne shone.

On the evening of 6 June 1966 the traffic in Ballyjamesduff was brought to a standstill as thousands of people flocked to the town to see their heroes.

Fifty years later, on Monday, 6 June 2016, we went back to Cavan to relive those memories one more time and met for Mass, fun and a cabaret in the Kilmore Hotel, Cavan. Jimmy Magee was there, as proud as punch. There was no football match that night – for obvious reasons. There weren't enough oxygen tents in the whole of Ulster to keep us alive.

Among the artists appearing on that Golden Jubilee All-Stars were the marvellous Daniel O'Donnell, Queen of Country Philomena Begley, The Indians, Matt Leavey, Johnny Peters, George Hunter, Billy Joyce, Kathy Durkin, Joe Doherty, Pascal Brennan, Frankie Kilbride, Harry Rambsbottom, the Conquerors and countless others. All the proceeds from the event went to the Irish Motor Neurone Disease Association (IMNDA) and Cystic Fibrosis Ireland – Cavan Branch.

Later we told tall stories of how we went on massive tours to Switzerland, Britain and, on a number of occasions, to the United States of America, including Las Vegas.

Over the years Father Cleary (now deceased) and I offered Masses for the group. They were the funniest and perhaps the most sincere Masses of my life. They were usually in hotel rooms and other places but hardly ever in a church. Jamsie O'Donnell – Daniel's brother – always ended up preaching to the converted.

For me the Jimmy Magee All-Stars became a way of life that kept me fit and in touch with reality. I learned far more wisdom from those guys than I did from any book of theology. In the toughest of times they remained my closest friends.

CHAPTER 11

TRIBUTE TO JIMMY MAGEE

On 22 September 2017 a massive cross-section of Irish society gathered in Kilmacud Church, Dublin, to offer the funeral Mass and mourn the passing of a true legend and a lifelong friend – Jimmy Magee. Losing friends like Jimmy means that life will never be the same again.

In years past Jimmy himself had been there as we did the same for his lovely wife Marie. Then, tragically, Jimmy spoke movingly and unforgettably at the funeral rites for his son Paul, who died so young from Motor Neurone Disease. Same church; same family; three wonderful people.

But this was different. The Memory Man was gone. It was now our turn to share some of the memories that Jimmy himself created.

I remember sharing with the overflowing congregation in Kilmacud a thought inspired by the great Kerry poet Brendan Kennelly. When the poet's father died, Kennelly, displaying his artist's soul, wrote about his own memory of his father. He pictured him dancing on the flagstones of the kitchen floor in their Kerry home, whistling a tune that was echoed by the rhythm of his dancing feet. He was dancing to his own music, and, as Kennelly concluded: 'Always in tune with himself'.

Kennelly then gave us the key to unlock the door of hope; as long as a man's memory lives a man will never die. Intriguingly, Brendan himself told me that was why the good Lord himself commanded us, on the night before he died, 'Do this in memory of me'.

It was impossible to accept now we were offering that self-same Mass for the Memory Man and doing it in memory of Jimmy.

Some symbols of Jimmy's life were carried to the altar before Mass. His family could have carried a cartload of symbols and still not have captured the essence of this extraordinary man who was loved by the nation. These are some of the memories his children had of their famous father:

First, they carried a picture of a dashing young man with a microphone in his hand. That was Jimmy Magee, the disc jockey.

Then they brought up a parchment he had received from the International Olympic Committee. It was to recognise that he had served as a working journalist for a record eleven Summer Olympics.

Inevitably one of his grandchildren brought up a pair of boxing gloves. Of all the sports that Jimmy did, soccer and boxing stood out. But Jimmy was an enthusiastic fan of all sports. He often said the greatest day in his broadcasting career was covering the All-Ireland final live for UTV. That completed the journey from an innocent boy in his back garden in County Louth pretending he was Mícheál Ó Hehir, kicking the ball and commentating on it up and down the garden, playing his own All-Ireland.

Another of his family carried a special broadcasting award that RTÉ had presented to Jimmy. It was the Mick Doyle Golden Memory Award. Jimmy had given his life to RTÉ and was often taken for granted there too.

There were, of course, the books that he had written, particularly his autobiography. And, finally, there was a small Stars and Stripes flag, symbolising the place of his birth, New York.

There were so many poignant memories of the Memory Man himself. Jimmy was, of course, an entertainer, a writer, a broadcaster, but the two sides that weren't always obvious to the public were his love of family and his enduring faith in a merciful God.

A couple of weeks before Jimmy died a special meal was arranged at the County Club in Dunshaughlin in County Meath. It was organised by Seán Reilly and Brian Peters. Seán was a lifelong friend of Jimmy's and probably the man Jimmy trusted most in life. Jimmy loved music and not many know he was the person who compiled the first ever Top Ten to be broadcast on RTÉ. Seán and he had shared a small office in Lombard Street in Dublin where both of them worked for Release Records and managed the mighty bands of the era, including Larry Cunningham.

Seán went on to manage Daniel O'Donnell and bring him to the pinnacle of his career as a world-class star. He, too, had retired a few weeks earlier. Brian Peters was the inspiration behind the meal and the one who ensured that his chef had a meal that pleased Jimmy, and that was no easy task. I was lucky to be there too, and we chatted about our friendship and life and solved the problems of the world over a most beautiful lunch. Little did we know it was to be our Last Supper.

It was a wonderful conversation and we completed a virtual tour of the hotels Jimmy stayed in, the flights he took, the meals he enjoyed and the people that he met. For Jimmy everyone was a person of interest. He thought as much of the amateur boxer in the National Stadium as he did of his hero Mohammed Ali. He got as excited about an awkward corner-forward playing for or against the Jimmy Magee All-Stars as he did about an eight times All-Ireland winner who played in the same team. That was Jimmy. He had a story about every person he met because he was interested in every person he met. Jimmy's life was about people, about joy, sport and decency.

He was as proud of the fact that he was born in New York as he was of being reared in Cooley in County Louth. When he was fifteen his father died. His mother wanted him to be a pharmacist, but he ended up working for the railway so that he could support the family. That took him eventually to Dublin where he met and married Marie Gallagher, and they had five children – Paul, Linda, June, Patricia and Mark.

Jimmy wrote for The Sunday World for forty-three years, and never missed a Sunday. As it happens I've gone one better this summer when I began my forty-fourth year in The Sunday World. Since Jimmy died it's getting lonely at the top.

Jimmy witnessed the greatest sporting events in Ireland and in the world and could recount them with perfect accuracy and from a unique angle – his great gift as an observer of humanity. A conversation with Jimmy inevitably rolled back those years and uncovered Gaelic games, soccer, rugby, boxing, athletics, anything that was ever called a sport. He was unquestionably addicted to sport.

Jimmy lived the events he commentated upon. Who will ever forget the Atlanta Olympics when, as John Treacy came in to claim his silver, on the run-in, off the top of his head, Jimmy reeled off every single Irish person who had ever won an Olympic medal?

In his life he covered over 200 international soccer matches, thirty European Cup finals and every Olympics from 1972 to 2012. If ever there was a man who embodied Irish sport it was Jimmy Magee.

He made his knowledge and his connections in sport count. On 6 June 1966 (6/6/66) he founded his All-Stars. Over the years we played 250 matches and were never beaten. We never won either because all the matches ended in a draw. The important thing was that we raised millions for charity in every one of the thirty-two counties of Ireland.

Jimmy was the first to bring ecumenism to sport. He knew every single Irish entertainer personally and through their pulling power the matches and concerts drew the crowds to have fun and make money. He also brought stars from Gaelic football, hurling, soccer, rugby and boxing on to his All-Stars. We all played Gaelic football for fun, though if you didn't pass the ball to Jimmy, you soon realised it wasn't that much fun.

Jimmy had a devilish sense of humour that was pointed but never hurtful. For many years I wore the Number 7 jersey on the Jimmy Magee All-Stars football team. And for every one of those matches I was introduced in the following way: 'And when great left-half backs of the GAA are mentioned, there won't be a bloody word about Brian D'Arcy.'

Of course he also sent himself up. On one occasion he interviewed Spike Milligan. Spike was notoriously difficult to interview. Jimmy opened the conversation. 'It's great to have you here, Spike. You're welcome to Ireland.' To which Spike answered, 'On a day like today you're welcome to Ireland.'

Jimmy also interviewed the great Ella Fitzgerald, whom he regarded as the greatest jazz singer who ever lived. He was working for the sponsored programme called The Glen Abbey Show. He began the interview with, 'Ella, you're welcome to The Glen Abbey Show.' To which Ella replied, 'I'm very pleased to meet you, Glen'.

It is true Jimmy was blessed with a great memory. Thankfully he died whilst his memory was still intact, though he recognised that it was just beginning to fade. The fact is Jimmy had a good memory because he worked tirelessly gathering facts. He had a voracious appetite for sporting facts and trivia. I can honestly say that in all the years we travelled the country together, I never witnessed him being beaten by a fair question. He often reminded me of Goldsmith's famous poem: 'And still the wonder grew that one small head could carry all he knew.'

Jimmy was a man of faith. He was philosophical, and although he didn't overpower you with his religious beliefs, he was never afraid to state them when asked. A couple of times a year when the All-Stars met, we always began with a Mass. We said Mass everywhere and anywhere except in a church. We laughed, we chatted, we encouraged and, most of all, we got to know loving people who needed forgiveness from a loving God.

Jimmy was extraordinarily lucky in that he had a family who adored him and fans who respected him. Like many of us men, he wasn't good at caring for himself. But he had friends who cared for him with love and friendship.

It's sad when a legend dies. And it was sad when Jimmy departed. But there is a time for everything and even Jimmy knew that it was time for him to go. He was still working; he was still lucid; still independent; his work was done; he fought the good fight and was not found wanting.

I was lucky to share the stage of life with a friend, a father, a special human being, a brilliant, unique, gentle man. And there's only one description of Jimmy – different class – as he once famously said about Maradona.

With stories like these we'll never forget the Memory Man who left us so many beautiful memories.

CHAPTER 12

GOOD FRIENDS - My Brother Gaby

I have lost many good friends since I wrote the first part of my memoir in 2006. In fact, I sometimes say that if I don't die soon there will nobody left to come to my funeral. Not that it will matter much to me.

When I looked at the photographs of the launch of 'a Different journey' which took place 13 years ago, I was shocked at the number of close friends who have died since.

Jim Aiken. Dermot O'Brien. Albert Reynolds, Joe Dolan, Tony Loughman, Big Tom, Frankie Byrne, Jimmy Magee, Bill O'Donovan, Larry Cunningham, Nelius O'Connell and dozens more too numerous to mention. Whilst I was proof-reading this book, Arthur Ryan, Brendan Grace, Seamus McMahon (from Big Tom's band) and the lovely Danika Mc Guigan all left us for a better place.

When I think about friends from Mount Argus and The Graan I become sad; so many have just slipped away so quietly.

Close friends who die leave a hole the heart. I really appreciate friends, even when I'm not always in touch with them.

Naturally family members affect us even more; maybe that is why the biggest shock of all was the sudden death of my brother Gaby. Sudden death has become the norm for the male members of my family.

Both my father and my brother were exactly seventy years of age when they died. Neither of them got any warning. My father was working on the very day he died and was in the best of health. He dropped off watching Saturday night football on television.

My brother's death had many similarities. He was in the best of health, still active and, in fact, had bought a new pair of working boots the day he died. It was October, winter was coming and he was preparing for the wet weather.

His sudden death was a massive shock for our whole family, but particularly for his wife Maura and their two sons Desmond and Gerald. I got a phone call from Gerald in the middle of the night telling me to go to the hospital in Enniskillen because Gaby was having a heart attack. Maura realised that Gaby was having a bad turn and was not responsive. She called her sons, who both live nearby. An ambulance was called immediately, but it was too late, and by the time it got there the crew was unable to resuscitate him.

Meanwhile, I went to the hospital and searched everywhere for Gaby. I knew the staff well so they told me he had died at home and I went out to Gaby and Maura's home in Bellanaleck. My only brother was dead.

Personal bereavement takes time to penetrate. When sudden death happens, most of us are protected by shock, which mercifully numbs awareness. We slip into automatic mode. There are so many arrangements to make, so many plans to think of. That is what we all did.

It's truly amazing how news travels in a country district. By six o'clock the next morning the whole countryside arrived at my brother's house. It was as if they were waiting for it to happen. Without thinking they took over. They looked after us, did all the heavy lifting and allowed us all to get our thoughts and our plans together. That's community.

My brother was involved in most things that happened in his local community. He was involved with the GAA, with his parish, with a community centre, card games on a Saturday night and anything else that happened.

The area I come from is blessed with many journalists. Apart from myself, there is Martin O'Brien, Irish News, Irish Catholic and BBC Northern Ireland. Derek Thornton has made numerous successful documentaries; Marion Maxwell is a historian and writer and her sister Jennifer was a BBC producer. Then there is a famous family of journalists, the MacConnells. Cormac, Sean and Michael were full-time journalists for their entire lives and are recognised all over Ireland as brilliant, insightful and gifted writers of prose and of songs. Cormac wrote 'Silent Night, Christmas 1914', and Michael has a barrow-load of popular songs, including 'Only Our Rivers Run Free'.

In the old days we played football together, hunted rabbits and served Mass for the bishop, no less. Cormac once wrote that Gaby was far more suited to the priesthood than I was. He was right, of course. Gaby was quiet, gentle, thoughtful and gentlemanly, especially on the football field. The MacConnells rightly held that I could be as stubborn as a mule on the football field.

I was the younger brother who was more like my father in that I played football reasonably well, even though I would never be as good as my father was. Who is? Gaby was more a volunteer than a player. He was the club chairman and an ardent supporter of our local team Bellanaleck. He encouraged youth by supporting the coaches in the club who brought young players through. Their groundwork is now producing a host of top-class players for our rural club and for the Fermanagh county team.

The GAA would do well to remember that the dedicated club volunteers are the soul of the organisation, not the paid professionals higher up the administrative ladder.

Gaby was also one of the many dedicated lay people who supported the parish priest day and daily. He knew everyone in the area because he spent his entire life there. If a visitor wanted to find a grave of a long deceased relative, he knew in which plot that particular family buried their dead.

Every area is blessed with men and women like Gaby who love their community. They leave a legacy of generosity, good neighbourliness and decency behind them. They hand on practical faith and good customs and they watch their children take up the mantle of quiet leadership as they themselves grow older and wiser.

If such a spirit of community didn't already exist, it would have to be invented.

Gaby's involvement in his local area was the reason the entire community came together in an instant as soon as news of his death spread. They showed their respect through their generosity. Everybody in the community seemed to know their place. Tea and sandwiches were made, extra stools to sit on were stacked up, boxes of biscuits were unwrapped and, most of all, a willing army of helpers dug the grave, organised the house for the wake and distributed hi-vis vests to the people directing traffic. They kept going for three days non-stop and the family was able to get on with the grieving, unwittingly allowing the community to take care of them.

I hadn't noticed it before because in other cases I would have been part of that army who automatically helped out. Now, on the receiving end of it, it was humbling, consoling and extraordinarily helpful to the grieving process.

A huge crowd came to the wake, to the removal and to the funeral. So many of my friends from journalism, entertainment and football, especially the Jimmy Magee All-Stars, as well as my Passionist brothers and priest friends, all made heroic efforts to be there and I will never forget it. When someone is helpful in times of trouble, especially in bereavement, they will never be forgotten. It's also true that a harsh word when we're vulnerable will never be forgiven.

For a priest, presiding at family funerals is the most difficult of all. Without a doubt the saddest funeral I have ever had to do was when my nephew Brian died at five years of age. I just about stumbled through it. Somehow we get strength when it's most needed.

I wasn't ordained when my mother died. All I remember about that funeral was helping to collect the offerings. Offerings are, thankfully, long gone. But when I was a youngster, they were the talk of the country, particularly north of Dublin.

As far as I can remember the custom of collecting funeral offerings during the Mass started out as a charitable gift to the family of the bereaved. During the Great Famine so many people died, and the people were so poor, that the community made a reasonable money offering to help the family pay for the funeral expenses. As time passed, families were better off and didn't want to take the money for themselves. Instead they handed the money over to the clergy. The clergy naturally kept the tradition going for well over a hundred years.

My mother died in 1965. On that occasion I was assigned to stand with the priest and the undertaker at a table inside the altar rails. Those who attended the funeral lined up as if receiving communion, and left their offering on the table. The priest then called out the name of the donor and the amount given. It was awful. It was presumed that the priest, the family member and the undertaker would know everyone present without having to ask for names. But if a stranger came to throw down his few shillings, he would be asked for his name and address and that information would be announced – along with the amount he contributed.

Everyone went back to their seats and waited to hear the amount 'made' on the dead person. When the people finished making their contribution, the money was gathered up in a large tablecloth and brought into the sacristy. It was counted, added up and taken away. The priest then came to the altar rails and announced: 'The amount taken up at the funeral of Mrs D'Arcy was the sum of … '.

Next day the talk would be how much they 'went' for. A large sum meant the person was popular; a small sum indicated the person had few friends or relatives left. If a person missed the funeral, they could leave an envelope with the priest and he would read it out at Mass on Sunday when the new total was announced.

The fact that I remember nothing of my mother's funeral Mass, other than the offerings, shows what a brutal, awful system it was. A custom that began as a Christian act of charity ended up like a cattle mart. Thankfully, offerings disappeared in the 1970s.

By the time my brother died everyone had found better ways to show their appreciation. It is funny that at the time of the funeral you can remember almost everyone who shook hands with you.

I notice in city areas wakes and community funerals are not what they used to be. However, I am glad to say that in most rural areas a funeral is a time to grieve with the family and to console them in their great loss. I believe that if we didn't already have the Irish wake, American counsellors would create it. It's the best possible process to ignite healthy grieving.

Wakes and funerals bring out the best in a caring community, allowing neighbours to wrap a blanket of love around their broken-hearted friends.

For me, though, there is a more obvious lesson to be learned from grieving communities. In times of crisis, people know exactly what has to be done; they know their own role and they are not afraid to just do it; they don't ask the priest or anyone else what should be done or what is allowed. They carry out their tasks and responsibilities themselves.

When are we going to realise that this is the Church in action? This is the living community practising their living faith. This is 'love your neighbour' spirituality at its very best.

In my view there is no reason for us to fret about what will happen when there are fewer priests. The people, led by the Spirit, will mature and grow, will take their Church back into their own hands, and will build a stronger community-based faith from the roots up.

I just wish I were young enough to be part of it.

CHAPTER 13

IAN PAISLEY

Patriotism is not a short and frenzied outburst of emotion but the tranquil and steady dedication of a lifetime.' Those words from Adlai Stevenson, the former United States ambassador to the United Nations and one of John F. Kennedy's political advisers, came instantly to mind when I heard of the death of Dr Ian Paisley.

Over the years I met most of the Paisley family socially and professionally. I worked on radio and television with Ian Junior and Rhonda.

The first radio programme was a series I hosted for BBC Radio Ulster called Be My Guest. We had great fun, good chat and plenty of good-humoured jibes. It was a major surprise to the suits in the BBC that a priest and the Paisleys even sat in the same studio.

The next time I met Rhonda was in very different circumstances. She is a talented artist, an innovative writer and an effective communicator. Some years after the programme, she contacted me again. She had been selected to research and collate an exhibition of religious objects and symbols from different religious traditions in Northern Ireland. When completed it would help each group to respect and understand symbols which, up till then, had been a source of division.

She went about her research with enthusiasm. When she contacted me she was getting co-operation from the main Protestant churches and groups but was unable to make contact with a Catholic diocese that would loan her religious artefacts to display at the exhibition. I invited her to lunch with me at The Graan monastery in Enniskillen. We had a friendly and useful conversation about her project. I thought it was a great idea and agreed to help in any way I could. It turned out to be a successful exhibition and was well publicised. When it ended we met again and true to form she handed back everything I gave her in pristine condition.

Later Rhonda wrote and published children's books based on the Bible. She invited me to the launch in Martyr's Memorial, the Free Presbyterian Church in Belfast. Of course I went along. I was nervous because in those days ecumenism wasn't high on anyone's list.

The Paisley family welcomed me; Doctor Ian introduced Eileen, his wife, who said she had 'a crow to pluck with me'. I was relieved to learn that her only complaint was the day and time of my programme on Radio Ulster. It clashed with the times of their church services. Could I not change it to a more suitable time? I jokingly replied that if I did that 'the Catholics would never forgive me'. She enjoyed the joke.

Ian and I continued to send each other books we'd written and we exchanged Christmas wishes each year. It was no surprise at all to me that Ian and Martin McGuinness got on so well in Stormont. Chuckling came naturally to both men.

It was, however, sad to see how Ian Paisley's own church and his own political party treated him for doing what God and any sensible person would expect him to do, namely share power and bring peace and prosperity to the long-suffering people they represented.

When he died, BBC Radio Ulster asked me to deliver 'Thought for the Day' the next morning.

'The steady dedication of a lifetime led him – and us – down both frenzied and tranquil pathways,' I began. 'Dr Paisley led a full and complex life as a minister of religion, a powerful politician and a loving family man. It will be his family who will miss him most in the weeks and years ahead. There have been many judgements made about the man and the politician since he died. However, Ian Paisley stoutly "Preached Christ crucified" in season and out of season.

'He believed in the certainty of Resurrection. For him God's judgement is the only one that matters and God is a merciful judge. "When God acquits, can anyone condemn?" St Paul assured the Romans (8:35). None of us should be judged by our worst, or indeed our best, actions but somewhere in between.

'For those of us living in Northern Ireland, life has been a roller-coaster struggle for more than fifty years. Deep down we knew that nothing – good or evil – lasts for ever. "Peace came dropping slow"; we knew that only monumental change would break the cycle of hate. In the end, the longed-for change provided the hope that melted our despair. There is no shortcut to any place worth going.'

I explained how Dr Paisley once gave me a copy of the book he wrote whilst imprisoned in Crumlin Road. It was a biblical study of the letter to the Romans. His personal dedication to me on the fly-leaf ended with this reference: Ephesians 6:19 'Pray for me … that I may fearlessly make known the mystery of the Gospel.'

'Ultimately, the Gospel challenges everyone to change and live differently,' I concluded.

'John Henry Newman put it best when he wrote: "To live is to change and to be perfect is to have changed often."

'Ian Paisley changed much during his long life. For that we should be grateful to him – and to the God who saves.'

For Passionists, 'We Preach Christ Crucified' is our reason to be and is our motto. 'We preach Christ Crucified' is also prominently displayed in Free Presbyterian Churches throughout Northern Ireland.

St Paul in 1 Corinthians 1:23 continues to unite the strangest of bedfellows.

CHAPTER 14

DENY, DELAY AND DEFEND

Just before Pope Francis visited Dublin in August 2018, Columba Books organised a seminar in the Gresham hotel in Dublin called '5 Years to save The Irish Church'. The invited speakers were Sister Stanislaus Kennedy, Mary McAleese, Father Joe McDonald, Mark Patrick Hederman and me.

The full-day gathering attracted a capacity attendance. The hundreds who attended were enthusiastic and committed. They were genuinely excited that at last there is a realisation of the impending disintegration of the Catholic Church as we knew it, in Ireland.

Because I was asked to open the seminar, my task was to set the scene. So I attempted to highlight the major issues we should focus on.

I share these thoughts fully aware that I don't know the future. All I know is that God is always with us. There will be a future and believers will determine it consciously or otherwise. There is no single solution, other than to learn to listen to the Holy Spirit and be willing to let go of what hinders God's work. God will guide us to discern the shape of a church that allows its members to experience God's love, and that's the only church that matters.

It has taken centuries to get us to where we are and the journey will continue with or without us. However, it is our privilege and our duty to reflect upon the crises in the Church we love and it is our duty to admit, humbly, that we're lost, vulnerable and in need of guidance.

This is a time of major change in the world and in societies everywhere. As the Welsh religious poet David Jones observed in Anathemata: 'It is easy to miss Him – the living God – at the turn of a civilisation.' The age of Trent is over and done with and that is a great blessing. We've held onto its outdated model for too long.

This is an opportunity to let the Spirit breathe the Church of the Second Vatican Council into existence. What a privileged age to live in.

If I appear critical it is because I am utterly frustrated at how our Church, which I love, and to which I've dedicated my entire life, as layperson, religious and priest, is failing to care for its most loyal members. We shouldn't be in this present crisis; it was both predictable and avoidable.

Some of the most dedicated and gifted people, priests and laypeople, have walked away from our Church because of its failure to engage in the discernment process. Discernment is a necessary entry into the personal transformation we must embark upon for the simple reason that what we don't transform we transmit.

It is a pattern with human institutions. Inevitably attachment to power and position prevails to the detriment of the mission. Deny, Delay and Defend is how the malaise is described in secular terms.

Vocations are gifts from God. The shortage of priests is also a gift and is surely God asking us to be different in order to meet the needs of a different world. It is wrong to cling to a model that requires so many male celibate priests when we are being led to reach out to the special gifts of the laity.

It is not a problem. It is God telling us to affirm God's many gifted believers.

I am aware that my view of the Church in crisis is distorted by a deep guilt. Here's why. At the beginning of my priestly ministry fifty years ago, the churches were as full as the dance halls I attended nightly. More by accident than design, both became places of ministry for me.

In the dance halls I got to know ordinary people who were totally at home as they met, chatted, dated and danced. I was the one who was out of my comfort zone, initially at least. I went out of the monastery to discover what the real world was like.

People willingly shared their troubles, their joys, and their problems with me. I realised there was a silly game being played out in the Irish Church. People allowed the clergy to think they were in charge. They skilfully told them what they wanted to hear but blissfully lived their lives by making their own choices according to their own consciences.

The Church in Ireland was a whited sepulchre. We clerics thought the country was solidly Catholic and under control. Yet how could it collapse so quickly if it was built on a firm faith foundation?

I had to learn that they were good people but increasingly so only in their own way. They paid little heed to the rules, regulations, controls or customs of the institutional Church. They played the game when it suited and made their own decisions when it didn't suit.

Think Humanae Vitae, for example. Some couples obeyed it scrupulously. Some tried and failed. Eventually most decided that their loving relationship was more valuable than any prohibition could ever be.

In and around the dance halls (and a few years later in The Sunday World) people appreciated that I shared with them the healing Sacrament of Reconciliation in smoky corners of ballrooms. I did it because I believed that Christ would do exactly the same. I did it quietly because I knew the clerical Church never approved.

Life has many valid liturgies. Patrick Kavanagh (like Van Gogh) spoke prophetically about the Liturgy of the Seasons. The sower has faith that corn will emerge in summer.

'O give me faith
That I may be
Alive when April's
Ecstasy
Dances in every
Whitethorn tree.'

In the Church, on the other hand, I learned to be secretive, political, and 'safe' and, above all, presume I was always right. Increasingly I experienced unhealthy attachment to power, control, repression, and whatever the opposite of joy is.

In the dance halls I found joy and new life in happy people who were shaking off the shackles of oppression. I got the courage to do the same in my own life.

Anything I share with you here I could have told you thirty-five years ago. It was obvious then that the Church leadership had lost the trust of the people because we abused power and privilege; we used the sacraments as weapons to punish and control people – a heresy in itself.

The edifice was built on sand. Religious practise became external, rather than a living, loving relationship with the person of Jesus our Saviour.

I've learned that change happens. It can be threatening, but for people of faith it's an opportunity to experience life, religion and Church differently. It should be a privilege to embrace each new generation enthusiastically. We should look forward, not backward. New wine is to be stored in new wineskins. Be courageous about change – it's God's way of keeping us alive.

The sexual abuse of children by priests and religious is a scandal. However, I believe one of its most destructive characteristics was that it gave people who were already disillusioned with the Church a legitimate reason to quit. We asked people to believe in our Church instead of opening up a loving God to them – and who wouldn't believe in a compassionate God?

Here is the real reason for the growing guilt I struggle to come to terms with. During my watch as a priest churches have emptied. We've moved from overflowing congregations to empty buildings; from 90 per cent practise to 9 per cent. We priests have got older and more irrelevant; the people have learned that they can exist more happily without the kind of God, and the largely negative religious practices, we have to offer. We have distorted the saving Word of God.

I have every reason to be consumed by guilt. I spent my life trying to restructure structures when I should have restructured minds, mostly my own. Faith is not about surviving, it about thriving.

The tragedy is that nowadays so few people appreciate the marvellous gift of the Eucharist, which is the summit and the source of the life of the Church. This saddens me greatly, yet I know that on those special occasions when people share Eucharist they find comfort and hope when they are welcomed and cherished. That's the future right there. Faith in God's goodness is not dead. Faith in the clerical Church is fast disintegrating – and the sooner the better.

When people stay away from our churches they are making a mature decision. We clerics need to listen and we must change. They are more likely to be listening to the signs of the times than we are.

Seamus Heaney was once asked to contribute to a book (The God Factor: Inside the Spiritual Lives of Public People, by Cathleen Falsani) that outlined the spiritual lives of influential people. The poet honestly replied that spirituality was one part of his life about which he felt 'woefully inarticulate'. But, to show his good will, he included a poem he hoped might be of use. This is part of 'A Found Poem'.

Like everybody else, I bowed my head
during the consecration of the bread and wine,
lifted my eyes to the raised host and raised chalice
believed (whatever that means) that a change occurred.
I went to the altar rails and received the mystery
on my tongue, returned to my place, shut my eyes fast, made
an act of thanksgiving, opened my eyes and felt
time starting up again.'

The Eucharist is 'time starting up again'. We become what we receive. God is present in the joys and sorrows, forever offering hope and food for the journey. Yet we know the Eucharist now means so little to so many. How did that happen?

When we talk about saving the Church we often mean going back to those days of power, control, crowds, pomp and ceremony. We seem to want to return to the outdated times of Trent. That won't happen and it would be a disaster beyond words if it did.

I will not be alive to see any of the reforms and changes that I've longed for throughout my entire priestly life. There's a real freedom in accepting that they won't happen in my lifetime. It's also vital to admit the need for a different future, even though I don't know what shape that future will take. A better question for me to ponder is: What seed of a living faith will I leave when I'm gone?

I am certain, though, that change will happen. Indeed it has already come in spite of us. The toothpaste is out of the tube and it will not return. Transformation happens only when our old worlds fall apart. As Richard Rohr says in From the Bottom Up, 'The pain and the chaos of collapse invite our inner selves to listen at a deeper level and to move to a new place.'

Reformation is happening in a positive way whether we know/like it or not. The changes are not from the top down but from the bottom up. Not from the outside in but from the inside out.

Donal Harrington, in Tomorrow's Parish – a vision and a path, (1) uses the example of the journey from Dublin to Cork. A few years ago, it was Naas, Newbridge, Kildare, Portlaoise, Cashel, Fermoy etc. Now we go from Dublin to Cork without having to stop at a traffic light. The towns are bypassed so that we forget they're there at all and we visit them only in an emergency or for an occasional break. So it is with our churches; we're bypassed; our services are used sporadically and when it suits.

Our major sin was, and is, putting the maintenance of the institution before the gift of new life offered by the Holy Spirit. We already have form in this matter – didn't we protect the institution and abandon children to abusive predators?

You've heard it said that if you want to make God laugh tell him your plans for the future. Nevertheless, here goes.

I was reading some of what I wrote over the years on this topic recently. Before the election of Francis, I had outlined for Sunday World readers the kind of leader the people long for. I wrote:

The new pope must have the ability and the power to reform and reorganise not only the Curia but the way the Church is governed ... Most of all, the new pope will need to reinstate the practise of collegiality, because to fan the flame of collegiality would instantly involve people of talent in the decision-making of the Church, especially women. The new pope must welcome women as full members of the Catholic Church.

I'm eternally grateful that Francis was elected pope. Like all of us he hasn't been perfect, but I can assure you that had he not been elected I would not be a priest now. I would have been shown the door.

The kind of church that Francis struggles to create is the only credible plan available to us. Francis emphasises God's mercy. His image of church is summed up in simple words and in simple phrases.

In The Joy of the Gospel he writes:

A preacher needs to keep his ear close to the people and to discover what it is that the faithful need to hear. A preacher has to contemplate the Word, but he also has to contemplate his people. He needs to be able to link the messages of the Gospel to an experience which cries out for the light of God's Word. (n. 154).

Francis understands that radical change of necessity entails dealing with conflict. 'It is the willingness to face conflict head-on, to resolve it and make it a link in the chain of a new process.'

I feel lucky in that I've been in a position to experience the uncensored views of genuine people of all faiths and none. They trust me enough to share their doubts and their vision every week. Fifty years of broadcasting and over fifty years in journalism have given me a unique perspective.

The sacraments are where the people ought to meet a loving God. Yet too often we impose rules and regulations on grieving people, for example, because we'd rather be safe than helpful. We make marriages as loveless as our own lives often are. We reduce a gifted person's life to make it fit into our little minds. No wonder people increasingly arrange weddings and funerals outside churches now, away from mean restrictions.

The growing secularisation in Ireland is a result of many things, including clerical child sexual abuse, an intolerance of dissenting voices, an inability to understand the God-given beauty of sexuality and gender. These are areas where we need to be courageous to be relevant.

The Catholic Church is no longer held in esteem by most of the population because when the people meet the Church too often they experience canon law rather than the law of the Gospel, the law of love.

In short, for better or worse, people don't fully trust priests now. We should know that when trust is broken it can never be restored. It demands a new relationship altogether, not a patched-up version of what has failed.

Pope Francis aims to re-establish a synodal church. It will be a genuinely inclusive process of consultation with free and open debate. That's the opposite of what we've had for centuries. The emergence of a synodal church will take time. It will mean the destruction of many of the structures that block progress, including the Roman Curia itself.

I now firmly believe the faithful can no longer wait for permission to do things differently. That's the key to progress. We sometimes need to make change happen – to become the change we desire, as Gandhi taught. We must be brave, be hopeful, be different. We have nothing to lose and everything to gain.

Already, the people of God are working out their own relationships with God. They are organising their marriages and their funerals in a way that is meaningful to them, even though what they do is often condemned by the Church authorities.

We must finally begin to learn from the people. They have decided that what we offer is not life-giving. They are making a genuine attempt to celebrate their own beautiful lives and to acknowledge the working of the Holy Spirit in their own life experiences.

That is why one of the most helpful gifts we have to offer is the gift of genuine non-judgemental listening. Listening, not to come up with answers or to correct people, but so that we might learn what it is like to live in and to celebrate real life experiences.

Listening, though, is merely the first step. Change comes only with hearing. When we actually hear the cry of the poor we should be moved to respect their lives as genuine religious experiences in themselves – and something infinitely more valuable than what we offer them.

To put it simply – what we're doing is not working. Furthermore, it's not going to work. We are not coming up with solutions because we don't fully comprehend the problem.

That doesn't mean throwing everything out. But if we continue imposing our way of being Church on the faithful, people will continue to do what they're already doing – walking away. They are telling us that they want to build community more than parish; power has come to mean control.

When we listen we'll discover we have no shortage of vocations, just a shortage of male celibates.

We need to be courageous enough to tell those in authority that the reasons they give us for not ordaining women are simply not good enough. We are not simpletons. The arguments forwarded from on high are actually insulting. We must have a mature debate to discern what the truth is concerning the ordination of women to the priesthood. Women are second-class citizens in the Catholic Church. This is the major issue which must be tackled honestly, not in the future, but NOW. We must cherish womanhood in the Church, as is happening daily in wider society.

Women must be given a real voice; they must demand respect; they need our support in their struggle for equality. Anything less is spiritual abuse.

Nor is there any obvious reason why married clergymen could not be part of the ministry immediately. Married priests are part of the Catholic Church already. Why must it be restricted to Anglican converts?

We mustn't forget that, in the future, the Church will not be dominated by clerics – women or men - as it has been in the past. It will grow from the ground up, not hierarchically from the top down.

To conclude, if we're looking for a model for a Church for ever in need of reform, we find it in St Matthew's Gospel in the Beatitudes. The Sermon on the Mount is the blueprint for Christian living and is the heart of Jesus' teaching. It's the heart of the Gospel message.

The alternative reign of God, which Jesus teaches, overturns trust in power, possessions and personal prestige. To be changed by God's words in the Sermon on the Mount we need to have humble, open hearts.

Look at the way Jesus sets the stage for the Sermon on the Mount. He sees crowds following him and heads to the mountain, which itself is symbolic, pointing to the new law fulfilling the Mosaic law.

He begins with a simple message, which is the key to everything else – Blessed or happy are the poor in spirit; the Kingdom of Heaven is theirs (Matthew 5:3). What does it mean to be poor in spirit? It means an inner emptiness and humility. It is to be able to live without the need for personal righteousness and reputation. It's the powerlessness that is often framed in the first step of Alcoholics Anonymous. It is Jesus saying: Happy are you, you are the freest of all.

Most important of all, Jesus uses the present tense. 'The Kingdom of God IS theirs'. He does not say WILL BE theirs. God's reign is now, not later.

Blessed are the merciful; they shall have mercy shown them. The experience of mercy and forgiveness is where we meet God, who loves gratuitously.

Blessed are the gentle. To live simply is to live gently. To live gently in the Church is to let go of an old model so that future generations can experience the beauty of God's presence in our midst. It's to recognise, as all the great saints have recognised, that after a while possessions are what possess us.

The Beatitudes tell us that we must hunger and thirst for justice and, as Martin Luther King Jnr put it, 'Injustice anywhere is a threat to justice everywhere'.

Love is the foundation of it all. Jesus did not say, 'Thou shalt be right.' Jesus says, 'This is my commandment; love one another.' God's love is planted inside each of us as the Holy Spirit. Love is who we are. Richard Rohr wrote in From the Bottom Up that 'Only God in you can know God ... you cannot know or love God with your mind alone.'

Finally, I believe that we need to affirm genuine prophets in our midst. It has been said that a prophet is one who keeps God free for people and who keeps people free for God.

Could the biggest sin of our modern Church be that we have made God unreachable and, worse still, unlovable? An elderly man wrote to me this year pointing out that, 'Too many people are taught guilt to keep us clergy in business'.

Could it be that the sin of the clerical club is to make God less accessible instead of more so? Prophets have the courage to speak the challenging word; they understand where the signs of the times are asking us to go; prophets believe intuitively that God is trustworthy; that God is faithful.

Have we ever thought of what we're doing to people when we say you can come to God only through us, by doing the right rituals, obeying the rules and believing in the right doctrines? Do we not realise that this is telling God whom God is allowed to love?

The surprise of the Gospel is that God continually breaks the approved rules of God by forgiving sinners, choosing the outsider and the weak, and showing up in secular places.

Our job in Church today is to spend our lives loving others the way God loves us. But first we must be aware of how God loves us.

We must be aware of the twin evils of indifference, on the one hand, and of fundamentalism, on the other.

In my own spiritual life I spend more time fearing and trying to control God than actually loving God. The truth is the very opposite. In Jesus God becomes powerless. Seeing God in the form of a small baby indicates the shift of emphasis from power to powerlessness as no other story does, with the possible exception of seeing God nailed to a tree.

Pierre Teilhard de Chardin tells us, 'We are not human beings having a spiritual experience. We are spiritual beings having a human experience.'

Pope Francis says that 'Hope is the humblest of virtues, because it hides itself in this life.' It is a gift from God, he adds, and we must ask for it.

Vaclav Havel wrote that 'Hope is NOT the conviction that something will turn out well, but the certainty that something makes sense regardless of how it turns out.'

During my time in Enniskillen, The Graan monastery became famous for the Novena of Hope, which grew over a period of twenty-five years. The speakers were mostly lay people sharing their personal stories. All religions came, young, old, sick and well. The church was overflowing two and three times a day – about 3,000 a day, in the heart of rural Fermanagh. It was a celebration of the joy of being human. On the last night, we had to ask the PSNI to block the roads half an hour before the service began and to turn away the hundreds we could not cater for. We has to ask police to turn people away from our church; that's the power of Hope.

Hope – even the sound of the word is life-giving.

CHAPTER 15

NO SHOW LIKE A JOE SHOW

On the night 'a Different journey' was launched back in 2006, the room was full of good friends from all walks of life, especially the loyal entertainers who remained close to me all my life. I often reflect gratefully that I have a few close friends, many good friends and a multitude of acquaintances.

Lifelong show-business friends accepted me for what I was – a friend who would help them if I could. They knew I wasn't hanging on to their coat tails looking for reflected glory.

In our young days we lived as if we were immortal. It's part of the optimism the entertainer has to have. You're only as good as your last show. Don't look back; look forward to the next gig.

I began to notice attitudes changing immediately after the Miami Showband murders. Those funerals were heart-breaking.

Show business in Ireland never tolerated sectarianism; showbands kept on playing throughout the worst of the Troubles. They were able to bring people together when others were blowing them apart.

After the Miami murders fear crept in; trust was broken for ever. Some say the night those gifted musicians were cruelly murdered at a fake check-point was the day the music died. Others are convinced it was the day innocence died and we all had to grow up.

That same week, one of the true gentlemen of the showband era, Tom Dunphy, was killed in car crash on his way to a gig in Donegal. Tom was a founder member of the greatest showband of them all, Brendan Bowyer and the Royal Showband. Four funerals in three days is too much grief to cope with.

Yet we have to realise death is part of life. You can't avoid it. For the past decade I have helped to officiate at the funerals of dear friends, but in truth I am offering the last rites over an entire industry. I am getting close to being the last, lost, living soul. I'm now consulted as a historian, not as a fan. I watch programmes on television telling me what a special era the showband years were. They attempt to tell the history of a time most of them never knew or appreciated. It's hard to take because those pioneering musicians deserve better.

One of the most difficult funerals I preached at was in Mullingar in the last cold days of December 2007. That's when we laid Joe Dolan to rest in Walshetown graveyard in his native Westmeath.

As time passes it is more difficult to accept that I'll never see Joe Dolan on stage again. When friends die we go through a peculiar kind of grief. Something inside us says that we should not be as sad as we are because 'they were only friends'. Yet genuine friends are so rare that their deaths affect us as much as the death of a family member. That's certainly the way I feel about Joe Dolan.

Grief comes at unexpected times and at our most vulnerable moments. I was in the car on 3 February 2008. The mobile rang and it was a friend of Joe's. He said, 'This is the first year in living memory you didn't bring the oil of St Blaise to bless Joe's throat.' And so it was.

For thirty years or more on the feast of St Blaise I blessed oil, put it in a little bottle and brought it to Joe's home. If he was there I'd have a chat and a cup of tea and then I'd bless his throat; if he wasn't at home I left the oil bottle in the letter box and he blessed his own throat.

Joe had his private and deeply felt rituals. The only sickness he ever worried about was losing his voice. He had great faith in the oil of St Blaise and every time I met him he asked me to bless his throat. Joe knew where his gifts came from and how easily they could disappear. He knew who to give thanks to and he never took his incredible, unique voice for granted.

If we, his fans and friends, miss him so much, what must it be like for his family, especially his brother Ben? How could you get over the death of your brother beside whom you stood on stage for forty-seven years?

Joe Dolan lived life to the full. He enjoyed life. He was never a begrudger. He genuinely delighted in other people's success and was grateful for his own major successes, which he accepted with humility.

He was the most unique and most successful of the showband singers – of that there is no doubt. This is not to take away from any of the other stars, all of whom were my friends and all of whom contributed greatly to lifting the dullness from our youthful lives.

Joe kept on reinventing himself and attracting new audiences. It would be hard to find anyone with a bad word to say about him; fellow performers and fans all loved his genial, lovable, roguish character. He had a smile that would melt a heart of stone. Yet he was deadly serious about life. Over the years he and I had many conversations. He was a bright articulate man who was right up to date on current affairs.

Deep down, though, his greatest gift was that he loved the underdog.

Shortly before he died I went to see him in the Mater Hospital. He asked me to give him a blessing and for some reason the Scripture I read happened to be the same Scripture reading that his family chose for his funeral Mass. It's from the book of Ecclesiastes. In the 1960s it was set to music and reached the top of the charts when it was sung by The Byrds. 'For everything there is a season, a time to be born and a time to die; a time to weep and a time to laugh; a time to mourn and a time to dance; a time to keep and a time to throw away; God has made everything suitable for his time.'

In his hospital bed that night Joe knew it was nearing the time for him to say goodbye. Of course we didn't dwell on it; we both kept hoping there would be other happy days ahead. There was no need to meet the grim reaper halfway. I first met Joe and Ben fifty years ago. They called me into the band room in the Old Sheiling in Raheny in Dublin where they were pioneering the concept of showbands in cabaret. They told me one of their band members was thinking of leaving them to become a priest. Joe and Ben pleaded with me to dissuade the young pianist from throwing away a future in show business.

I think it was Joe who said, 'Sure he'll save more souls in the ballrooms than he will in a chapel.' And he was probably right. Ben was even more practical: 'It's far easier to get a priest than it is to get a good piano player.'

Of course I did not dissuade the young man and thankfully he went on to become a priest and remained a very good priest until his untimely death. Joe and I often laughed about it afterwards. God gets his way.

When, at Joe's funeral Mass, I mentioned that he always helped the poor, it seemed to come as a shock to many. Helping the poor came as naturally as singing to Joe Dolan.

Over the years I would go into the band room just before they went on stage. The ritual was always the same. There were cups of tea and big thick sandwiches if we were lucky. Mostly, though, the rooms were smoked-filled as the band members played cards to pass the time before going on stage.

Joe would leave the card-table and go to a quiet corner where he'd ask me if I had any good jokes. For good jokes in this case, read bad jokes. I told the ones I couldn't tell anyone else and then he'd tell me the best he had in his repertoire. He'd end up with, 'You'll have to give me absolution for that.' Which I usually did and then went on to spread the new jokes Joe had shared with me.

As the band members filed on to the stage, Joe hung back and shook my hand as he pressed a couple of large notes into it saying, 'I wish you'd take it yourself but I know you won't. You know who the poor are so make sure some family gets the help they deserve.'

When I lived in Mount Argus, dry rot infested the entire monastery and church. The roof and the walls fell in on us. Many of the showband stars, of their own free will, organised and promoted functions to help us restore the famous church. They were genuinely the most generous benefactors of all.

I organised garden fêtes in Mount Argus grounds for eleven years in a row. I'd ring some of my friends and ask them to pop along if they had time just to be seen there. It became a huge day in South Dublin. On many occasions 10,000 people crammed into the front fields on a Sunday afternoon in June.

I never once asked Joe Dolan to come along. I never had to ask him. Every single year without fail Joe arrived in the field, dressed immaculately in white. He'd sing a song if he had to. He'd sign autographs if he had to, he'd stand for photographs and patiently smile for half the day. Then he'd take a cup of tea, chat with a few of his friends and disappear. That's the way Joe did things. Next day he'd ring to see how I was and to know how much we made.

Joe loved a sermon he could relate to. He knew how hard it is to get up in front of a thousand people and hold their interest. He admired anyone – a priest, an entertainer, a politician – who could do it. He'd pass on snippets of sermons he heard in other churches.

There was no show like a Joe show. It was almost like a pilgrimage. There is a famous waitress, Caroline, in a Chinese restaurant in Navan, who lived for Joe's shows. Twelve years on she's still reliving those happy times every time I call. Even talking about the shows revives the happy memories. As long as a man's memory lives, a man will never die.

He loved telling stories against himself. One of his favourites happened when he was enjoying an after-christening party in a pub in Stillorgan, Dublin. One of the customers recognised him and persuaded him to get up and sing 'Make Me an Island' with the pub band – which he did. On his way back to his seat, an elderly man, a typical Dub, whispered out of the side of his mouth, 'Don't you be murdering that song! That's a Joe Dolan song and no one can sing it like Joe.' Joe hadn't the heart to tell him.

Joe's modesty worked against him. He was a world star who preferred to live in Ireland. By that I mean he underestimated his talents and his popularity.

Had he really believed in his abilities he would have been a major pop star worldwide. But Joe was a home bird. He earned enough money to enjoy life. He often told me, 'As long as I can sing an odd song, I'll never starve'.

I went on two working trips to South Africa. One day I was feeling lonely strolling in a shopping arcade in Johannesburg. Imagine my delight when I turned a corner and met a laughing Joe Dolan, arms outstretched and dressed in his white suit. I was about to greet the great Joe when I realised it was a cardboard cut-out advertising Joe's latest album. He was an idol in South Africa, popular with every race and culture.

In 1981 Joe and the band toured in Leningrad and Moscow. 'Make Me an Island' was a hit in seventeen countries, which shows how universal Joe's appeal was.

When I lived in Dublin Joe invited me to his home every Christmas night. It was always late when I finished my calls, yet I'd make time to be with Joe and his friends. He generally invited Traveller families in the afternoon. They'd share the meal, receive their presents, sing a song for Joe and go home happy. We had a much quieter chat and always a laugh.

Joe crossed boundaries effortlessly. Pop and country fans loved him, young and old flocked to his gigs, northerners and southerners came together to see him, and in the North Catholics and Protestants mixed to his music.

Not many from the showband era made it from ballrooms to cabaret and from pubs to theatres, but Joe did. He pioneered it. Joe was authentic. What you saw was what you got. He was a truly remarkable human being who died long before his time.

A few weeks before he died I was celebrant at the funeral of a mutual friend. I ended with a quote which made a deep impression on Joe, so much so that he asked me to text it to him. And I did.

I ended the homily at Joe's own funeral with that quote and I'll do the same here. 'Death leaves a heartache that no one can heal; love leaves a memory that no one can steal.'

CHAPTER 16

LEAVING THE GRAAN

I'm a nervous preacher; I cope by preparing well. I've always been that way. I still need to prepare for three hours or more to make sure the homily I preach is truly part of what I pray.

Preaching is God's word and God's work, not mine; the ripples of a compassionate word are humbling and beyond imagining, as I learned just a few months ago.

I was in the RTÉ studios in Cork doing an interview with Daithí and Maura. There were other guests in the Green Room and, as always happens, there was plenty of nervous chat and even more nervous laughter. I knew two of the guests from way back 'in old God's time'. We had endless memories to recall and relive about the showband scene of old.

The television show went on air live and my two friends were first on.

Meanwhile back in the Green Room there was just me and a man whom I didn't know. I thought he too was a guest but he was actually promoting the two entertainers. We immediately struck up a conversation.

'I'm delighted to talk to you Father Brian,' he began. 'The last occasion we met was very different to this one.'

I thought I'd never met the man, but he explained it was years ago in Mount Argus. Very early on a Sunday morning he lay down in the doorway of the monastery for shelter. He'd been drinking all night; he was exhausted, penniless and homeless due to this terrible addiction. It was the end of the road for him.

He remembers waking up and seeing me, then a young priest and the rector of the monastery, standing looking in at him. He expected me to be cross but he remembers instead that I asked if he wanted tea and something to eat. He was delighted to get anything. I, apparently, went to the kitchen and got a cup of hot tea and brown bread with butter and marmalade – he remembered those details. But it was the next bit that convinced me his story was true.

He clearly remembered me apologising to him; I hadn't time to talk to him, I explained, because I was saying the next Mass at eleven o'clock. I told him preaching made me nervous and I needed to go over what I had to say. I hoped he didn't mind; he could take as long as he wanted to finish the tea and brown bread. And off I went, to read over the sermon and say Mass.

I have absolutely no memory of the incident, mainly because similar incidents happened day and daily in the 1980s at Mount Argus. There were always homeless people sleeping at the side of the monastery, waiting for some food from the kitchen – we had a community of over eighty monks living there in those days.

He is convinced something close to a miracle happened then. For the first time in years he allowed himself to think. He says he came to his senses. He was shocked that someone as well-known as I was then, in Dublin, would be nervous about preaching. He began to accept that I was a human being with weaknesses and was struggling to manage the terrible fear of speaking in public. That's what made the difference.

He finished his food, dragged himself up and went on his merry way. Walking past the door of the church he heard singing and he made up his mind to change his life. From that day to this day an alcoholic drink never crossed his lips.

He managed to pick up the pieces of his life, went back to studying and eventually became a teacher. He told me he had just retired as principal of his school a few months ago and, in his retirement, he was back to his first love, music.

'I've always wanted to thank you for what you did for me on the steps of Mount Argus on that Sunday morning. I couldn't believe it when you walked into the Green Room today. It was like another miracle. We were destined to meet. I've had thirty-five wonderful years and I'm grateful every day that I took the chance to change while I was still healthy enough to do it.'

Kris Kristofferson's 'Sunday Mornin' Coming Down' comes to mind.

Honestly, I have no memory of any of the things he recalled so clearly. But I don't need to remember because it's not about me, it's about that lovely man and the miracle of 'coming to his senses', just as the Prodigal Son did thousands of years ago.

The key was my nervousness. It was my weakness, not my strength, that allowed God's mercy to work so effectively through me. Sometimes it's not what we say but what we do that makes the most memorable sermon.

That's why I have to prepare. It's an awesome privilege to preach compassion and mercy and forgiveness. It's a massive responsibility too. The very least I should do is to put time and effort into believing what I say. What I preach may not be worth hearing but at least I must know it was not due to any lack of effort on my part.

When I'm speaking, I invariably begin with whatever is currently making the news. I like to bring the Gospel into our world.

A case in point was the sermon I preached at Mass on the Sunday before I left The Graan in Enniskillen in 2017. My heart was broken at having to leave the place I call home. It was where I prayed before I entered the Passionists and I am aware of what The Graan means to so many people in that area – Catholics and Protestants.

Of course I was disappointed at being asked to leave Enniskillen at this time in my life. When you're over seventy years of age, it is not easy packing up and walking away from family and friends. The people of Fermanagh stood by me and got me through the Vatican debacle a few years earlier and many other hard times. That created a bond that only we understand or appreciate.

The Graan catered for a wide range of people then. We had a wonderful cross-community apostolate. It was hard for me to leave but it was just as hard for the people of Fermanagh, Tyrone, and surrounding counties. They were not pleased.

In truth, my heart was breaking. I didn't want to leave and I couldn't see any good reason why I had to. I was able to do good work around the area, particularly cross-community work. People were coming to our church in great numbers and most of them enjoyed the Sunday homilies because I tried to make them relevant to our lives. The people who came appreciated the way I spoke honestly about abuse. There were no excuses, no fancy words, just common sense, they always told me.

Having made those points to the superior, I then did what my order asked me to do. I packed my bags and left. I was out the door the next morning.

I had to be careful not to make my last Sunday there too emotional. It would not have been good for me and it wouldn't have been good for the morale of the people either.

I tried to make the sermon as normal as I possibly could by taking God's word to their world. I reminded them it was forty years since Elvis Presley died. I joked that most of them were too young to remember, knowing well that almost everyone in the church did remember it.

I've always been a huge fan of Elvis Presley's music. Elvis gave us the first taste of real freedom. To a narrow and repressed little world like ours the music of Elvis lifted us out of the dark ages. It was my generation who understood his music and that's why Elvis was such a threat to the generations who went before. Elvis died alone and a prisoner of fame – he gave his life so that we could be in touch with our inner freedom.

Telling the congregation stories they were familiar with helped me to integrate them with the Gospel.

I went on to talk about how Jesus gathered ordinary people as disciples and how he needed to go to a quiet place to rest and regain his strength. I was telling myself really that in the storms of life we should not act too hastily. We should not become consumed by our own troubles.

The Gospel on that day was teaching me, like St Peter, that when events happen it's wise not to waste your life and your energy fighting battles you cannot win. There's no point wasting a good life worrying about things we can't change. It becomes an excuse for not dealing with the things we can change. Deep inside me I had to hear the words Jesus spoke to Peter. 'Do not be afraid, have courage.'

The example that came to mind was Elie Wiesel. Most of us know his tragic but inspiring story. Eli's father, along with his mother and sister were arrested, put on a prison train and brought to the gates of Auschwitz concentration camp. There his mother and sister were taken to the women's camp and were never seen again. Elie and his father went to the men's camp. Once inside they were separated and a few days later the older prisoners told Elie, who was still a young child, that his father was also dead.

Elie survived the concentration camp and struggled ever since to comprehend the meaning of life. He wrote that when he looked back at that time in his life, he realised he lost everything on that day; but the most important thing he lost was faith in a loving God. How could God allow such a tragedy to happen? He explained why losing faith was the worst loss of all. Had he been able to keep his faith his other tragedies would have been handled better. Without faith nothing made sense.

It was a warning to me to process what I was being asked to do in a faith context. The temptation always is to hold on to hurts and perceived injustices. To do that is to allow the past to destroy your future. It's far better to move on, accept what you cannot change and find a whole vista opening out in front of you.

One of the readings proved helpful. The prophet looked for God in what he thought were the obvious places, namely thunder, lightning and fire. He could not find God there. Finally, the prophet thought he would find God in an overpowering storm, but he didn't find God in the storm. Eventually, he was forced to rest. And in the quietness a gentle breeze came. Unexpectedly he found the elusive peace of God in the gentle breeze. God is found not in power but in gentleness.

I held myself together until the end of Mass when I tried to say goodbye with dignity. I failed miserably and broke down. I left the people of The Graan just as I had lived with them – as a weak human being struggling to find a way to be brave. The tears, the hugs and the handshakes assured me that being human is just fine.

CHAPTER 17

BOXED IN BY JULIE

When I was a much younger priest, I had a steep learning curve in all areas of parish and pastoral life. When I was newly ordained, I was really enthusiastic. I thought I was God's gift to the world. It took me three years to realise I was not God; being human was good enough.

Initially, you're going to be the best confessor who ever lived. You're going to be the most sincere man saying a Mass who ever lived. You'll always help people in trouble. You'll never be hard when people come to you with a problem. You've all these lovely ideals. At least those were the ideals I had. And I wasn't alone. Many others in the class had the same vision.

But then, life teaches you that ideals are one thing and you must have them, but prudence in the application of the ideals is part of the learning process. Unusual people can teach you about life.

In Mount Argus, in the early 1970s, there was a wonderful lady who used to visit our church. I want to be respectful to this lady because as you'll soon see she had more faith than any of us. I don't want in any sense to demean her. She was a lady who perhaps wasn't mentally secure. But she wasn't mentally deranged, either, though she had her moments, shall we say. I think she lived in a hostel in Dublin. We knew her as Julie. That was not her real name but that was how we referred to her affectionately. She was a legend around Mount Argus.

Julie was no respecter of persons. She always knew when a vulnerable priest was around. She could pick us out and pick on us. Often as I sat in the confessional box I'd open the slide to find Julie there. And she'd land a list of curses on me and a list of sins and then she'd burst out laughing. 'I got ya there, didn't I?'

So who was the wise one?

For the first dozen times, I tried to be patient. 'All right Julie, one Hail Mary'. And then I'd pull the slide on the other side, with great relief, only to find Julie on the other side as well. She'd say: 'I'm here again'. I never understood how she managed to get to the other side so quickly. She had this great laugh and everybody would hear it ringing all over the church.

Julie would just break the rules with that freedom that I, only now looking back, see as cutting through all the arrogant nonsense we used to go on with. Back then, though, she was a nuisance. Did she not know her place?

Occasionally she came to funerals in Mount Argus. When everybody was sitting mournfully at the beginning of Mass, with the Mass cards decked on top of the coffin, Julie would come running up with her handbag and, as Mass was just about to start, swipe every Mass card off the top. It was not an easy action to explain. I'd whisper 'duine le dia' or some such phrase to explain her actions to mourners. If there was a wedding in the church, she'd meet the bride at the door with her handbag and green coat and headscarf tied tightly underneath her jaws. You could never see her face. All you saw was a protruding nose and mischievous eyes dancing out of her headscarf, which she wore like blinkers. Then she'd go to the bride and say: 'Are you preggers or what?' The look of shock on a bride dressed in white was wonderful to behold.

Julie had this unfailing way of bringing us all down to earth. Another inexplicable compulsion she had was receiving Holy Communion. Back then you could go to one Mass; you were allowed to receive Communion only once a day. This was a big leap forward from once a month, or maybe once a year, which had been the custom in the past.

Julie decided that she would, first of all, go to the Franciscan Church on Merchant's Quay and 'get' as many Masses as she could. At each Mass she would go to the far side of the rail, receive Communion, go to the middle section of the rail, receive Communion, go to the next rail, receive Communion, and do the same all along the rail. It was a big, wide church and she'd receive Communion five or six times at each Mass. This of course was a huge moral problem for everybody except Julie and Jesus.

She would then come up to Mount Argus, go to the ten o'clock mass and do the same thing all over again. At 6.15 in the evening, Julie was back to receive more Communions. Only priests distributed Communion and we had long discussions about whether we should give her Communion. If we didn't we knew she would create a scene.

I learned about her tricks early on. I went out to say Mass very nervously one Sunday when Julie planted herself underneath the pulpit and shouted: 'Would you look at D'Arcy; look at him laughing. What's he laughing at?' in the middle of the sermon. 'Look at the smile on him,' she says. 'Look at him, can you see him?' Try to keep your composure in the middle of that!

So you always knew that, despite the power you thought you had, Julie had all the authority. I dodged round her as best I could. Anything for a quiet life.

Move on to Ash Wednesday. I think it was Ash Wednesday 1972. I was a young priest in Mount Argus and editor of The Cross at the time. There was another young priest in the community now, Father Aidan Troy, who was a year behind me. The church was packed for Ash Wednesday Mass. Lent was taken seriously then.

I was giving Communion at the ten o'clock mass that morning and knew Julie had already received Communion from me twice. She had enough Communions to break her Lenten fast by now. I knew she'd also been to Merchant's Quay. I was saying the 6.15 Mass and I said to Aidan Troy beforehand: 'Julie was here this morning for Mass and she'll be looking for Communion from us again. We'll make a bargain – you give it to her once and I'll give it to her once and that's it.'

Picture the scene. The church was full. I see six nuns in the front row. I can see green-uniformed children from the Loreto behind them and I can see St Clare's children in the brown uniform. There were a thousand people in Mount Argus church for the 6.15 Mass that Ash Wednesday evening. We were doing well; I'd given out the ashes and given the sermon. I came to Communion now. Aidan Troy went to the far side and Julie went over to him. I was keeping a half eye on what was happening. She got Communion.

Then she jumped up and came over to me.

I moved across and she was in front of me again. I didn't make a scene. I just passed over her. I gave Communion to the person each side of her, but didn't give it to Julie. This happened three times and she was plainly annoyed.

Communion ended and everybody was sitting with their heads bowed, praying. Aidan Troy was back at the tabernacle replacing the Blessed Sacrament and the ciboria. I was purifying the chalice. Julie came up with her handbag, put one hand on the right-hand side of the altar gates and the other on the left-hand side. She looked me straight in the eyes and shouted at the top of her voice: 'D'Arcy!' I kept my head down. 'D'Arcy!'

Eyes were raised gently from the back of the church. 'Are you going to give it to me?'

I shook my head.

'Are you going to give it to me? Well, f*** you, D'Arcy, stick it up your arse!'

I collapsed with laughter. Aidan Troy was holding on to the tabernacle trying to keep himself from falling. The nuns' mouths opened in horror that their lovely little darlings were hearing such language in the church.

And Julie danced down the aisle, swinging her handbag over her head triumphantly and still shouting: 'F*** you D'Arcy, shove it up your arse!' She disappeared out the main door with a shriek of laughter. I laughed so much I cried. I couldn't say a prayer. I couldn't open my mouth. All I could do was give a silent blessing and we all went into the sacristy.

Very shortly after that, Julie disappeared and none of us knew where she went. We never saw her again. We heard rumours that she was in various mental hospitals, but I didn't know her real name, and didn't know anything about her.

As we grew older we began to appreciate her more and to see that maybe she was correct and we were arrogant little clerics trying to impose a regime. Maybe she had understood the essentials a little better than any of us. The next time I met Julie was a happier occasion altogether.

Move forward sixteen years to 1988. I'm still in Mount Argus for what turned out to be one of the greatest days in my life – the Beatification of Father Charles of Mount Argus. It was a marvellous day in Dublin; thousands of pilgrims from all over Ireland came to Mount Argus, filling not only the Church but the car park as well.

Most of the community wanted to go to Rome for the beatification ceremony. I made a conscious decision that the last place I wanted to be was Rome. Father Charles's remains are in Mount Argus. We organised a suitable service for the people he loved in Dublin. As the elite gathered in Rome his real devotees were able to celebrate in the church where his body lay.

Cardinal Ó Fiach came to Mount Argus, as did the papal nuncio and other dignitaries. At my suggestion, Cardinal Ó Fiach and I went outside to bless the people in the porch of the church. Amazingly we found thousands upon thousands of people standing out in the cold on a dark October evening. Cardinal Ó Fiach was blessing the sick in wheelchairs, parked at the hall door. That really annoyed me. Had I known they were outside I would have brought them into the sanctuary.

There was one frail little plump lady sitting in her wheelchair at the church door. She shouted to me, 'Do you not know me, D'Arcy?' And I suddenly recognised the voice. I went over and I said, 'Julie!'

She said, 'That's not me name, but that's me.'

'Where are you?'

'St Loman's.'

'God, Julie, I'm so glad to see you. How did you know about this big day?'

'Ah sure, poor old Charlie kept me going for years. I'm delighted to see this day. I saw it in the paper and I wouldn't miss it. They brought me over here and I'm delighted to be here and to get blessed with the relic of my aul' Charlie.'

I have to say, I cried like a baby. In my youthful arrogance I regarded Julie as a nuisance, always looking for more and more Communion, but now, wiser and older, I knew how wrong I was. Julie was the one with real faith.

I will never forget her.

CHAPTER 18

CARDINAL DALY AND THE LATE LATE SHOW

A quarter of a century after it happened, I'm still asked about the 'confrontation' Cardinal Daly and I had on The Late Late Show in November 1995. Many of the details are well known, yet it's a memory of a tussle, not a dialogue, that persists.

It all began when there was an entire Late Late Show dedicated to the impending crisis in the Catholic Church in Ireland. It was in the early days of the collapse of the Catholic Church's position in Ireland immediately after the horrific revelations of child abuse by the late Father Brendan Smyth.

In the mid-1990s the Church was still an influential institution. The vast majority still believed that it was a small minority of priests/religious who abused children. The damaging revelations about what happened in industrial schools and orphanages, not to mention mother and baby homes, and indeed the cover-up of wholesale abuse by bishops and religious superiors, had not yet taken place.

Initially I was not invited on The Late Late Show on that night because I had appeared discussing the very same sensitive topic the previous Friday with Gerry Kelly on UTV. However, I was in the Radio Centre to record my weekly insert, The Gig Guide, when John Masterson, the Late Late producer, asked me to sit in the audience, since, he said, Gay Byrne, the host, would feel more secure if he could turn to me on occasion. I reluctantly agreed to sit in and was given an audience ticket to do so. I had nothing prepared and hoped to be an observer, not a contributor.

The first half of the show had a small panel of religious experts, priests, a laywoman and a bishop, who were in discussion with Gay Byrne. There were many other vocal experts in the audience, which was obviously hand-picked too. They were all involved in the discussion.

At one point Gay talked to me about the Church. I believed the anger created by the Church's misuse of power was now coming back to haunt us with a vengeance. We had to realise the world is changing; we could not go back to 'the good old days'; the Church was no longer seen as merciful, compassionate or pastoral. Too many in leadership were seen as dictatorial, oppressive even; there was no obvious empathy for the struggles people have. Not everyone agreed with me. Some of the panelists and many of the audience had quite a different view. To be fair, the discussion was reasonable and insightful up until the first major break for adverts.

What we in the audience didn't know was that Cardinal Daly and the Catholic press officer were looking in on this discussion in an upstairs room. They were able to take notes and decide which topics to take up. It looked like Big Brother in action once again. They held all the aces.

After the break, to the surprise of those of us in the audience, Cardinal Daly suddenly appeared on the panel ready to answer all questions. In a flash the audience became angry and rightly so. This was the Church at its worst. It gave the impression that those of us with problems were a minority and any question raised could be easily dismissed as the work of cranks.

The theme was: There is no problem, just a few malcontents.

The atmosphere in the studio plummeted. I could hear people behind planning to boo Cardinal Daly. I thought this was immature.

However near the end of the broadcast Cardinal Daly began to sum up, at pains to pour oil on troubled waters. He summed up what he thought he heard us say. Then he resorted to that well-worn phrase which I had heard a hundred times before. 'We have taken it all on board.' He would bring it to the Bishops in his own good time. Things will change. I knew that was shorthand for 'Go home now, be quiet; we know best'.

Just then, Gay Byrne looked around at me. To my surprise he said, 'Brian, you want to say something don't you?' I didn't really. Yet if I said nothing, the booing would begin. If Gay Byrne had not asked me, my life would have been different for sure. But because he asked an honest question, I knew I had to give an honest answer.

'Cardinal,' I said, 'how come there are so many good priests and so many good lay people and yet nobody believes that they are seen as good? Nobody believes anything will be done. What's the problem with communications there?

'Most people looking at this tonight will say, "That was a talk shop. It's nice to have a talk shop, but we will go to Mass on Sunday and next year and our parish will be the same."

'So why can't we break that down? Why can't we do something on a practical level that will give people that hope and encouragement which you speak about so eloquently?'

The cardinal answered, 'I wish I had some members of my own pastoral council here with me or some of my own clergy here to tell us about some of the things they are doing. I think some of us have been very hard on the clergy. There are some of them working very, very hard along the lines you desire. And getting there, too.'

I said, 'I don't think so, Cardinal. I don't think what you have said is fair. Cardinal Daly, you and I have had arguments many times before and I hope we will have them again in a friendly sort of way. But, Cardinal Daly, what I'm trying to say is that I know there are good priests holding the Church together and I know there is a lot of goodness. But at the end of the day, the Church is perceived as heavy-handed and out of date and lacking in compassion. Now why is that? You can't dismiss it because it appears to criticise clergy.'

He said, 'Brian, if I may say so, the Church is also you, and I don't think anyone would regard you as lacking in compassion. But you are the Church; the caring face of the Church. And many other priests and a few bishops too. Just a few, but we are trying. Don't dismiss the whole clergy.'

I answered, 'I'm not dismissing it, Cardinal. That is precisely the point. Nor am I dismissing the whole clergy. But they have been let down.'

Cardinal Daly said, 'Yes, I have been let down. Bishop Bill [Murphy] and Bishop Willie [Walsh] have been let down, but what do we do about it? We go and try to do better.'

I said, 'Perhaps the system is wrong. If you're hurting and I'm hurting, and it's a good thing that we should be hurting, and the people are hurting and the victims who have been abused are hurting, and those who feel they are locked outside the Church because of rules and regulations, they're hurting. If that is the truth, and you have admitted it and I have admitted it, where's the compassionate Church?'

The cardinal replied, 'The Church is in the compassion business day by day round the clock and priests who are living in ghettoised areas are the caring presence of the Lord for those people.'

Cardinal Daly was clearly flustered and I spoke more loudly than I normally do because I was in the audience and not beside him. In my own mind I was not angry but I was not going to let what could have been a wonderful dialogue be stifled by someone pulling rank.

The whole country was disgusted by child abuse. Priests were supposed to be leading sinless lives – they condemned those who 'lived in sin' from the altar. Real honesty was needed and real dialogue; we certainly didn't need an arrogant hierarchy ordering us to be quiet little subjects who pray, pay and obey. Somebody needed to acknowledge the elephant in the room. In other words, I knew we had to have a different way of governance in the Church.

In religious life this form of dialogue was commonplace for a decade or more. For me it was the proper way to behave. It didn't seem offensive to me. What I had forgotten was that within the secular clergy no such dialogue was taking place at that time. Instructions came down from the top. Rome told the hierarchy, the bishops told the priests and the priests passed on the orders to the laity. Everyone thought they knew their place. But that day was gone for good.

My speaking frankly to the cardinal created pandemonium, not only in the studio itself but in the country as a whole. After the show, no one in the studio or on the panel made any effort to speak to me. I was an outcast. Even good friends there avoided me. I seemed to have created a new agenda, one that was not to their liking.

Gay Byrne sensed their coldness. He said I should come to the Green Room and make it up with Cardinal Daly. I felt there was no need for me or Cardinal Daly to make up, since the whole purpose of the show was to have an honest mature conversation. Nothing more, nothing less. However I agreed to go to the Green Room as I always do after the show.

On my way to the Green Room, Maura Connolly, who was Gay Byrne's assistant, asked me to take two urgent phone calls. She was clearly upset. I presumed they were people who wanted to complain about me having an argument with Cardinal Daly. I agreed to take the calls.

The first caller was a woman who was clearly distraught. She described to me how she had been sexually abused as a child by a priest while she was in hospital. He came in every night, she sobbed, pulled the curtains around the bed, read his office with his breviary in one hand and abused her under the bedclothes with his other hand.

The abuse went on for many nights; indeed, it lasted as long as she remained in hospital. It had devastated her life to this day, she told me. She had failed relationships, had a major drink problem and now suffered from severe depression. As she relived her life story I was utterly heartbroken listening to her. The discussion on the Late Late brought it all back for the poor woman. I'm not at liberty to give many more details because it eventually went to court.

The second caller was a man who had been abused in a school run by brothers. It wasn't just sexual abuse in his case. He had been brutally treated by a number of brothers and teachers. He, too, was a broken person who had experienced alcoholism, broken relationships, and periods of homelessness – the usual symptoms. His family hadn't a clue because he could never get the courage to reveal how his life had become such a disastrous mess.

The calls lasted for almost two hours. At various times I saw Gay Byrne, many of his team, Cardinal Daly and the entire audience, walk out past me.

It was early morning when I arrived home at The Graan. I have no memory of the journey but I do know I never once thought of the confrontation with Cardinal Daly. I was consumed with worry as to how I could help those victims. I had arranged for them to phone me on Saturday morning.

I couldn't sleep, not because of what had happened on the Late Late, but because of the phone calls afterwards. I got up early, went for a walk, prayed, looked up contacts I could give to the two callers and hoped they would phone me.

Yet, when I listened to the news on radio at nine o'clock I was shocked to hear that the tiff between me and Cardinal Daly was headlines. It even dominated What It Says in the Papers. I knew I was in trouble.

Thankfully the victims phoned and I was able to put them in touch with appropriate help and they began the long journey to regaining their dignity and their lives.

By midday on Saturday The Graan was a disaster zone. An avalanche of phone calls created havoc with our normal busy weekend. It was the beginning of a shocking week for me. Unwittingly I had become, on the one hand, a demon for upsetting Cardinal Daly and, on the other, a spokesperson for the thousands of voiceless people who agreed with what I said. It was not a comfortable position for me to be in.

Thousands of letters were written and delivered to RTÉ, The Graan and Ara Coeli. Opinion split almost half and half between those who supported Cardinal Daly and those who supported my viewpoint. In all we reckoned about 5,000 letters came to me in the following weeks.

Since I had not met Cardinal Daly after the Late Late, I needed to have a quiet conversation with him. When I rang Ara Coeli on Monday, I was told he was on a break and would not be back until Friday. I made an appointment to meet him on his own on Friday night at his home in Armagh.

I went to Ara Coeli on that dark November night. Cardinal Daly himself ushered me into a small room with two low chairs, a glass table and a two-bar electric fire. He invited me in, had a cup of tea ready and was as gracious as I had expected he would be. He wanted to know what this meeting was about.

I explained that the whole of Ireland thought he and I were fighting. The papers were full of it all week. It was marvelled that an upstart of a priest would take on the cardinal. Not a comfortable position for an ordinary priest from a religious order to be in!!

He was adamant we were not fighting and that I was being oversensitive. Because he was away all week he was not aware of the extent of the controversy. I explained as best I could and said that it was not charitable for us not to attempt a proper dialogue. He agreed fully with me but then wondered why I had been so angry and so critical of the Church on television. He knew me to be a quiet, even shy priest, for years.

Twenty years previously, as editor of The Cross, the then Bishop Daly regularly wrote articles on the Common Market for me. Furthermore, on numerous occasions I had the task of putting popular language on some of the hierarchy's pastoral letters that he had written. We had a friendly working relationship. He disagreed with me writing in The Sunday World, even though his predecessor Cardinal Ó Fiaich had repeatedly encouraged me to keep writing in that paper. Cardinal Daly realised I was not an enemy of the Church. So why was I so angry?

I then outlined some of the scandals currently bubbling under the surface about priests and bishops in Ireland. There were rumors of a paedophile ring involving priests in one diocese. In another western diocese a national paper was sitting on a horrendous story of abuse; they were waiting for an opportunity to publish. I asked him if he knew where Bishop X now was. That he was receiving treatment for an addiction? He knew nothing about any of them.

It was obvious that those who advised Cardinal Daly about the state of the Church were falling down on the job. He was trapped in an ivory tower. As we spoke, I became aware that he was sinking deeper into the chair as the blood drained from his face. I worried that he would suffer another heart attack. It was bad enough fighting with him on television one Friday night, but to bring on a heart attack the following Friday night was all I needed!

I explained that I did not want to upset him further. When we crossed swords on the Late Late, it was out of a deep love of the Church. It was clear that Cardinal Daly sincerely believed nothing derogatory should ever be said about the Church in public. I disagreed. We have to be honest; we are not a perfect society; we are not always true to Christ; we are not always true to our calling. If we are not humble enough to admit our failings and to ask pardon for them, how can we preach mercy and reconciliation to the faithful?

We agreed to differ and parted amicably.

It was the kind of conversation we should have been able to have with Gay Byrne; it was friendly even though we failed to agree on the way ahead. I explained to him that many priests, including some from his own diocese, had been abusive to me because I had confronted him on the Late Late. He assured me they were not acting on his behalf. He understood that I had a point of view, though he disagreed with washing dirty linen in public.

He promised to talk to those priests and assured me the threats made against me and my order were without foundation. I was grateful for that. On the way home I just hoped nothing would happen him that night but I was shocked to realise that he, a man in his late seventies, was left to carry such a heavy burden alone. I couldn't comprehend how out of touch with the real situation in the Church he was.

That section of The Late Late Show has been shown many times on television. In many ways it defines my life. The Church of Ireland Gazette commented that what seemed like a promising career for me in the Church was now in ruins. The Irish Times proclaimed that my Father Trendy image was now gone forever. I had grown up overnight, they wrote. Little did they know that I never was Father Trendy and that coming to terms with sexual abuse had made me stronger than I or they realised.

Months after the incident with Cardinal Daly I met one of his senior bishops at a function. He asked me how I was since being publicly rebuked by Cardinal Daly. He explained that as soon as I spoke that night, he knew from his armchair that the cardinal would fight back. He said that is how he treats the bishops at their meetings in Maynooth – he treats us like little boys. I asked the bishop if anyone dared to speak truthfully to the cardinal at their meetings. Of course no one would dare do any such thing, he assured me.

Then they deserved to be treated like little boys, I told him. No wonder we're in such a mess. I was appalled to hear that none of these so-called leaders had the guts to speak truth to power.

Another bishop explained to me that they were appointed bishops precisely because they would not rock the boat and would do as they were asked. They would defend the indefensible when they have to. The Church's image must be kept intact.

That is what happens when an institution becomes so dysfunctional that it cannot trust the Holy Spirit to discern what is best for God's people on earth. That is what is called systemic dysfunction.

Since that night I can honestly say my life changed forever. Many priests (though by no means all) treated me as an enemy. I was frequently refused permission to preside at funerals or to celebrate weddings around Ireland.

The clerical church never really trusted me again. I was isolated when priests met.

It was the opposite with the people though. Even those who thought I was wrong on that fateful night gradually realised I was not an enemy of the Church. To this day, people repeatedly tell me, 'If the leaders had listened to you then, the Church would not be in the mess it is today.' They recognised that I was not in it for the short term; that I could be trusted to speak the truth.

Looking back, I can say with certainty that I didn't choose to cause a storm that night, but I don't regret it.

CHAPTER 19

THOUGHTS ON JOURNEY

Life is a journey and life takes us on many journeys. At my age I'm only too aware that the journey is nearly over for me.

As a priest I've been with hundreds of dying people. It's a privilege that I never take for granted. Helping people to leave this world behind in exchange for the beauty of eternal life with God brings faith into focus in a way that nothing else can.

Sadly, too many of those I prayed with as they died, were young people on the side of the road, killed in road traffic accidents. My very first experience of that was ten days after ordination. In early January the monastery got an urgent call to send a priest to an accident on a dark country road. I had just returned from my ordination holidays that evening, full of joy that I had achieved the only goal I ever wanted. I was asked to go on the call because I was the only priest available who could drive.

The police were already there and in the lights of their car I could see the body lying on the road. I was ill-prepared for such a tragic scene yet I knew automatically what to do.

I asked the police if I could touch the man, who seemed to my inexperienced eyes to be dead.

They nodded. I knelt beside him. I held his hand as I whispered an act of contrition into his ear. I anointed him and spoke consoling words to him. I remember his hand was cold but then it was a winter's night and he was coming from milking in an old-style, primitive byre.

The ambulance arrived just as I finished the prayers. The ambulance crew made a quick examination and concluded the man was dead.

'He got a bad knock,' the ambulance man said. 'He has injuries all over.'

Then they all turned to me. His elderly parents were sitting on either side of a turf fire in their thatched cottage across the road. Somebody had to tell them. I was unanimously volunteered to break the news. I hadn't a clue how to approach them but I prayed for inspiration before knocking on their door. I walked slowly up to them and in the light of the blazing fire introduced myself.

'You're a very young priest, Father, what has you in these parts on a night like this,' the mother asked.

I wasn't brave enough or foolish enough to tell them. I could feel tears on my cheek so I explained who I was and asked them had they any relatives nearby. The father said their son was feeding cattle across the road.

Were there any others? A daughter lived about a mile away. I went out to the crew and asked if the police would collect the daughter. In January 1970 there weren't many phones in rural Ireland.

I went back inside and by now the couple knew something was wrong. Bit by bit I explained how their son had been knocked down crossing the road from the byre to their home. It was a dark night and he was carrying a meal bag. The ambulance was there and had taken him away. I consoled them by assuring them everyone did all they could, that I had anointed him and he didn't suffer.

It took the lovely old couple nearly half an hour to get the story into their sad hearts. I offered to pray with them if it would help. The mother got her rosary beads and we went into a peaceful mantra praying the Sorrowful Mysteries.

The daughter arrived, breathless and hyper with grief. She already knew the worst. They all consoled one another with words of comfort handed down through the generations.

'He didn't deserve that;' 'He was a great worker;' 'He'll not be able to go to the cards tomorrow night now.' 'We better let the neighbours know.' 'He was in great form this evening.' On and on they went, sipping tea, crying, putting turf on the fire, sweeping the floor to have it clean for the wake.

By the time I left, the house was full, their son was on his way to the morgue and his cousin, the driver of the car that killed him, was being taken away in a police car. He was, the neighbours told me, very drunk and didn't know what he had done.

I drove slowly and carefully back to the monastery where I found the monks gathered for supper. Everyone wanted to know what kept me so late. 'You're only back from ordination today and you missed evening prayer already,' the rector said sternly.

I went to the bathroom. I washed my hands over and over. I splashed cold water on my face to hide the puffing beneath my eyes.

It was morning before I could tell them that I shared the most poignant evening prayer ever with the grieving parents of a dead son.

The journey had begun.

Often in the Gospels Jesus learned about life and about himself on his daily journeys. We, too, may need to climb to the rugged mountaintops if we are to trust God enough to discover there is something beyond the clouds. Journeys of self-awareness are harder than physical journeys. Scott Peck wrote a famous book, which became a world bestseller, called The Road Less Travelled. The title came from a poem by Robert Frost.

Peck began his book with one short sentence of three words. 'Life is difficult.'

So it is. No matter what road we travel we discover life is difficult, but with God's help, not impossible.

In the Bible going up mountains has a special significance. It is the place where God lives; the place where we meet God. Moses got the Ten Commandments on a mountain. Elijah had mountaintop experiences. We found Jesus on the Hill of Calvary abandoned and neglected.

Journeys are necessary. There is no map for life. There is no satnav to keep us out of danger. Life is a constant search and, as Robert Louis Stevenson said so truly, 'To travel hopefully is a better thing than to arrive.'

I think that's what Elizabeth Barrett Browning meant when she wrote so beautifully:

Earth's crammed with heaven
And every common bush afire with God
But he who sees takes off his shoes
The rest sit around and pluck blackberries.

Looking back I realise I seem to have many of St Peter's bad attitudes. Peter was so anxious to do the right thing that he missed the most important thing.

The disciples were often paralysed by fear. It took Jesus to touch them as he did every sick person to heal them.

Today we are afraid to risk or to change. The Second Vatican Council told us the Church is in need of constant reform. Yet we are silent when we should be speaking. We defend the indefensible. We cling to what was and deny ourselves the future God wants.

How come we are afraid of too much mercy when God says mercy is the centre of his heart? Why is it that we judge more than we reconcile? Why is it that we don't embrace the sinner as Jesus does? Jesus was put to death with the accusation that he was 'a friend of sinners'. That certainly could never be said of today's Church.

I remember Archbishop Desmond Tutu in South Africa putting it brilliantly. He was speaking to thousands upon thousands of very poor black people. He urged them to become transfiguration people. I thought he was mad when I heard him preach it. But then he explained. 'We should transfigure injustice into justice. We should transfigure condemnation into compassion. We should transfigure harshness into care. We should transfigure sorrow into laughter and despair into joy and hope.'

That's our vocation.

One Wednesday in 2017, a few days before I had to leave my home in the Graan, a group of about twenty men and women who had worked with me there in prayer and self-development groups for fifteen years or more came together for a final inspirational day out.

We went to visit the Seamus Heaney museum in Derry to honour a poet who was part of the spiritual vision we grew into. We drove to Bellaghy to his HomePlace. We received a warm welcome from the staff there. They made sure we got into the right spirit from the moment they met us in reception. Checking in beside us was Declan O'Driscoll, who introduced himself as the brother of Dennis O'Driscoll, the glorious poet who did the biographical interviews with Seamus Heaney in the book Stepping Stones.

The centre is a brilliant place. Each visitor is given a phone-like implement which helps to make the visit personal and unique. On the visit we got to know Heaney from boyhood to death.

It's his life story told through the bits and pieces of Bellaghy. There Heaney was able to see the spiritual and the mystical in local symbols which became universal through the language of poetry.

There are anvils, ploughs, turf spades, buckets, typewriters, all the things we have around us but never see their mystical qualities. Heaney was able to make ordinary things symbols of a greater life.

Here the voice of the poet himself recites the poems he wrote about the anvil or turf spade or a knife that peeled spuds with his mother.

One poem that jumped out at me focused on relationships. Relationships outlast time and place, Heaney wrote in 'Scaffolding'. It came about after he and his wife Marie had an early marriage tiff that wasn't easily resolved. On her own admission Marie ran upstairs in a huff. Seamus didn't sleep at all but next morning he gave her 'Scaffolding'.

In it Seamus explains how when a wall is being built it needs scaffolding to keep it safe, but when the wall is finished you can take down the scaffolding in the certain knowledge that the wall will not fall.

'Never fear my dear, we may let the scaffolds fall, confident that we have built our walls,' he concludes. The poet reassured her that their love was greater than a mere tiff.

At the end of the day we moved to the graveyard where Heaney is buried in a simple grave behind the church in the village. A local explained that if we looked four feet over in the other direction we would see the family plot. There his parents and grandparents are buried, as well as his brother Christopher, who was knocked down and killed by a car and who was buried in a coffin four foot long – 'a foot for every year'.

On Heaney's headstone we are encouraged to 'Walk on air, against your better judgement'.

Martin Luther was an Augustinian monk who recognised that his Church was in need of reform. It's often said that if the Second Vatican Council had been held when Luther called for reform, there might never have been a Reformation.

However, it seems that Luther was a man with little joy in his life. When he left the Augustinians he married. His wife had a tough time communicating with him, perhaps because he suffered from depression. One day, the story goes, she went upstairs and came down dressed in black from head to toe. Luther was shocked and asked her why she was doing this.

'Because God is dead,' she answered.

He flew into a rage, insisting it was blasphemous to say such things. She told him it was no different from him leading a joyless life as if God were dead.

Martin Luther learned two good lessons on that occasion: a) the woman is always right; and b) the woman always has the last word. It's good for us to remember that joyless religion is the most damning form of atheism.

It reminds me of this Sufi story. Once there was a man who sincerely searched for a healthy spiritual life. All his life he sought to find a community where he could touch the presence of God. He found a learned guru who had a reputation for being wise. He was impressed by the guru but, like many searchers, always had to ask one more question.

'In this community does God listen to your prayers and work miracles?' he asked.

The guru proved his wisdom with his answer. He said, 'There are two ways of praying. One is when we pray so that God changes his mind. Many consider it a miracle when we change God's mind and get what we want.

'However, in this community we consider it a miracle when the community, through their prayers, learns to listen to God.'

That's what journeys are for.

CHAPTER 20

MICHAELA HARTE PRAYER

None of us will ever forget the tragic circumstances of Michaela McAreavey's (or Michaela Harte's) murder when she and her new husband John were on honeymoon. It was one of the saddest times for all who knew the Harte and McAreavey families. I was privileged to know both families and often enjoyed John and Michaela's company – usually at football matches.

At our Novena of Hope at The Graan near Enniskillen, I also asked people who had been through turmoil to share their journey with us. Incredibly, on different years I asked Michaela's famous father Mickey to speak, as well as her husband, John McAreavey, and also her brother, Mark Harte. On three different years, they each spoke of their own personal experience of grief and how they each coped with such an unspeakable tragedy.

All three packed the church to capacity and held every single member of the congregation spellbound with the sincerity of their lives and their religion.

They spoke explicitly about where their faith came from and how it helped them survive such suffering.

At the end of his sharing, Mark read a prayer which he told us Michaela recited every day. The prayer is actually printed on Michaela's memoriam card. This is the prayer that gave so much strength to Michaela herself and continues to give hope to her family, her friends and to all who take part in the Michaela summer project:

Lord every day I need you
but especially this day.
I need some extra strength
to face whatever is to come

This day, more than any other day,
I need to feel you near me,
to fortify my courage
and to overcome my fear.

By myself I cannot meet
the challenge of the hour,
I need you to sustain me
in all that life may bring.

And so, dear Lord,
Calm my trembling hand.
Be with me this day Lord,
so that I may know your guiding hand
At work in everything,
And know your guiding presence
with me always.

CHAPTER 21

THE POWER OF WORDS

Poets, songwriters, journalists and orators continue to inspire me to change my outlook and change my life. Without them I'd still be a lonely, self-righteous, dogmatic old bachelor.

I've written often about generations of great songwriters. But poets like Carol Ann Duffy, Patrick Kavanagh, Mary Oliver and Seamus Heaney never fail to inspire me with the raw courage to tackle new challenges.

Two weeks before he died, I went to hear Seamus Heaney read poetry in the Millennium Theatre, Derry. The piper Liam O'Flynn was also performing with him on that night. They often performed together and always magnificently. Both of them are now gone and the world is a poorer place. It was a night made for history; it was the first time Seamus had performed in the Millennium in Derry (amazingly!) and the first time the Fleadh was held in Derry. The atmosphere was mystical and magical.

Immersed in the poetry and music, it turned out to be the most spiritually awakening experience I had in years. Little did I know then that it would be the last public appearance made by the Nobel laureate in his native heath; the last time I would hear his unique solemn rendering of his own magnificent works of art. I shall treasure the memory forever.

It's not just with hindsight, but I recognised a real sense of vulnerability in the poet, especially as he recited in his distinctive soft voice:

> You are neither here nor there,
> A hurry through which known and strange things pass
> As big soft buffetings come at the car sideways
> And catch the heart off guard and blow it open. ('Postscript')

Three of Heaney's poems have propped up my spiritual life for decades. I came to him through Patrick Kavanagh – the first poet I really understood. Kavanagh highlighted the deep significance of the apparently insignificant. Heaney himself acknowledged that he found in Kavanagh 'details of a life that I knew intimately'.

Seamus Heaney's universally known 'Mid-Term Break', which he wrote in a bedsit ten years after his brother Christopher's tragic death, made me cry when I first read it. It has done so many times since, when I helped parents to bury their children in little white coffins. I prayed it nightly after my five-year-old nephew died in the mid-1970s. Tears rolled down my cheeks when Seamus Heaney read it that night in the Millennium, in the certain knowledge that it will have the same power to 'blow open my heart' every time I pray it.

That was when I recognised Heaney's miraculous ability to knock you sideways with a last line that seems to slide in, bringing the poem to a stunning end while simultaneously kick-starting a new beginning of a lifelong, personal, reflective search for meaning. Heaney's endings always create new beginnings with me.

When my mother died at an age when she and I were too young, I wish I had known his wonderful sonnet 'When all the others were away at Mass'. How such an ordinary chore as a mother and son peeling potatoes could become a symbol of warmth and love fully conveys the mysticism of poetry.

By the time my father died suddenly, I was lucky enough to be familiar with 'The Follower'.

All those evenings I spent working beside my father in the bog spreading and clamping turf; all the back-breaking summer nights weeding potatoes – and every other vegetable that would thrive in mossy ground – were summed up succinctly by Heaney. I wondered how he knew

I was a nuisance, tripping, falling,
yapping always. But today
It is my father who keeps stumbling
Behind me, and will not go away.

There's that 'shocking' last line again.

I heard Seamus Heaney say in an interview that one of his greatest poems came as a gift almost. As I remember it he and Marie, and Brian and Anne Friel, were driving in County Clare one especially windy day and stopped to take in the marvellous sights, sounds and smells emanating from the bracing Atlantic Ocean. The experience was mind-blowing and immediate. Later that evening he went to his room, began to capture the magic from his memory, put together the first version of 'Postscript' and read it for his companions at dinner that evening.

And I hope these pages might encourage both you and me to make the time to 'drive out west', to escape and reflect on the beauty of life and God's creation. Then, we too will be able to experience what we need to experience – big soft buffetings coming at you sideways, 'And catch the heart off guard and blow it open.'

For it is only when the heart is broken open that we can know the need for healing.

CHAPTER 22

REMBRANDT'S PRODIGAL SON

The first time I saw a reproduction of Rembrandt's 'The Return of the Prodigal Son' I was aghast. In front of me was the most moving explanation of the Gospel story of the Prodigal Son I had ever encountered.

I really understood the meaning of the Gospel story for the first time. What stunned me was the realisation that I don't have to be perfect to be loved by God. It was Rembrandt's genius that broke open my heart.

Rembrandt painted The Return of the Prodigal Son towards the end of his life. Repeated personal tragedy and his own wayward life had fractured his relationship with God. But he found reconciliation as he worked on this 'spiritual' masterpiece.

The Gospel has the patient father welcoming home a wayward son, whilst at the same time, placating an elder son who never left home.

I'm told Rembrandt worked hard to find a friendly, compassionate face for the father, who embodies God's forgiveness for all our sins.

In the painting the Prodigal Son's shaved head is buried in the father's breast. It is the head of a carefree young man; but at the same time the head of an infant, a foetus really, on a journey to rebirth from the father's bosom.

This Prodigal Son is dressed in a pilgrim's outer garment. His left foot has no sandal. The bare foot highlights that this is a penitent in need of forgiveness. The right foot, with its well-worn sandal, tells us this is a pilgrim with many miles still to travel.

The conclusion is that reconciliation is both the end of a journey and the beginning of a new life.

However, the hands of the father are the most striking. Those used to studying Rembrandt's paintings recognise both hands from previous works. The father's left hand is placed on the shoulder of the returning Prodigal Son. It's a strong supportive hand, a trusting hand – a man's hand.

Amazingly, the father's right hand is completely different. This is a woman's hand. In Rembrandt's other works this woman's hand is often used to recall a caring, forgiving, loving person. Just as the feet represent both penance and pilgrimage, so the father's hands represent strength and gentleness.

The saddest person in the painting and in the story is the elder son who looks on from the margins. He never made a mistake so he can't know the need for forgiveness. His self-righteousness locks him into his begrudgery.

At first sight, I saw myself as the Prodigal Son and in a sense I am. Yet I am also the elder son, the begrudger, the self-righteous one. The truth is that I need to become more like the father. I need to learn to embody the father's gentleness, strength, love, forgiveness and wisdom. I need to 'leave home' and leave the safe place of habit.

This painting taught me that for a Prodigal Son to return, he first has to admit his mistakes. I now know that all of my inner speeches of justification for my life are but repetitions of the Prodigal Son's, 'I will go to my Father and say … '

I've learned that the father has to love both the Prodigal Son and the begrudging elder son equally. Most of all, Rembrandt's two beautiful hands – the masculine and the feminine – assure me that God is both a father and a mother. This painting made me realise that I can never earn God's forgiveness; I simply must be humble enough to accept it. That's another reason to be grateful.

Chapter 23

WAKE UP WITH WOGAN

When I wrote the first volume of my memoir 'a Different journey', the publisher wondered if Sir Terry Wogan would pen the foreword. I thought about it for a long time. I hate asking friends to do favours and I rarely impose on them. But since I thought there would be only one memoir I plucked up courage and shyly asked him to write 'a few words'.

This is part of the much too generous email he returned next day.

Fr Brian D'Arcy has been there for all the important events of life in the Wogan family: my mother and father's funerals, the weddings of my three children, and he'll probably see me off the premises as well, because he hasn't aged a day since I first met him.

Maybe he loves life too much, and music, and sport, but what a Bishop he would have made!

He has crossed forbidden boundaries again and again in Northern Ireland, risking all to temper hatred and bring tolerance and understanding. He has toiled in the townships of South Africa.

He is devoted to his Community and his flock in The Graan, County Fermanagh. He writes for newspapers and magazines, he joins me at the microphone regularly for BBC Radio 2's Pause for Thought.

Brian D'Arcy's not doing it for fame or fortune, reward or applause. He's doing it for good. Thank God for him.

There is no better example of the generosity, the thoughtfulness or the dignity of Sir Terry than those sincere words which he penned and returned within a day of being asked.

Furthermore, when we launched the memoir in England, Terry came with his Radio 2 Breakfast team to perform the launch with the same humour and enthusiasm he brought to hosting the Eurovision. He, Eamonn Holmes and Barry McGuigan sparked off each other on a morning that would make you proud to be Irish. The many English people who attended, especially colleagues from the BBC, were in open-mouthed admiration.

Terry had a huge influence on me as a person and as a broadcaster. He was a true legend who was the most popular broadcaster in Britain at a time when the IRA was bombing innocent people on a regular basis. I know there were many mornings when he had to wake up Britain, not knowing whether his Irish blarney would add insult to injury as more IRA atrocities made headlines on the news bulletins every half hour.

When it came to fame he often joked that the line between popularity and hatred is fine and fickle. On one occasion he was voted The Most Popular Personality on Television AND The Most Hated Man on Television in the same year. He knew that had to be the peak because everyone knew him and had an opinion about him. Actually Terry won Television Personality of The Year on ten occasions.

There was a massive outpouring of grief when he died. I was prepared for the bad news because I had been with him a few days before; still, I was heartbroken. His kindness to me over nearly forty years was literally beyond expression. You can only imagine the devastation it caused to his beloved Lady Helen and their family. Now when I go to London to broadcast with Chris Evans who took over from Terry and, indeed, was kindness personified, and Zoe Ball, the Radio 2 Building is named Wogan House. That's a measure of his true greatness.

Terry had no equal when it came to broadcasting. His advice to me was: 'The secret of successful broadcasting, Brian, is to be able to hang around long enough to become a habit. When you're a habit you can't be done without.' That's exactly what Terry became – an unforgettable morning addiction.

In the end he had eight million listeners every morning. He was delighted to hand over to his friend Chris Evans, telling him: 'My listeners are loyal. You'll lose a million or two, maybe, but you'll gain a few more million younger listeners.' That's how it turned out. The listenership at first went down and then up to ten million. And when there was nowhere else to go, Chris too moved on, remembering Terry's advice: 'There may not be a right time to leave, but there certainly is a wrong time to stay.'

I was lucky enough to be part of his programme for almost twenty years. Pause for Thought at a quarter past nine has a huge listenership. I realised the power of his show when people arrived from all over the British Isles to our monastery, The Graan in Enniskillen, simply because they heard me broadcasting from Enniskillen on Terry's show.

One story in particular is worth retelling. In the 1990s the British army were everywhere around Enniskillen. Often half the congregation would come in to Mass well after the sermon and collection because they were being held up by a futile British Army patrol near our church. It was bloody annoying for them and for me. But what could you do about it?

Then, out of the blue, I got a specially delivered invitation to attend the Christmas party in the nearby British army barracks.

It was the last thing I expected or indeed needed. But I thought about it for a day or two and decided I'd accept the invitation. After all, my role was to build bridges within the community.

I told no one about the invitation – not even the men who lived with me. I went to the barracks hoping nobody would see my car going through the gates. Many a person was murdered for less.

Inside I was greeted warmly by the commander in charge. He immediately made his way across to shake my hand.

'I'm so glad you came Padre. I was going to call up to The Graan to see you but I thought this would be the perfect occasion to thank you for helping my wife to consent to my coming here.

'I had just been told I was being changed to Ennisillen in Northern Ireland on a sunny Monday morning. I knew my wife – we were only recently married – would never agree. I was listening to Terry Wogan as I drove down to break the bad news to her.

'You came on and Terry asked you what it was like in Enniskillen today. You painted an idyllic picture of cows, sunshine, green rolling hills, peaceful waters, conjuring up an oasis of calmness.

'I knew my wife always listened to Terry. So when I got home and broke the news to her, she immediately agreed I should go because "I heard Father Brian telling us what a peaceful place Enniskillen is on the Terry Wogan Show."

'I can never thank you enough. I will be leaving soon and I'll tell my wife I met you and perhaps I can visit you in The Graan before I return. It would mean so much to her.'

He came to see me, we had tea, a little chat and then he said, 'Is there anything I can do for your community before I go?'

I immediately jumped in to tell him there was only one thing I wanted him to do. 'Please tell your soldiers to stay off the roads when people are on their way to church. It rightly upsets them and seems to be a bigoted, discriminatory act.' He was shocked but instantly realised it was the soldiers who were creating the bad feeling in the area.

He thanked me and promised it wouldn't happen again. And it never did. Our collections went up instantly but nobody knew the real reason – Terry Wogan's popularity and my ability to make Fermanagh beautiful.

I have been privileged to broadcast with almost all the legends in Britain and Ireland over five decades and without insulting any of them, the easiest to broadcast with was Terry. He truly welcomed you to be part of his programme. He made sure he helped me in every way and he did all in his power to make Pause for Thought the most listened-to religious programme in Europe. He was utterly selfless as a broadcaster.

For Terry, Helen and their family always came first. He kept his private life and his public life separate. I utterly respect that. The only Terry you'll hear about from me is the public persona – and his kindness to me

Over the years I had the honour of being with Terry and his different producers solving the world's problems over cups of coffee – and the occasional bacon butty – looking out over the London landscape. It was then you realised what a brilliant mind Terry Wogan had. He had an incisive mind, and articulated the fruits of his reading and reflection with charm, wit and humility.

Frequently over the years we talked about religion. Terry was one of the most Christian people I have ever met. He received many gifts during his Jesuit education, but perhaps someone fell down when it came to communicating a God of compassion.

In one of his many self-penned books, Where Was I? Terry had a dissertation on what the Catechism taught us about sin. What a memory!

When I was a lad ... everything was a sin ... Sin was a cottage industry where I came from. You could hardly open your mouth, or go outside your front door, without committing one. There were Grievous ones. Deadly ones, Mortal ones and Venials. The first three categories were Biggies, and if you did a Mortal, you were toast condemned to the eternal flames of Hell – unless, of course, somebody threw you a life-line by way of Confession, or an Indulgence.

Venial sins were like walking on egg-shells, trip-wires at every turn: Lies, Disobedience, Bad Language, and Impure Thoughts – you couldn't get through five minutes of a normal day without a handful of Venials to your name. In the fullness of time, these would guarantee you a light frying for several aeons, in Purgatory. And you were getting off lightly at that ...

The Big One was Sex. You couldn't even think about it. And in the Ireland of my youth, thinking about it was all you could do. There wasn't a lot of it going. The next Worst Thing was Vanity (Murder came way down the list). You could get into trouble looking in the mirror. You grew up learning not to boast, push yourself forward, preen or show off. And you know, as I look around me, that wasn't such a bad thing.

Today, all is Vanity: if you've got it, flaunt it. The Wannabes are everywhere: wannabe rich, wannabe noticed, wannabe famous. And they're prepared to do anything, no matter how degrading, to strut their stuff in front of the cheap seats. The sound of this millennium is a shriek for attention, Me, Me, Me. And if that's not a sin, it's a shame ...

These are my observations on the passing parade, and it's surprising how little the parade has changed on its weary way by. Oh yes there have been wars and famines, sub-prime lending and billions borrowed, but these need not detain us here ... (2)

I once did a series of sixteen programmes on the history of showbands for BBC Radio Ulster/ RTÉ Radio One. Terry loved and admired the showbands. He was one of the first to play them on his famous Hospitals Requests and he frequently played them on his morning Radio 2 programme as well. I asked him if he'd ever been involved in Payola.

He jokingly recalled he was involved in payola when he worked with RTÉ. Payola in those days was called dropsie. (You dropped the disc jockey a few quid for himself to play your record. Drop. Dropsie? Get it?) This is how Terry remembered it.

One afternoon I was preparing to broadcast Hospitals Requests for Radio Éireann. We were in the GPO in O'Connell Street then. Before going on air I went to the downstairs toilet. A man came into the toilet and we stood side by side at the urinals. Greetings were exchanged, and after the statutory ten minutes of pointless blather, the reason for his visit became plain. He had the latest record of his band, especially for me. He wanted me to listen to it, because he respected my opinion above all others, and he personally would be amazed if I didn't think it was the finest thing of its kind since Count John McCormack kicked the bucket! A natural for Hospitals Requests and a crowd pleaser that would have the patients leaping from their beds.

I said I would certainly give it a listen, and, shaking his hand, I excused myself to the bathroom. Luckily, I had finished my simple toilet, when your man entered. He moved swiftly, even surreptitiously to my side. 'Now,' he said, as he pressed a packet of twenty Sweet Afton cigs into my hand, 'that's for yourself.' He left as swiftly as he had come. I never played the record. I can't be bought!!!

Terry often told me that story and I know who the manager was. He was a decent man who has gone to his reward. The record went on to become the most iconic hit of the whole showband era. Terry should have known that any record about a gentle mother couldn't fail.

CHAPTER 24

THE LUNATIC AND THE CHERRY BLOSSOMS

A wise man with a sense of humour is a dangerous person to meet, especially if you're feeling a bit vulnerable. I was sauntering along Church Street in Enniskillen when I spotted the wise man on my side of the road. He had a smile on his face as bright as a harvest moon. I should have known he was up to no good. He complimented me on how well I looked. I thanked him. 'You know, Father Brian, you'll never get old,' he said. I thanked him again. 'At your age you'll just get older.'

Cherry blossoms continually remind me of the brevity and the fickleness of life. You look for their buds in early spring and your heart lifts when they burst into a cloud of glowing colours. Their beauty brightens creation in a magical display. Then, suddenly, a blast of wind comes on a stormy night and their blossoms lie miserably on the ground, gone and soon forgotten.

Fifty-seven years ago, when I first entered The Graan monastery to join the Passionists as a seventeen-year-old boy, I tried to be a good novice. I accepted that the 'old' (though very young) Brian D'Arcy had to die to the world and its dross and to mark that death to the old I had to accept a new name, which was Desmond Mary. My worldly clothes were left at the novice master's door and I put on used penitential clothes, a hand-me-down habit and sandals. I've told the full story earlier in the book.

I accepted that the food was both awful and scarce. I accepted that I had to get up in the middle of the night to pray and then go back to bed before getting up again at six in the morning. I didn't question any of those things.

I reluctantly left my family and my football behind. I was not allowed to write to my parents and I could not speak to them if they came to Mass in The Graan, as they sometimes did, hoping to get a glimpse of their prodigal son. I went from being a teenager who knew everything that was happening in world affairs to an unquestioning novice who was forbidden to look at, never mind read, a paper or listen to a radio – there were hardly any TVs back then.

Looking back on it now, I morphed into a spiritual zombie. It was tough but I accepted it all. I knew it was what I had to do to be a priest. Now I realise how seriously damaging it was to me as a human being; a young man who gradually accepted the destruction of his 'self' could be made accept anything.

One day when I was a malleable novice, the rector of the monastery called me to his cell. This rector had been in Africa and was very close to being made a bishop. He had been educated in Rome, and was then regarded as a bright intellectual who was secretary to the Passionist General for a term. When he came back to Ireland he served as provincial superior and was now rector at The Graan. He was a man of some standing.

The master of novices was away so the rector was in charge of us. One morning he called me to his room after breakfast – dry bread and thick coffee. He asked me if I could use a cross-cut saw. I could, because my father had taught me. He then asked another strong burly novice, if he could use the saw. He said he could, even though he couldn't, because he was afraid to tell the truth.

The rector then gave us a task for the day. We were dispensed from all novitiate duties and instead we were to work on the land. Outside the monastery there was a row of twenty beautiful, mature cherry blossom trees, planted as shrubs fifteen years previously. They were well-shaped and were beautiful in full bloom.

He then ordered us to cut all twenty of them down as close to the ground as possible. They were, in his words, 'useless trees that gathered dirt'.

We went to the farmyard, got a cross-cut and I explained to my companion how it worked. We started to cut the trees and by twelve o'clock we had all twenty trees cut down with just ground level stumps peeping over the grass. The other novices came out after lunch and carried them to the dump where they were left to dry out before they were burned.

I wasn't happy that I'd cut down the trees – what country man would be – but the rector knew best, and I was happy to be an obedient novice, praised by the rector.

Some of the priests in the community berated us through open windows for daring to cut the trees, even though they knew we had to obey the rector. They had not been consulted, yet they were afraid to talk to the rector so they rounded on us instead.

All went well until the next day when I was in the gardens doing solitary walk – a time when we walked around for thirty minutes and every now and then stopped to recall the presence of God. It was a reminder that we shouldn't be distracted by nature but instead we should contemplate God. Another example of the evils of dualistic spirituality.

Whilst I was walking, Charlie Keenan, who was the gardener, stuck his spade in the ground and walked straight over to me. I didn't realise that Charlie was the man who had originally planted those trees, carefully nurtured them and was rightly proud to see them blossoming. It was his lifetime's work.

He looked at me with anger in his eyes. He spat on his hands and said, 'Are you the lunatic who cut down the cherry trees?' Since I was not allowed to speak I nodded in assent.

'Well it's jail you should get. Only a lunatic or a criminal would cut down such beautiful trees.'

He went back to his work.

The presence of God was far from my mind.

Only then did I realise the enormity of the mistake I'd made!

But I was seventeen, about the same age as the trees, innocent, eager to please and under obedience. If I hadn't cut the trees I could have been sent home.

Today I genuinely think it's probably the most serious sin I have committed in my entire life. How could I not understand that it is a sin to destroy God's beauty? How could someone reared close to nature in the country not understand how stupid and malicious it was to saw down cherry blossoms? That's how bad spirituality demolishes a person. I have confessed the sin on many occasions, yet I cannot forgive myself.

The poet Thomas Bracken has a line: 'Poor souls with stunted vision, oft measure giants by their own narrow gauge'. The rector, who was educated in Rome, in the midst of the greatest art treasures of the world, and who had travelled the world, decided that a beautiful creation like a cherry tree was dirt. Charlie Keenan, a man of nature, a man of the soil, a man in touch with God's power, knew that it was a work of art and should not be destroyed.

I have meditated on this incident for a lifetime. A religion that becomes so detached from God is capable of carrying out terrible deeds in religion's name. That's the kind of brainwashing that enabled deviants to justify abusing children. It dehumanises gullible idealists and makes them cowards, afraid to speak out against sin for fear of upsetting those who put themselves in God's place.

I can't claim I understood exactly the implications of it all at the time. But as I think of it now I recognise that God was teaching me a valuable lesson about the limits to human obedience. I did the wrong thing for the wrong reasons because of blind obedience to a false god. It's why I resist 'blind obedience' every since.

CHAPTER 25

THE VATICAN AND ME

The monastery known as The Graan is situated about three miles from the centre of Enniskillen, County Fermanagh, in Northern Ireland. It's been part of the community for 110 years.

All told I lived there for close on twenty-five years, the vast majority of them as its rector/superior. I spent the best years of my life there and don't regret a second of it. The people who attend The Graan are my friends and my family. We have been through good times and bad; we matured together through Church scandals and devastating violence. As a community we grew up together. We learned to trust each other.

When I returned to The Graan as rector in late 1989, I had just completed twelve years running Mount Argus in Dublin. I was parish priest there as well as chief fund-raiser for the massive restoration project. I was very aware how attitudes were changing in the Church and we needed to prepare for it. Nothing stays the same and the best time to prepare for the trying times is when you are strong, not when you're falling apart.

When I left Mount Argus, there were eighty-three in the community, the largest Passionist community in the world at that time. There might be twenty or so there now.

As soon as I settled in at The Graan I knew we needed to make radical changes if this monastery was to survive. I set about restructuring the building and farm and then rethought the pastoral service we provided.

I had already helped to pioneer the Novena of Hope in Mount Argus where it was a blessed relief for the people to hear positive preaching, not only from priests but from lay people too. Old style missions were on the way out. The people of Ireland had had their fill of hell and damnation; they needed to have hope in their lives.

The theme of hope was even more needed in the troubled North of Ireland. Right from its beginning in 1990, people from around Fermanagh, Tyrone, Leitrim, Cavan, Donegal, and further afield put the nine days of the novena in their diaries and, come hell or high water, turned out in their thousands.

I was guided by the people and made it a genuine festival of hope with days for the sick, penance services that worked, joyful, welcoming liturgies and music everyone could enjoy. We laughed, we clapped, we prayed, we were comfortable in God's house and we worked ourselves to a standstill. Not only that, we developed a massive cross-community coming together. Young and old, people of every creed and none knew they were welcome. I invited speakers from every walk of life and clergy, both men and women, from all of the Christian churches.

It was truly amazing how enthusiastically people reacted to positive leadership. Boundaries were crossed successfully and even politicians reluctantly followed in the wider community.

What we did on the outskirts of the town, by joining up with our neighbours in the Rossorry Church of Ireland community under the guidance of Archdeacon Cecil Pringle, was then replicated in Enniskillen itself. So much so that Her Majesty Queen Elizabeth II visited St Macartin's Church of Ireland cathedral and then, in a historic act, crossed the street to worship in St Michael's Catholic church.

President Michael D. Higgins also came to Enniskillen and went from St Michael's across to St Macartin's. Both acknowledged the impact of what we started at our novena in The Graan, along with Archdeacon Pringle's worshippers in Rossorry.

The last night of the novena was always special. My friends in the music business came every year and helped us celebrate appropriately with joy and gratitude. You couldn't find a seat in the church hours before Mass began. In later years we had to ask the PSNI to help us with traffic control to prevent latecomers jamming up the car park. It must be the only church in the western world where we had to hire the police to keep people away from Church.

When I was changed from The Graan in 2017, it nearly broke my heart. The sense of failure was so intense as to be almost irrational. When I think about it now, it was total grief. It was a reminder that in life, nothing is permanent. It's all a journey and the journey is the achievement. The Graan was my home. I was born a few miles up the road. I walked in the doors to give my life to God as an idealistic seventeen-year-old.

When I left Mount Argus I felt I had achieved something because, against all the odds, I managed to convince people it was worth saving, even though many of the monks living in it had no such conviction. When I left it I learned to leave it behind. Even though, when times changed and attendances began to dwindle, I often wondered if I should have put so much of my life into it. But I knew in my heart that I did it for the right reasons. Those wonderful voluntary lay workers who helped me, found immense fulfilment in what we achieved in Mount Argus.

I was younger, too, and knew I couldn't stay there forever. Like many another person I had to learn that life was teaching me a valuable lesson; what you dedicate yourself to building up, others will be happy to dismantle. Do not build personal kingdoms. God must be the centre of everything I do and when God is in charge, whatever I leave behind is in safe hands.

Old Pope John XXIII used to pray each night in his oratory: 'Lord, it's your Church and you are in charge of it. I'm off to bed now and while I sleep soundly I leave your Church in your hands.'

In my early forties, I was able to do just that with Mount Argus.

The Graan was different, though. It became the only place on earth I've ever called home. I was happy to be with my own people and they were at home with me. Mostly they trusted me. Together we went through the worst period in Church history since the Reformation. We spoke openly about the scandals, the secrecy and the lack of leadership. They knew my seed, breed and generation. I couldn't fool them and never even thought of doing so.

The Graan was in danger of closing in 1989. Many in the area thought I was being sent to them to oversee its closure. They soon found out that was not on my agenda. I tried to give them the respect they deserved and they soon recognised that I was working from a different model of Church than the others.

I was so at home there that for the first time I admitted to myself that I was a broken, vulnerable man because of the abuse and opposition I had lived through. It was the first time I felt safe enough to be myself. Had I not found a home in Fermanagh, I doubt very much if I could ever have admitted the abuse itself, never mind the personal consequences of it.

That's why the Novena of Hope was so helpful to me and to others. I was not bringing hope to a community. We were journeying towards hope together.

The last night of the 2011 Novena of Hope was special. More people turned up than could get into the church. Those who couldn't enter stood outside and joined in the spirit of hope which the novena inspired. The atmosphere around Enniskillen was electric; everyone agreed it had been a truly grace-filled occasion. The whole community was on a high, as they should be after a spiritual revival.

I went to bed after midnight exhausted but utterly at peace. Little did I know how much I would need hope in the weeks that followed.

Next morning I got up early and prepared to go for a quiet walk in the countryside, as I did every morning, to pray in thanksgiving and to chill out in the fresh air. I noticed a call on my mobile. It was from the provincial superior – the person chosen by us to lead the Passionists in Ireland, Scotland and Paris. He wondered if I could meet him at a neutral venue; he had something important to discuss with me. He'd like to meet me today if possible. I called him back. He wouldn't say why he wanted to meet and he seemed uncharacteristically distant.

We settled on a halfway place, which was Quinn's Corner near Dungannon. I presumed it was another emergency abuse case affecting someone in our order. I was one of four elected consultants (or advisers) with whom the provincial had to discuss almost everything. During our term of office we had to tackle numerous historic abuse issues which surfaced during the eight years we were in office. It was a trying and depressing time. I knew it had to be something very serious if he needed to talk about it so urgently.

I was anxious when I pulled into the empty car park. He was already there. I suggested breakfast inside. He said he feared someone might overhear our conversation. So we sat in his car like two suspicious drug pushers exchanging booty. He asked me to listen to what he had to say first and to keep calm. By now I was convinced that someone had made a false accusation of sexual abuse against ME. There was no danger of me saying anything; I was shocked into silence.

He carefully took an official-looking envelope from his inside pocket and held it in his two hands away from me, making sure I couldn't read it.

'The Vatican is not pleased with you for criticising them. They don't like your attitude,' he said nervously. 'I just hate having to do this to you, Brian, but I've been sitting on this letter for nearly a week. I didn't want to disturb you during your novena. But I can't hold off any longer', he told me.

He began to read out the two and half pages of legal jargon, awkwardly constructed sentences liberally sprinkled with Latin phrases and canon law references. There wasn't a single reference to Christ or the Gospels. I'd like to quote it all for you but I never got the letter from the Vatican and if I had it, I could not publish it, under pain of excommunication.

When he finished reading I was no wiser. So he read it again … and again. He was not permitted to let me read it myself.

It was a letter from the CDF in the Vatican. Apparently they were sent copies of my articles from The Sunday World as well as copies of other articles, broadcasts and interviews, which they claimed proved to them that I was overcritical of the Catholic Church. The Catholic Church, in their definition, meant the clerics and the Vatican. This apparently was their 'credible evidence' that I was the cause of serious scandal to believers everywhere, especially the laity.

I was to be severely restricted in what I could communicate in future. I asked if I could continue to offer Mass. The provincial was at pains to point out that I was still 'a priest in good standing', which basically meant that I could continue my ministry as a priest as before.

Strictly speaking I was not technically 'silenced'. Instead I was censured for my past comments and censored for all future communications. I was to have all my articles etc. passed by a reputable theologian. As you can imagine, I wouldn't have many readers left if I did that.

In essence I could only praise everything the bishops and the Vatican did or said.

The way in which the censure itself was communicated, tells you everything you need to know about the way the Vatican works – or doesn't. The institution is all that matters. Fairness, justice, proper procedures, care of the individual or even good old compassion does not count. The institution itself and the careerists who run it are all that matters. It is precisely why they are incapable of ever dealing effectively with child abuse. They will always protect their jobs and the institution. They will abandon the victim. They always do.

In my case, as far as I can ascertain, they ordered the superior general of the Passionists to come to the Vatican to collect the letter ordering him to order the provincial superior to order me to stop criticising the Church leadership in general and the Vatican in particular. They would not reveal the source of the alleged complaints against me or indeed the exact nature of those alleged complaints. To this day I have no idea what exactly I had done/said that was wrong.

They refused to have direct dealings with me because it's not about me or any individual, it's all about them. They didn't ask for or consider hearing my side of the discussion. If they had I would have been able to tell them that I was writing what every decent believer was thinking. I've always been careful not to contradict dogma. It's dogmatism I despise.

Everything about the censure was shrouded in secrecy. When I asked for a copy of the letter the provincial told me he was forbidden to let me have a copy. He had no idea who reported me to the CDF either. He was genuinely upset and I have no issue with him or with the superior general in Rome.

The superior general, who had been summoned to the Vatican to receive the letter, did not know who reported me. He himself had read many of my books to help him learn English. He could find nothing objectionable in any of them, he assured me.

There was to be no appeal, no discussion, no publicity, no defence and no rights. I was not to make any public statement about it. I must suffer in silence. That's what they consider to be just procedures.

When I read condemnations of injustice from the Vatican now, 'practise what you preach' instantly comes to mind.

The provincial was as shocked as I was. I had great sympathy for him because he was carrying out the imposition of a censure which he knew to be unjust. If he hadn't done as he was told, he too could have been removed from office. It also meant that if I refused to accept the censure, he would be held responsible. Naturally, I didn't want to make life difficult for him so it limited what I could do about the censure to precisely nothing.

I knew in my heart that anything I said or did in the past was an honest attempt to force the leadership of the Church I love to change their attitude. As an abused person I was offering them advice from the inside. In conscience I had no choice in the matter. I firmly believe that to be silent in the face of evil enables evil to thrive and is as culpable as the evil act itself.

Can they not understand that if an institution claiming to speak in God's name would not or could not protect innocent children from its predator clerics, then such an institution is culpable for the abuse? That was precisely what they didn't want to acknowledge or to change.

When we waded through all the jargon the letter warned that if I failed to accept this censure, according to canon law, I would be excommunicated – meaning that I could not even receive Communion, never mind preside at Mass.

I joined the Passionists in 1962 as a seventeen-year-old. I endured sexual abuse as a young boy and later as a gullible student because all I wanted was to be a priest. Not just any priest either. I wanted to be the kind of priest my mother and father would be proud of. I would have to be approachable, in touch with ordinary people. I would help the sick and the poor.

My parents would have wanted me to go out of my way to welcome the people those in authority turned away. That was why I spent night after night gliding around the edges of ballrooms, chatting to people who'd usually run a mile from a priest. It's why I write in The Sunday World. It's the paper ordinary people read. Rather than be the People's Priest, I preferred to be a priest the people could trust.

When I was a parish priest in Dublin, a very angry priest colleague spoke harshly at a deanery meeting of priests. He said that because I wrote for The Sunday World I was lowering the image of the priesthood. If I continued to write for 'a rag', the archbishop should insist I resign from being a parish priest. Most of the others agreed. Two elderly priests, however, spoke in my favour. 'The only person he's disgracing is himself,' they argued.

To my shame I seriously considered resigning from the parish. In fact, I was sure the Passionists would take me off the parish to placate the authorities. They weren't always happy with my chosen ministries either. One of the community, whom I thought was a friend of mine, was so embarrassed by a fellow Passionist writing for the World that he asked me not to use the letters CP after my name (CP signifies Congregation of the Passion). Ever since, I write as just plain Father Brian D'Arcy in The Sunday World. I would not want to embarrass the order.

I neither sought approval nor cared much about it. I knew I was privileged to be asked to write for such a widely read paper. If the community didn't like it or understand it, it was okay with me as long as they didn't try to stop me.

My parents admired priests who were more interested in people than in money. They spoke highly of priests who were comfortable sitting in the corner of a country kitchen dining on strong tea and home-made bread. That's where I'm most comfortable anyway.

On a different level, I had chosen to remain a priest rather than live out a loving relationship in marriage. Without boasting I can honestly say, hand on heart, that I dedicated my life to being the most relevant priest I could be. I could never sleep at night if I didn't. Yet here I was, forty-nine years after I entered, being told by the Vatican, no less, that I was a danger to believers! As far as they were concerned I should now put up and shut up.

By the time I got back to The Graan on the fateful morning, I had aged ten years. I couldn't tell anyone why I was distraught. The lovely people who worked alongside me in The Graan and in the BBC were the first to notice – strangely the religious community didn't.

Coming back to reality, it was Tuesday morning – the deadline for the following week's article in The Sunday World. I had to decide if I'd write about my predicament or not. I decided to keep writing as normal. I'd write something safe and not submit to a censor.

I was broadcasting for the BBC, hosting the iconic Sunday Half Hour on Radio 2, presenting Sunday with Brian D'Arcy on Radio Ulster and contributing to Pause for Thought on the Chris Evans Breakfast Show.

There were hard choices coming up. I could not possibly allow the Vatican to impose their censorship on the BBC, The Sunday World or, indeed, any other outlet. I would not ask them to cooperate in censorship because no self-respecting communications outlet would tolerate it.

Early morning and late at night I walked miles and miles along the country roads of Fermanagh pondering my future. To say I was devastated would be putting it mildly. I never felt as useless or as alone in my life. At first, I thought I'd have to leave the priesthood so that I could continue speaking honestly about the dysfunction at the heart of the Church I loved and to which I had given my life.

Nothing made sense anymore. I could find no peace within me. I continued to offer Mass and preach to the people at The Graan as honestly as I could. However, I was acutely aware deep down that I was a fraud. Until now I was always honest with the congregation and I knew they appreciated that honesty. That's why they came to The Graan. They trusted me even when they disagreed with me.

I couldn't continue being a fraud – that much I knew. Night after night when everyone was asleep I had to get out of bed and march around The Graan car park, hoping nobody would see me. I met foxes in the graveyard and hungry stray dogs knocking over bins. I prayed at the grave of Father Angelo – the Passionist priest who put the idea of becoming a priest into my head in the confessional in 1960. I stood before the blue and white Calvary in the car park, begging for guidance. Not much in the way of inspiration came my way except that when I returned to bed I usually slept for a few precious hours.

One dark night I was in despair. I began to doubt myself. Perhaps I was too outspoken. Maybe I should be the same as most other priests. Would it be better to huff and puff in conversations with other clerics and pretend everything would pass if we kept our heads down? I couldn't talk to anyone about how I was feeling so there was no way to break the vicious circle of self-hate and depression. I was exhausted living a pretence.

For the only time in my life I felt utterly out of place in the world. I convinced myself that life wasn't worth living, that everyone would be better off if I wasn't around. It wasn't just a fleeting thought. I was convinced I had outlived my usefulness. In the dark of the night I had to force myself to choose to live because getting out of this world seemed an easier and more logical course of action.

I'd never been a hypocrite, yet I was being forced to live this double life by the CDF in Rome. Would it be such a tragedy if I disappeared for ever? The clear answer was: No, it wouldn't.

Thankfully, I recognised this as suicidal thoughts entering my head. The alarm bells rang loud and clear. I simply could not allow this negative line of thought to continue. I had to change my way of thinking. Self-pity, 'victim thinking', were distorting the picture. When I cleared my head I realised that I was giving the CDF permission to take away, not only my priesthood but my life as well.

Next morning I drove to the Marian shrine at Knock in County Mayo. It was where my mother took me before I made up my mind to enter The Graan. Neither of my parents wanted me to be a priest because we were not a well-off family, and they had such a high regard for priests, that they believed I was not good enough to be one. They spoke openly to me about it.

My mother gave in first, saying that she would take me to Knock to pray about it. If after the pilgrimage I still wanted to enter, they would not stand in my way. That was the crucial moment in my choosing to be a priest. Now it seemed to me Knock was the proper place to go to seek guidance about whether I should remain a priest.

To be honest, I didn't find much solace in Knock, probably because I was too disturbed to hear any voice other the Vatican's. However, on the way home, listening to music, the Holy Spirit whispered some thoughts of hope and enlightenment. The BBC had asked me to do a documentary on my life and times. I thought that the process of my decision to remain or to go would be a good theme. They agreed.

I decided I had to share my dilemma with some objective people who could point me in the right direction; I realised I had handed my life over to people working in a dysfunctional system, who were treating me unjustly. I was giving them the power to bully me to the point where life wasn't worth living. But life is God's gift, not theirs. They had no right to that power yet I was just as guilty for handing over control of my life to them. It was time for me to take my own God-given life back and face the consequences.

I was no longer prepared to silence myself – for that in effect was what I was doing. I began to make what should have been the obvious connection between being abused as a child and becoming a victim of clerical abuse again. Clerics stole my childhood. That was their fault. Now as an adult I should be thinking and acting differently. I was determined these Vatican clerics would not abuse me all over again.

On the way home I visited my parents' grave at Arney chapel. In my mind I could see both of them smiling back at me, telling me, as it were, that their child was at last an adult. I got a new lease of life at the foot of their grave. But then isn't faith all about new life being the product of death?

Gradually I began to reflect more rationally on the whole sorry mess. I couldn't talk to my superiors because they would be compromised. There was nothing helpful they could offer me.

In one attempt to discuss my position with other Passionists one colleague suggested that I wasn't 'cute' enough. He said I should be like him and play them at their own game. Don't say anything in public that upsets them, he advised smugly. I exploded angrily. Imagine a priest believing being 'cute' was the answer to abuse, suppression and injustice. How could any self-respecting human being think that being 'cute' is the fruit of the Holy Spirit? That's the clerical club mentality.

I had to look elsewhere. I gathered my family together. Years earlier, they heard about my abuse for the first time on a news bulletin on RTÉ. I had never told them anything about it. News about it leaked out when Joe Jackson asked me straight out in a Hot Press interview if I had been abused as a child and wondered if that was why I spoke out against child abuse so forcefully.

Counselling helped me to manage the effects of abuse in a healthy way. I reached the point where I felt no need to reveal past abuse but that if I were asked an honest question I would give an honest answer. So I did. That's how you signify that abuse is not a reason for the survivor to be ashamed.

Jackson was respectful but, understandably, Hot Press knew they had a story and passed it on to a daily paper to get their share of publicity. Their story appeared in The Daily Star and The Evening Herald and was subsequently lifted on RTÉ when Gerry Ryan asked me to talk about it on his famous radio programme.

That's how my family and friends found out. I was really annoyed with myself for allowing my shame to prevent me telling them something they had a right to know. It was wrong of me and I was determined not to let it happen again. So I called a family meeting and revealed to them as clearly as I could that the Vatican had censured me five months ago. I explained what the possible consequences might be and that if it ever got out, it would be front page news. I would be the subject of all sorts of innuendo and they might be embarrassed that their uncle/brother was publicly condemned by the Vatican as a priest who scandalises good Catholics.

They were upset and puzzled. They are good people who help out in their parishes and couldn't understand why I was being silenced for telling the truth. One of the younger generation spoke up.

'Uncle Brian, why are they condemning you when everyone knows you are one of the few priests who is trusted by lay people to tell it like it is? You are the reason we still go to Mass.'

Then my only brother intervened. 'What exactly are they asking you to do? Do they want you to tell lies about what's going on? Don't ever make little of yourself by telling lies. If you do that mammy and daddy will turn in their graves.'
That was all I needed to hear.

He then asked what the implications of being removed from the active priesthood would be. I explained, jokingly, that if he died I wouldn't be able to say his funeral Mass. We all laughed. Sadly, within a few months my brother died suddenly in his sleep at seventy years of age.

Once my family knew, the spell was broken. Secrecy is the enemy of truth. I confided in a few close friends to whom I could speak with in confidence. Most thought I should just leave the priesthood and live a normal life. I was sixty-six years old. I had done enough. Forget about them. Don't allow them to bully you and insult you, they insisted.

It seemed sensible and attractive, yet it wasn't sitting well with me. Then a friend who is an experienced therapist helped me shape my thoughts. (This formed a central part of the BBC's 'The Turbulent Priest' documentary.) 'First of all, whatever you do, DO NOT walk out,' he insisted. 'If you do, it means you don't believe in your priesthood at all. You are walking away from a life for which you have sacrificed everything and for which you have endured abuse and humiliation. That does not make any sense. If you're tired of the priesthood, and if you think you have nothing more to give, then leave the priesthood on your own terms.'

'But do not make their task easier by walking away now. They'll be able to say, with some justification, that you were never committed to priesthood anyway. Don't do that. Become a better priest instead. Be the voice the people trust. Go on doing good as you have always tried to do, and if they still throw you out everyone will see they are wrong and spiteful.'

'Furthermore,' he went on, 'You haven't fully integrated what this has done to you. When I see you now, I see a broken man. It seems to me you are living your abuse all over again.'

Suddenly the light went on. I spoke to the editor of the Sunday World and told him as much of the story as he needed to know. It appeared the CDF concluded that what I wrote in The Sunday World was shattering the Catholic faith in Ireland. The editor laughed and, ever the optimist, was thrilled to hear that they read The Sunday World in the Vatican! It didn't matter what the Vatican thought, he assured me. I would always be welcome to write for The Sunday World as I had done for the previous forty years.

The BBC was the same. They appreciated that I didn't go on broadcasting hiding behind a Vatican-appointed censor.

It was time to have confidence in my own abilities, to stop wallowing in victimhood, to stand up for myself and for those wounded people who put their trust in me. If I walked away from priesthood why shouldn't they walk away from the Church? I had spoken and written for years that we should not allow a small percentage of abusing priests and cowardly bishops to hijack the Church we love. We should discern our own goodness and we should discover a loving God who never stops loving us – the only God there is.

Even if we cannot find solace or peace or hope in the Church, don't give up on God. Don't abandon the life-giving gifts of the sacraments and the Mass because some paranoid, power freak of a cleric is driving you out. It's far better to just ignore them. Find some other place to worship and some other way to work out the long and lonely journey back home. God has been saving good people long before churches existed.

I preached that sermon to myself and decided to get on with my life as best I could. The CDF is not where God lives. God lives where love lives. I knew that the CDF would make life difficult for me and they might throw me out. So what? If they took away my ability to act as a priest in good standing in the morning, I'd go on doing the same things for the same reasons. They don't have the power to take my priesthood. Only death and me have that power. The saintly C.S. Lewis wrote: 'The prayer before all prayer is; May it be the real I who speaks. May it be the real Thou that I speak to.'

I slept better after that though I never really got back my good health or my self-belief. For thirteen months I lived in that limbo of censorship and kept the Vatican's secret locked inside me. People noticed I wasn't myself. I wasn't telling it like it should be told.

Then one day I got a call from Sarah MacDonald, who specialises in Church-related journalism. There was a story doing the rounds, she said, that the Vatican had censored five or maybe six Irish-based priests, all belonging to religious orders. She had it on good authority that I was one of the six. Would I confirm it? A few days before I had heard a whisper that the names would be floated in the press because we were still writing and broadcasting. It was thought it might be better to release the names and so make the censures known. That would surely destroy our credibility and silence me by another means. That's what the authorities thought would happen if they outed us.

Anyway, since Sarah had asked me a direct question I was duty bound to give a truthful answer. Sarah published her story and that's how, thirteen months after the furtive meeting in Quinn's car park, the news hit the headlines.

As I've said earlier, well before Sarah Mc Donald's article, BBC Northern Ireland approached me to do a documentary on my life. I have broadcast an hour-long, easy listening, music-based programme every Sunday morning for over twenty years on BBC Radio Ulster. I love doing the music programme as well as dropping in helpful reflections to inspire listeners on a Sunday morning.

The documentary department knew some of my story but did not know the detail of the CDF censure.

On the day Sarah McDonald's story broke, all hell broke loose in the media. The people around The Graan were shocked and very angry. They came out to The Graan in person. It was a hectic day. All the local TV stations arrived uninvited on my doorstep. I had a good relationship with many of our local radio stations dotted around Ireland because I helped them out when others didn't answer the phone. They all wanted me to tell the story in person. I had to be careful because I still wasn't supposed to talk about it in public. However, I was in a much better place now and I wasn't going to play silly

Vatican games. When I was asked a question I was able to answer, I did so as honestly as I could.

When they asked why I was censured I had to answer that I didn't know. I told them I was allowed to offer Mass and was still 'a priest in good standing'. On and on it went.

Thankfully I was on confessional duty that day at The Graan. I continued doing what I was supposed to do – blessings of people and cars, listening to those in trouble, confessions. Somehow I got through the day. I had encouraging phone calls from many people in every county in Ireland: politicians, friends in the GAA, entertainers and two bishops. People are thoughtful in times of trouble.

I was celebrant at the eight o'clock evening Mass. A big congregation turned up just to show their support. On the way to the vestry, I got a call from Mary McAleese, phoning from Rome, where she was studying canon law. She was kind, incisive, encouraging, understanding and, most of all, compassionate. It was a call I'll never forget. It lifted me and put good thoughts in my mind before going to the altar.

When I went to put on my vestments, I noticed that Natalie Mayne had a TV camera set up, un-obtrusively, at the back of the church. Natalie was producing the BBC documentary. She came in to the sacristy to tell me that she just wanted to record how our local community was reacting. It would, she thought, make a fine beginning to the documentary 'The Turbulent Priest'.

I agreed. But as I reached the altar, I saw one of elderly lady angrily leaving her seat and marching down to Natalie, who she told in no uncertain terms where to go with her camera. I was their priest and no one had a right to intrude at this sensitive moment. Then she calmly walked back to her seat, giving me a wry protective smile on the way.

By now I was teary, full of emotion and, if I'm honest, relieved. At least I was no longer hiding the Vatican's secrets from our people.

I began Mass. 'In the name of the Father … '

Just then, a member of the congregation, Aideen McGinley, an able, well-known, dedicated member of our praying community, appeared at the microphone.

'Just a minute, Father Brian, excuse me. I want to say something.'

She then addressed the body of the church.

'We all heard the news today. I want to say how unfair and how unjust this censure is. We know Father Brian better than the Vatican does. We know the work he does for everyone, no matter who they are or what their religion is. We know how honest he has been about abuse when other priests pretended it didn't happen. We know the hope he gives us.

'I hope I speak for you all when I say that we will stand beside Father Brian and we will support him as he has supported us. We will pray for him and with him. Thank you.'

She went back to her seat. There was a huge round of applause and we all cried together.

Aideen McGinley was immensely brave in what she said. She knows I will never forget her kindness, which was simply an articulation of the compassion of the entire congregation.

Despite her telling off, Natalie kept her camera running too.

My father and mother, Hugh and Ellie D'Arcy and baby Marie

The original homestead in Bellanaleck. Mammy and Joan in the doorway.
Daddy's bike taking pride of place!

My First Communion Day, 1952. That's me on the right. Gaby Maguire (left) and Matt Snow are alongside. Peter Nolan, Bridie Maguire and Eugene McHugh are at the back

An old school photograph

The D'Arcy family in 1963: (from left) my brother, Gaby, myself, my mother, Ellie, my sister Marie, my father, Hugh and my sister Joan

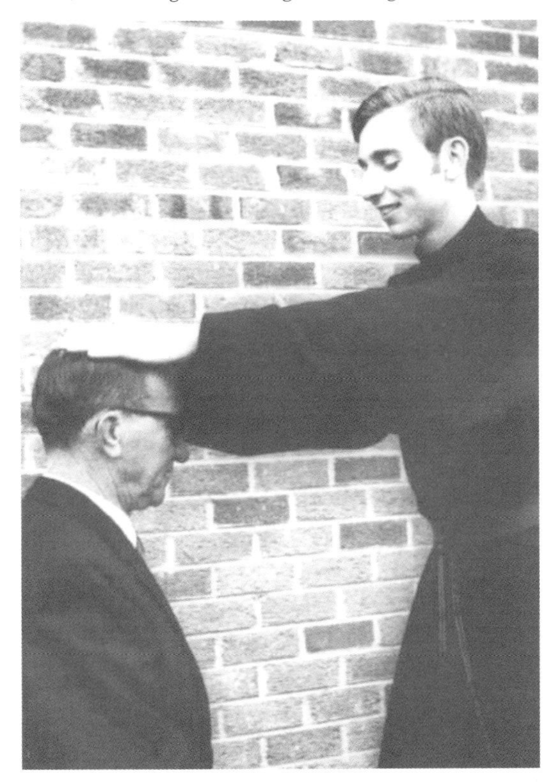

Blessing my father on my Ordination Day, 1969

Family occasion: My brother, Gaby, myself, my sisters Marie and Joan.
University of Ulster Honorary Degree

November 1970, with Fr Edmund Burke CP – admiring my first edition as editor of *The Cross*, with the Beatles on the cover

Profession Day, 1963, with my mother and father

The fight to save Mount Argus

Earliest picture I have of my father Hugh D'Arcy as a 14 year-old. St. Michael's, Enniskillan school hurling team 1926. Back Row: Bro Regis, H D'Arcy, J Bradley, C Fox, B Quinn, J Cassidy, D Love, Bro Joseph. Middle Row: J Devanney, O Mc Teggart, T Donnelly, Bro Avolino, T Quinn, B Day, A Breslin. Front Row: B Dorothy, E Quinn, T Sheridan.

Mount Argus, Dublin

Daddy, shortly before he died,
cutting the cake on his 70th birthday

Fr. Brian's family meets President McAleese and her husband Dr. Martin in Áras an Uachtaráin - 2006

Still friends after *that* "memorable" *Late Late Show*. Bishop Cathal Daly and myself at the launch of his autobiography

Studying at the Franciscan School of Theology in San Francisco with Dr Kenan Osborne, 1981

On my Ordination Day, 20th December 1969, with Eddie Masterson (left) and Brian Coll

Brian with Big Tom and Johnny Gallagher of Boxty Fame at a Mass for entertainers in The Céile House

Man of peace: with Bill Clinton at the Clinton Centre, Enniskillen

Mike Murphy

Brian Peters, Fr Brian, Jimmy Magee and Sean Reilly shortly before Jimmy's death

Fr. Brian D'Arcy with Tyrone football manager Mickey Harte

Kenny Rogers

The Men in Black

The *Late Late Showband Special* – (from left) Eamonn Monaghan (Capitol Showband), myself, Brendan O'Brien (Dixies), Derek Dean (Freshmen), Paddy Cole, Joe Dolan, Joe McCarthy (Dixies), Sonny Knowles, Seán Dunphy and Earl Gill (Hoedowners), Eileen Kelly (Nevada)

Simply the best: Tina Turner

Reba McEntire

Face to face with the Duke (not John Wayne!)

Duke of Kent

Fr Brian and the late Brendan Grace

Fr Brian with the late Big Tom and Rose

Attending Julia O'Donnell's 90th party with Eddie Rowley (Sunday World) and Daniel O'Donnell

Chris Evans points the way

Henry Shefflin

Declan Coyle

Fr Brian and Hugo Duncan at Outside Broadcast with BBC Radio Ulster

BBC Radio2 Presenter

Fr Brian with Brendan Bowyer and Val Doonican, who both received the Freedom of the City of Waterford

Flanked by Daniel and Sir Cliff

Preaching at The Graan Church

Nathan Carter at The Graan Novena of Hope

Sir Terry Wogan and Eamon Holmes

Fr Brian with Archdeacon Pringle with his wife Hilary and Mary Kennedy

Church of Ireland neighbours Archdeacon Cecil Pringle and Canon Ian Ellis

President Mary McAleese and Dr Martin attending the Centenary celebrations for The Graan Monastery

Joe Dolan

Sir Terry Wogan and Barry McGuigan

With Sir Terry Wogan on Lough Erne

Fr Brian with Keelan, Johnny Brady, Lisa McHugh, Nathan Carter, Philomena Begley, and Cliona

Gay Byrne and Fr Brian
(from Independent Archives)

Joe Duffy and Fr Brian at Trocaire concert in Mount Argus

Brian meets Beth Nielsen Chapman

Fr Brian supporting Fermanagh and Tracey Concrete

Fr D'Arcy Honorary Doctorate

Jimmy Magee, Fr Brian, Kathleen Reynolds, Albert Reynolds and Brian Carthy

Fr Brian with a cherry blossom which survived the axe at The Graan in Enniskillan

St. Joseph, pray for us

CHAPTER 26

THE VIEWS THAT UPSET THE VATICAN

When Cardinal Lavada, on behalf of the Congregation for the Doctrine of the Faith (CDF), signed the letter censuring me, he attached photocopies of articles and comments that were considered offensive. I'm led to believe my Sunday World column of 10 January 2010 was used in evidence against me. The CDF objected in particular to the headline, for which, of course, I had no responsibility at all.

I admit it was a hard-hitting piece. I'd spent many days over the Christmas period getting it right. I wrote and rewrote it to ensure I was as honest and truthful as possible about the evil that was destroying the Church I love.

It was based on weeks of reflection as well as hundreds of letters from believing Catholic readers who were utterly frustrated by the multiplicity of terrible scandals, over decades, which had eroded their faith. Worse still, their children had long given up going to church, deciding that the Catholic Church was beyond redemption. My article attempted to open a dialogue about those scandals and to collate the reforms the readers thought to be necessary.

Ten years later I feel frustrated. So little has been achieved, even though Pope Francis has put forward many of the same proposals, especially the evils of clericalism; the pope's language was much more critical than mine was.
Here are some of the relevant points from my article.

'It's time to reflect on where we are in the Catholic Church in Ireland,' I began. 'And Rome's influence for good or bad needs to be examined.'

'The clerical church is falling apart (a positive sign) … Diarmuid Martin knows he has the support of most lay-people in his efforts to finally clean up the arrogance of the past but is criticised for needlessly humiliating his clerical colleagues in such a public way.

'The result is that many bishops are discovering for the first time what most of us know from bitter experience – the institution in Rome demands to be preserved at all costs. Individuals, whether they happen to be the victims of abuse, and including bishops and priests, will be sacrificed to protect the institution.

'To be fair, some progress on behalf of the survivors of abuse has been made. But beware of making too much of it. Survivors have welcomed the resignation of the bishops. Yet those who reflect at all must recognise that the hierarchical Catholic Church is just as ruthless as it always has been. Institutions protect themselves at all costs. Individuals and victims were, and still are, disposable …

'The might of the Vatican continues to quash the individual without any radical change to its own structures … those are the very structures which need to be demolished because they are at the root of the dysfunction. A reader asked recently: "Why does Rome think it can provide the answer when we know it is part of the problem?"

'It is a mistake to conclude (as the media often does) that the sexual abuse of children by priests and religious has its roots only in bad management. Institutional hypocrisy is not the only cause of the sexual abuse of children – though undoubtedly it did enable abusers to continue their criminal acts.

'At the heart of the problem is a more deep-seated malaise. A combination of bad theology, the dysfunctional abuse of power and an outdated concept of what healthy sexuality entails, have contributed to what the Murphy Report repeatedly refers to as "the systemic failure" to protect the most innocent and the most vulnerable children.

'I believe that the evil clerical culture which pervades our institution right up to the Vatican bureaucracy itself needs to be dismantled. This present crisis may not be all bad therefore. If we are humble enough to ask for help it can still offer us the opportunity to become a Church based on Gospel values – helping the poor, encouraging the sinner, walking with the powerless, welcoming failure and finding new life in the passion of suffering.

'The bad theology comes from forty years of rejection of the principles of the Second Vatican Council. Pope John Paul II and Cardinal Ratzinger, now Pope Benedict, must accept most of the responsibility.

'The real issue was partially addressed by Diarmuid Martin in one of his Christmas messages. He spoke of a "false understanding of the place of the priest in the Church" and "a totally impoverished understanding of the Church as a community of the baptised". He's absolutely correct in what he says, but, sadly, we all know that nothing is likely to change.

'If we were serious, passing on real power to committed believers, an end to compulsory celibacy, accepting the possibility of ordaining women, blessings for people in good conscience living in second relationships, new forms of the sacrament of reconciliation allowing for general absolution, an end to treating women as second-class citizens, an admission that few Catholics live out the precepts of Humanae Vitae; compassion for gay people who want to live a spiritual life, a real voice for people in choosing their priests and their bishops and, critically, a limited term of office for both parish priests and bishops, would form some part of the agenda for change …

'A power-hungry institution which claims to be answerable to God alone, yet which persistently and deliberately acts in a sinful and criminal way, needs to be radically reformed. Rearranging bishops on a board is simply too pathetic to take seriously.

'Perhaps those in Rome don't realise how rightfully angry we are. The Vatican so far shows no ability to begin the kind of repentance and honesty required to make their leadership credible. The utter arrogance shown to the Murphy inquiry is a case in point.

'Furthermore the Vatican itself appointed the bishops it is now publicly humiliating. The kind of person they sought out to become bishops, and then imposed on the faithful, failed to protect children because the system discouraged honesty. In short it is Rome itself which needs to repent and reform.

'A letter from on high (i.e. the proposed special letter from Pope Benedict to the Irish Church) will add fuel to our anger unless it realises that the Catholic hierarchy on its own is incapable of doing what is needed in the matter of child abuse. Don't forget that we clerics have spent fifteen years attempting to get it right, yet it took the Ferns, Ryan and Murphy reports to spell out the most basic principles. Even now, many clerics still don't get it. Unless the pope is humble enough to accept an inquiry into the Vatican's own procedures, he will not be taken seriously.

'It is ten years since I first wrote that many believe covering up is part of the Vatican's policy. "Part of the human structure of the Church is rotten to the core" is what I said then and still believe. No amount of wriggling will convince us that those in charge of running the Vatican civil service are acting in an open and honest way even now.

'One of the major problems is that ordinary believers no longer trust clerics to do the right thing. Good people who trusted the clerical Church and the Pope in particular, now know that the clerical Church, and perhaps even the Pope, were not worthy of their trust.

'As we know it is impossible to repair trust once it is broken so deliberately and painfully. Perhaps it may be possible to attempt to build a new relationship. That will demand a different way of being church. It cries out for a true sharing of visions and futures. But it cannot be built on the discredited structures we now have. The end has come for autocratic, hierarchical rulers answerable to no one. The game's up.

'So it's time to make an opportunity out of a crisis.

'We clergy have caused the crisis, but God's people can turn it into a blessing. As a church we need to be more humble; to stop being so pompously self-righteous. We need reform from the top. We should take less notice of the Vatican and more notice of the parish council. There is hope; there is a future, but it will not be found in this mess of our own making.'

After it was published in The Sunday World I received hundreds of letters agreeing with its sentiments and adding many more grievances which I'd omitted. There were perhaps three or four dissenting voices, as there always are. Its value was that it put words on what people thought.

I have no idea who reported me to Rome for those views. Was it a cleric or a layperson? At the time, there were Vatican 'spies' in congregations around the world reporting on what they considered to be errant views.

Right-wing lay organisations kept Rome busy. Sadly, they were listened to while those who took on people's issues were branded as heretics.

Two years after my censure became known I met a high-ranking Irish churchman socially. He said he was sympathetic to my plight and took it upon himself to offer helpful advice.

He told me I made two crucial mistakes when I wrote that article (and in subsequent interviews on TV and radio).

Firstly, I communicated in a way that ordinary Catholics not only understood, but fully agreed with. I succeeded in putting into words what the vast majority of them thought. 'That's how you start a revolution,' he quipped.

Secondly, and even more damning, in his view, I was absolutely right in my analysis.

Sadly, I'm now convinced the bishop himself got it absolutely right too. I was rapped over the knuckles because (1) the people understood me and trusted me, and (2) I was right.

CHAPTER 27

MAKING THE TURBULENT PRIEST

The whole world knew I was teetering on the edge after the news of the Vatican's censure broke. To be honest, it seemed as if they had left me with no choice. How I arrived at the decision to stay in the priesthood unless I was pushed was discerned in an unusual way. I allowed the documentary team to eavesdrop on part of the discernment process. This was one of three ways guiding my ultimate choice – the other two were spiritual direction.

The BBC assigned Natalie Maynes to be the producer of the documentary. She was enthusiastic and wanted to get inside my head. It would be done with one camera and a small team who would film hours in my company. They were willing to spend a day with me to get three minutes of usable material. It was close up and personal as well as being more likely to be authentic.

They recorded hours upon hours of material. Senior producers constantly looked at the footage and were ensuring that Natalie asked the difficult questions to get the truth about Brian D'Arcy and his struggle to remain a priest. She was always fair but not easy to please. She knew early on that I would be as open as possible and always truthful. I answered every question she asked me – several times. However, there was one exception. She wanted to see the letter that the Vatican sent to my superiors, but I couldn't show them the letter because I hadn't got it.

She was alert to what was happening. If I was to appear on a radio or TV show she was there with her camera to capture the moment. She followed me everywhere, including hospitals and nursing homes. I had a struggle to maintain professional confidentiality. It was an authentic reflection of my struggle, so much so that I was sad to see how despairing I was when it was first broadcast. It got a huge audience and a massive reaction in other outlets in the days and weeks afterwards. The BBC were surprised there was such an intense interest in a priest's life.

I had to find out if I should remain a priest. As part of the documentary I asked people with different views to help me solve the dilemma of whether I should remain a priest and be forever silent or speak freely and run the risk of being dismissed from the priesthood.

Right at the beginning I had to admit the Vatican was treating me as a deviant. Furthermore, I was a danger to ordinary Catholics. I found it both heartbreaking and insulting.

The camera opened with me on the way to offer Mass in The Graan Church on the evening the censure was made public. It was filmed exactly as it happened. On my way to Mass the phone rang. It was the former president of Ireland, Mary McAleese, ringing me from, of all places, Rome. She had heard the news and wanted to give me encouragement to keep going despite the threats. It was typical of Mary and Martin's kindness.

Mary and I both agreed the Church was becoming increasingly fundamentalist in its approach. It happens to all major institutions. In times of difficulty and when they lose their influence, they conclude that when they strictly adhered to their traditions they thrived. Go back to the old ways and everything will be fine again, they think. In fact they become even more detached from the world they are supposed to serve. Big institutions find it impossible to change, yet unless they change they die.

During the filming I sought advice from people I respected. The film crew came with me to Vienna where we met Helmut Schuller. He had helped to found an outspoken association of priests in Austria which called for wholesale reform in the Catholic Church. His association had a major influence all over the world and prompted Pope Benedict to make a public statement about their claims. I asked Helmut what my approach should be.

He was well acquainted with my position and his advice was that I should not allow myself to become isolated. Individual voices are easily picked off. There is strength in a group. Don't allow yourself to become a lone voice, he said.

I pushed Father Helmut on whether he thought he was a divisive influence within the Austrian Church. There are definitely times when I feel I'm divisive here in Ireland. He explained that the real division within the Church is between the laity and the leadership. The laity does not have a voice. If we speak on behalf of the laity we are not being divisive, rather we are giving hope to the laity.

He understood that in Ireland people know that I have 'told it like it is'; that in itself is a unique position. I have an obligation to those people who trust me. It is not simply a matter of walking away from priesthood any time I feel like it.

'Accept that you are a leader and take that role seriously,' he concluded.

As part of the documentary I also wrote to Cardinal Seán Brady. I wanted him to be part of the process because I believed that he believed in a pastoral approach rather than a legal one. However, he felt that the BBC had been unfair to him in an earlier programme, so he declined.

When I wrote to him he did, however, invite me to lunch, where we had a rare opportunity to talk through the various options. As always, I found Seán to be personally agreeable. He said that instead of appearing on camera with me he would put on paper what he thought the role of the Church could be in the future. He, too, said I had a definite role to play within the Catholic Church as a priest and as a communicator. He agreed that I spoke for many lay people and had unique access to the media here. He was convinced I should not even think of leaving the priesthood.

The same couldn't be said when I went to meet Father Brian McKevitt, the publisher and editor of the conservative paper Alive. I went to Father McKevitt with an open mind. I debated as honestly as I could. But Father McKevitt was convinced I should preach only what the Church wanted me to preach in the way the Church said I should – or be forever silent. Even when the Church is wrong I should not say so. I should praise the Church, promote the Church. I should not be negative in public about the Vatican, despite its many failings.

I was shocked he couldn't see that no sensible person could do any such thing. This is a fairly classic description of brainwashing at its worst. I have no doubt Father McKevitt is convinced he is right. In his own way he was helping me to make up my mind to do what I had always done because his position was untenable.

Then the BBC team discovered I was a friend of Frank Kelly who, sadly, has since died. At the time Frank was a famous actor who came to prominence as Father Jack in the hit series Father Ted. Frank Kelly was a practising Catholic. He had two uncles who were Passionist priests. He was more than willing to help me.

We arrived at his Dublin home to record his opinions. Frank made it clear that censorship was a despicable punishment. It is even worse when it is used as a weapon. As a Catholic he despised many of the decisions being made by Church leaders to protect clerics instead of innocent children, and its lack of compassion for its own people struggling in the modern world.

Frank made a pertinent point. He said that as people become more educated, the lack of democracy within the Church will be untenable.

He said I needed to look at my life honestly. 'Look at it sensibly, Brian,' he said. 'If you don't know what you are being accused of, and if you don't know who your accuser is, and if you do not have a voice to express your opinion, then it is time you realised you are being bullied. There is no other word for it.'

For him my future couldn't be clearer. Do not allow myself to be bullied.

Lastly I went to visit a friend and former colleague in the priesthood who now lives in the south of England. Michael Carroll entered The Graan the same day as I did. We were ordained at the same time and we were close friends as students. Both of us took our studies seriously and we studied far more than the syllabus required. Michael was changed to Scotland after his ordination and I was made editor of the order's magazine The Cross. Michael trained in psychology and I trained in journalism.

After fifteen years as a priest Michael met his wife Cathy. He left the priesthood and went on to be successful in his chosen career, rising to the rank of professor in Roehampton University. I trusted Michael to understand the choices I had to make. He was aware of the journeys I made. When I published 'a Different journey' thirteen years ago, I asked Michael and Cathy to read it before publication to ensure my emotional health was sound. I wanted him to make sure I wasn't playing the victim or the hero; that it was the real Brian D'Arcy who was speaking. I needed to be sure that I wasn't contaminating the atmosphere with toxic attitudes.

Michael explained to me that he chose a different path from me because after he was ordained he began (a) thinking and (b) feeling for the first time in his life. Feeling was the disaster, he joked. Celibacy and religious life meant he was close to death on the inside. Nobody should freely choose to die emotionally for any cause or any church, he assured me.

He insisted I had to live my life with integrity. I was right to see that the institution was expecting me to sacrifice myself to protect the organisation. On the other hand I had an inner authentic voice that needed expressing. He told me I had 'to own' my life to ensure I lived authentically and with integrity. To do otherwise would facilitate my own destruction.

He said that there was a connection between my abuse as a child and the Vatican's unjust treatment of me now, that in my eyes this was another episode of clerical abuse. Once again, the Institution was prepared to protect itself at all costs. He said that I must stand against it with dignity now, in a way I couldn't do as a child.

It's essential to claim your own voice if you are to live with integrity. It means that you cannot ever be silent in the face of wrongdoing. You never allow yourself to be so silent that you have no voice of your own. You can only make responsible choices when you have the freedom to express your opinion about those choices.

Michael said I had to adopt what he called a deflector shield – to live my life doing what I know to be right. He advised me to tell them to send all the letters they want; to make all the threats they want. Tell them you will be authentic and will continue to be so until they respect you or kick you out. Even then, continue to speak the truth from your heart because that is the only way to live responsibly.

Coming home from visiting Michael and Cathy I was able to say sincerely that I was going to remain a priest; I was going to speak the truth. I am not going to be silent; I owe it to the people who depend on me to be a voice that is both truthful and hopeful. What I'm doing is legitimate and is a response to God's personal call.

That's where the documentary ended. They followed my journey as I discerned my future in front of the cameras. There was nothing underhand or hidden about it. It was obvious I got the affirmation I needed from those I trusted most.

CHAPTER 28

'FOR GOD'S SAKE HANG IN'

I'm lucky in that people feel free to talk with me anywhere and anytime. One day I was stopped in Navan, County Meath, by a well-dressed woman who crossed the street to give me a lecture. She directed me into the doorway of a shop. She stabbed my chest with her pointing finger.

'Fr Brian, has someone got to you?' she began. Before I could tell her the true story, she went on, 'I have always respected your honesty; most of us Catholics, hanging on by our fingernails, are relying on you to tell the truth. I have watched you on television and read what you write and listened to you on the radio. You have kept me going. You are the reason I still go to Mass.

'But in the past few months you've changed. It's as if you're afraid to speak truth to power. I don't know what it is. Maybe you are disillusioned like the rest of us. For God's sake, hang in there! Don't let them get to you. Keep telling the truth.'

I never got a word in. She shook my hand and walked on.

I knew she didn't know the truth about the Vatican's censorship and I couldn't tell her. However, her insight disturbed me deeply and reminded me that one cannot deceive genuine believers.

Keeping silent about the censure, I realised, was playing into the hands of the CDF. Worse still, the people knew I'd been got at. By playing according to their rules I was letting myself down and failing the people who'd supported me for decades

The blame for the sorry state of our Church today lies directly with Church leadership – as well as with docile clerics who, by playing safe, have become part of the problem.

No matter how many reforms, apologies or new regulations we introduce there is a sneaking suspicion that the clerical Church is still not revealing everything it knows. Efforts to get at the truth are frustrated; statements of repentance are grudging; every layer of truth exposed points unerringly to a system that shields abusers.

It would be foolish to presume that there is no abuse taking place right now. My fear is that we could face decades of worldwide revelations as the exposure of the abuse widens and the crisis deepens.

The German bishops have admitted that once trust is broken, it cannot be repaired. It will take a radically different model of Church. The gulf between the clerical leadership and the faithful laity is now immense. It will be necessary to dismantle much of what we held sacred. Crucially, it will be a from-the-roots-up church built on the faith of the laity who will take ownership of their Church – which is how it all began and how it is meant to be.

CHAPTER 29

ENDA KENNY

When Enda Kenny, as Taoiseach, addressed the Dáil castigating the failure of the Catholic leaders in Ireland for their lack of cooperation and lack of openness, he put words on the angry thoughts and feelings of the vast majority of Irish people, north and south.

Enda Kenny, as the most experienced politician in the Republic, knew he was safe to speak the truth about the sharp practise of some Vatican officials. He knew it would do him no electoral damage whatsoever.

It was a time when we thought straight talking would foster a new and better relationship between the Irish state and the leaders of the Catholic Church at home and abroad.

Judge Murphy first put words on the essence of the problem when she highlighted the 'systemic failure' within the structures of the clerical church. Then she 'outed' the deliberate interference of Vatican officials in the civil process.

At the time I was not surprised by Kenny's speech. He was merely standing up for his people.

Mr Kenny said: 'Clericalism has rendered some of Ireland's brightest, most privileged and powerful men, either unwilling or unable to address the horrors cited in the Ryan and Murphy reports. This Roman clericalism must be devastating for good priests, some of them old; others struggling to keep their humanity, even their sanity, as they work hard to be keepers of the Church's light and goodness within their parishes, communities and human heart ... Thankfully for them this is not Rome.'

I mention this for a reason. A few years later, Mr Kenny and his wife went to Rome to meet the recently elected Pope Francis. It was interpreted as a diplomatic attempt to foster better relationships between Ireland and the Vatican.

I read all this in the newspaper and thought no more of it.

On a Sunday afternoon in the Autumn of 2016, I was driving to Belfast airport on my way to London to broadcast a Pause for Thought with Chris Evans on BBC Radio 2.

The phone rang. I answered.

'Hello. Is that Father Brian?'

'Yes, it is.'

'Brian, this is Enda Kenny, Taoiseach, and I'm wondering if you have a few minutes.'

'Of course, Taoiseach.'

'I'm going to Rome to meet Pope Francis tomorrow. I have been asked to bring up with him the fact that some priests in Ireland have been censured. I know you are one of those priests. If the opportunity arises, how should I bring up the subject and what would be the most effective approach?'

I was most grateful that he even thought of me and the other priests in a similar position. I presumed he had already had more direct conversations with some of the other priests who were closer to him.

I thanked him and told him I realised we priests were not the most important item on his agenda, but that perhaps the best approach would be to let Pope Francis know it was foolish for the Vatican to become involved in such a minor and local dispute.

It was also disastrous from a PR point of view. Because of his impending visit to Ireland, the pope didn't need to be constantly reminded of the previous administration's foolishness. The whole country is aware all of us have given our best years to the priesthood; we are not enemies of the Church; when we point out the obvious mistakes being made by Church leaders at home and in Rome, it's because we are loyal citizens of both the Church and the state.

Mention to the pope, I advised, that he himself is highlighting the very same issues. We support him in what he is attempting to do. At any rate it's always prudent not to silence loyal opposition voices. The Vatican should listen to and encourage any priest whom the people in Ireland still trust because they are few and far between.

The Taoiseach thought this was a practical approach and said that he would make those points if the opportunity arose.

I wished him luck and thanked him for his kind consideration. I meant it too.

On his return he rang me again to say that he wasn't able to speak to the pope himself about my position but he certainly did put all those points to his officials in strong but diplomatic terms.

Later, when I met Enda, he explained in person how it had turned out.

The fact that I'm still writing this means that Enda's words didn't fall on deaf ears. I'm even more grateful for his intervention now.

CHAPTER 30

WHAT I SAID TO HOT PRESS

I'm used to interviews now. I prefer live interviews because there's less risk of what you say being distorted by poor editing.

I did a major interview for the influential Irish pop magazine Hot Press. I spoke with Jason O'Toole in 2016 for a solid five hours and he produced two question-and-answer features in the magazine. He published in excess of 13,000 words from our conversation in the 28 September issue.

Jason himself wrote that 'the interview is probably the most honest dialogue ever between an Irish Catholic priest and a journalist.' It is the only major interview I've given since the Vatican's censure in 2011.

"Brian D'Arcy was warned by the Vatican that he risked being expelled from the priesthood if he refused to remain silent. Theoretically, now, he could be booted out of the Church for speaking to Hot Press. Being condemned by the Congregation for the Doctrine of Faith (CDF), (made him feel) like he was being abused again."

Jason then let me put my own words on it.

You're absolutely right about that, Jason. I wondered why it had such an effect. It devastated me.

Anyone looking at me would know that I was physically unhealthy at that time. It was only when I tried to reflect [that] it seemed to me and to others, the reason I took this censure so seriously was … it brought back my previous sexual abuse as a child: I saw this quite simply as another abuse by the clerical Church, on me …

And I still see it that way. There was no need for it. It was unreasonable, not only for me, but for each of the other priests as well, particularly Sean Fagan, who died recently. The way he was treated by the Catholic Church that he loved was horrendous. An organisation that treats its loyal members like that doesn't deserve to have dedicated members.

But most of all, the process was un-Christian and not worthy of a body that calls itself Christian – and that is the most important issue. Whether I was hauled over the hot coals or not is irrelevant … what upset people most was that they did not see me as a heretic. They knew I was saying precisely what they were feeling. And that's why I got such incredible support from people across the world. But, of course, none of that mattered because the hierarchy doesn't listen to people.

In my view, it certainly wrecked my physical health … But, then again, I have to take responsibility for that – I shouldn't have let them do that to me. I should've been strong enough to say, 'No, this is not right', and to stand up against it and to make sure that I would not risk my health by trying to live a lie …

Of course what they did was wrong, but my reaction to it – by allowing it to have such an effect on my health – was also wrong, and I've learned from that. I wouldn't let them do it to me now.

Jason then drifted into more interesting territory.

You inspired the late comedian Dermot Morgan's Father Trendy character, on The Live Mike Show - which was a precursor to his iconic role of Father Ted.

[Me] He [Dermot] said the most outrageous things with a pious face. The extraordinary thing was that I was stopped hundreds of times on the street and called Father Trendy and then halfway into the conversation they'd realise, 'Oh, my God! It's not Father Trendy! It's Father D'Arcy!' It became the bane of my life. And everything I said became parodied. I could see people laughing at my sermons because they thought, 'This guy is Father Trendy.'

[Jason] Did you hold a grudge against Dermot?

[Me] Dermot and I became good friends. And very quickly afterwards I realised, 'If that's all the Church ever did wrong, wouldn't it be easy to live with it now?'

[Jason] Were you ever offended by the caricature of Father Jack, in Father Ted?

[Me] (Laughs) Father Ted was a cartoon. Everybody was exaggerated and that's the best part of a cartoon. And it was hilariously funny. I don't think it was at all damaging. I knew Frank Kelly, who played Father Jack, exceptionally well.

[Jason] Frank Kelly had two uncles in your religious order.

[Me] Frank himself had some difficulty doing Father Jack. Frank was a very loyal, practising, solid Catholic, who went to Mass every day. But to me, it was merely a form of exaggeration. It had a certain truth in it and that's what made it funny ...

[When] Dermot Morgan started off doing his Father Brian Trendy act it was obvious who he was imitating. And that happened because the late Kevin Marron – God be good to him – was editor of The Sunday World [Kevin died in a plane crash in 1984] and was very good to Dermot Morgan, as he was to Brendan O'Carroll, long before others recognised their genius. Kevin Marron was always plugging the two boys. Dermot was going to call himself Father Michael Cheery, obviously because of Father Michael Cleary ...

Kevin said, 'He's too old! Why don't you call yourself after our guy?' So, the two of them came up with the name Father Brian Trendy. We had a picture taken: Dermot was dressed as a priest and I was dressed as a priest. And the initial article telling us he was going to do the priest thing in the nightclubs and on the television was published in The Sunday World. The headline was: 'A Good Kick up the D'Arcy!' Kevin was a genius …

Jason and I talked about celebrity and how other clerics see me.

Within the Church I was always looked upon as a maverick … When I'd go to a funeral, it was almost like I had AIDS! Other priests just disappeared around the corner, away from me, in case they'd been seen talking to me!

Recently, I met a bishop I've known for years … He said, 'Holy God! There'd be some scoop for a photographer if he sees Brian D'Arcy shaking hands with a bishop!' And I said to him, 'Actually that wouldn't be half as big a scoop as if they saw a bishop shaking hands with Brian D'Arcy! [Laughs].

Jason moved on to discuss some of the burning issues of the day.

You make a mistake, marry too young and the marriage doesn't work out. Yet you cannot get remarried in the Catholic Church. I want to remarry and will never be afforded the opportunity. I think that's sad.

[Me] Yes, I feel the same. I hope the Church, through Pope Francis, is trying to work on that. No matter what the Church says, the couple have to work out their own relationship [according to their] conscience. My view is: where love is God is – and where God is, sin cannot be. I work with couples to do as much as I can for them. And even though I cannot have a marriage ceremony in church, I welcome them to our Church …

[Jason] [on homosexuality] 'Is the Church's attitude changing?

[Me] The Catholic Church's official teaching on homosexuality was gravely lacking and gravely misinformed up until now. I do think there's a growing willingness to recognise that we need to change. As society develops and our understanding of complex problems develops, we need to change our position, to ensure that we do not cause unnecessary suffering to any person of good will.

One reason people voted against same sex marriage was because they didn't like the idea of gay couples adopting.

I don't think it makes the slightest difference. Adopting a child is a very serious responsibility and to hand a child over to a couple who are not the biological parents is a huge thing. We should take precautions for the benefit of the child, and make sure that the couple are capable of what they're taking on – whether same sex or heterosexual. We must make sure that the child has the possibility of a balanced, good upbringing.

[Jason] Would you like to do it? [Marry them in church]

[Me] If I were allowed to do it, of course, I would do it. I cannot now do a public marriage on behalf of the Church because the Church doesn't allow that. But that doesn't mean I can't do everything possible to help them. It's not an evasive answer. I do everything I can on a pastoral level to help the couple grow in their love. But if the Church allowed it I would be the first in line to do it for them.

[Jason] Do you believe that women should be allowed to be priests?

[Me] I have to be very careful how I answer this. If I answer a straight yes – which is how I feel – then I could get the second yellow card and be silenced for ever ...

This is one of the issues which got me into trouble with the Vatican. I actually do believe that women could become priests. That's my view after studying it for years. [Officially] the Church has come to the conclusion that it's not a question we can even discuss ... If it's so obvious that women cannot become priests there must be very good reasons theologically, scripturally and culturally for that. So, let's hear them.

But I can't say, 'Yes, definitely, women can become priests,' because that would be counter to what the Church teaches [presently].

You asked me a different question: you asked me, 'Do I think we're going to see women priests?' I long for the day when it might happen. We must have a real discussion, not just about ordination, but about the role of women within the Catholic Church. I think the prohibition on ordination is a symptom of the disrespect which has been shown to the vocation of womanhood in the Catholic Church for centuries upon centuries.

[Jason] Do you agree that women are treated like second-class citizens in the Church?

[Me] I do. Women are the backbone of the Church yet have absolutely no say. This male, clerical, celibate club known as 'the clergy' is the ruination of the Church, in my view. It's not the priesthood – that's a different thing. It's the clerical club, which is this male hierarchical structure that is 3 per cent of the Church and has 93 per cent of the power in the Church.

[Jason] … Why do good men in the Church not rebel against the discrimination and insist on the equal treatment of women?

[Jason] … What you said is a good point: why do good men in the Church not rebel against it, as well as good priests? But then again, why should women have to depend on men to get their freedom?

After more than five hours of conversation Jason concluded by introducing the topic of euthanasia.

[Me] It is going to be a big thing in the future. More than any other pastoral work, I spend most time … helping [people] to die. All life [from conception to death] is sacred and we do not have the right to decide that a little unborn baby is useless or an old person is useless. We have to care for them and they must be comforted in the best possible way. And mostly we do. It's a beautiful experience when it happens. It's one of the most treasured privileges I have in my whole life and I do it all the time. Life is sacred. We shouldn't take unnecessary means to keep people alive, but we should never directly and intentionally kill a human person at any age.

[Jason] No matter how much pain they're in …

[Me] That's not what I'm saying. It's not an argument either, because with proper care and with proper medication there are very few people who have unbearable pain. I have rarely come across it in my work. If we could use our energy and expertise trying to find ways to protect them from pain, then that would be much more helpful than saying, 'We won't waste money on drugs and we'll just kill them off!' Life is sacred. And pain is part of life too. And pain is part of our journey. Mental pain, physical pain, spiritual pain, which is probably the worst of all. All are a necessary part of our journey.

CHAPTER 31

POPE'S MASS IN PHOENIX PARK

I fulfilled one ambition in the Phoenix Park in August 2018. I concelebrated Mass with Pope Francis.

Six years earlier another pope had censured me, essentially for telling the truth about the true extent of the scandal of sex abuse itself and for highlighting the Vatican's role in it. Had Francis not been elected pope I would have been banished from active ministry years ago.

I found the papal Mass in the Phoenix Park a deeply emotional experience, and that took me by surprise. I was touched in a painful inner place by it all. I still find it difficult to find peace. Most days I live my life as if the abuse never happened. But I have to be vigilant lest I get caught up in a pointless trap of resentment. To harbour resentment is like consuming poison myself and expecting my enemy to die. Managing bitterness is an ongoing process but it is entirely possible.

A priest friend who is member of AA explained to me once that the acronym HALT is a helpful reminder of the danger signs. Never allow yourself to get too Hungry, too Angry, too Lonely or too Tired.

Pope Francis has not been able to change much in the Vatican set-up but he has highlighted the evil effects of the clerical club; he has tried to change the ethos there. As a result some of the cardinals and bishops have dismissed him as a heretic. They try to condemn him unjustly in the same way they tried to silence priests and theologians under Benedict.

I believe Francis is a good man and a sensitive pastor. He's human and he's not afraid to acknowledge it. That's why he's liable to make mistakes. He's aware he needs prayers and guidance. Yet I know he's sincere. His vulnerability keeps him humble. His humility shone through when he visited Ireland, especially in the Phoenix Park.

His words of apology at the beginning of Mass were inspirational. They could become a paradigm of pastoral care for victims and survivors. He left aside the formal ritual of the liturgy and spoke from his heart. It was exactly what we needed to hear. Here's why.

On the Saturday evening before the Mass, survivors were invited to meet with Francis and were given the opportunity of directly telling him the horrific truth about their abuse; the insults, the pain, the struggle to be believed, the lack of compassion shown to them, and the suffering they've endured since, often at the hands of senior Church people. Pope Francis listened to them for ninety minutes. Their stories left him deeply disturbed and it showed.

Next morning he prayed for guidance at Knock shrine. He realised he couldn't attempt to celebrate Mass without first asking for forgiveness, not only on his own behalf but for the crimes and sins of priests and religious everywhere. It would have been sheer hypocrisy to ignore their plight. He shocked his officials when he decided to compose and write out by hand a special penitential rite based on the stories the survivors told him. It was powerful.

When I realised what he was doing I was both shocked and grateful. I felt so weak that I had to sit down. I was moved to tears because the pope not only acknowledged decades of abuse, but, as the head of the Church, begged God for forgiveness. He was acknowledging all survivors of abuse. I felt sad and alone sitting at the foot of the altar, but I knew then why I was so keen to concelebrate Mass with Francis.

'Survivors of abuse of power, conscience and sexuality … ,' he prayed in that sincere tone he has made his own, 'I would like to put these crimes [NB: not sins!] before the mercy of the Lord and ask forgiveness for them.'

Those are the words of a pastor, not a canon lawyer or clerical careerist.

'We ask forgiveness for the abuses in Ireland. Abuses of power, conscience and sexual abuses perpetrated by members with roles of responsibility within the Church,' he went on.

That's bishops, priests and religious he's talking about. Victims have been woefully betrayed by these people. Rome has much to answer for; Francis was acknowledging the crimes and sins of the shepherds he depends on.

'In a special way, we ask for pardon for all the abuses committed in various types of institutions run by male and female religious and by other members of the Church.

'For those cases of exploitation through manual work that so many young women and men were subjected to, we ask for forgiveness.'

It became obvious the pope actually listened to, and was moved by, the sufferings of generations of vulnerable victims. He acknowledged that it is priests and religious who need forgiveness, not the abused people struggling to survive.

'For the time in Church we did not show the survivors of whatever kind of abuse, compassion and seeking of justice and truth, and concrete actions, we ask forgiveness.'

It was a far cry from when he accused the victims in Chile of making false claims, telling them they were in need of forgiveness. The pope has moved away from the sheltered world of Vatican diplomacy and has come down on the side of the hurt and the vulnerable. He's asking Church leaders to do the same.

He didn't spare bishops either.

'We ask forgiveness for some members of the Church hierarchy who did not take charge of these painful situations and kept quiet.'

He could have added that 99 per cent of the clerical club shamefully kept silent too. Their career prospects were more important than defending innocent victims.

He moved on to other forms of abuse. Single mothers were abandoned by their families and communities and were sometimes maltreated by religious.

'We ask forgiveness for the times when many single mothers were told that to look for their children who had been separated from them … was a mortal sin. This is not a mortal sin. We ask forgiveness.

'Sustain and increase this state of shame and give us the strength to work for justice. Amen.'

It was a powerfully graced moment from a man deeply disturbed by the shameful actions of 'holy people' supposedly acting in the name of Jesus. Francis named it for what it is – a scandal, a crime and a serious sin.

I was so overcome by the heartfelt prayers of Pope Francis that much of the rest of Mass was a blur. I'm certain of one thing though – I was meant to be there.

CHAPTER 32

VICTIM OF ABUSE

I have made countless attempts to put down on paper a hesitant description of two events in my life which were short enough in duration but which have governed every aspect of my life since – for better or worse, mostly worse. I have struggled and failed to describe my feelings for more than twenty years now. I don't know if I will be able to tell my story now; if I do, it will be an inadequate retelling. I will not communicate even one per cent of the devastation I felt in those dark days over fifty and sixty years ago respectively – and, far too often, still feel to this day.

In fact I'm setting myself up to experience the horror of abuse all over again. That's what sexual abuse does. It can cripple you emotionally, physically and spiritually. Still, I have to do it. Any time I've tried to share these experiences, friends tell me not to go there if it's so painful. Yet for the first time I want to take control of my own emotions and give those who don't know, a tiny glimpse of the devastation sexual abuse brings.

'Hell is pandemonium,' John Milton wrote. I know what he means.

There is a painful knot in my stomach just thinking about it and it will not go away. My heart is beginning to race now. I've sat in front of this laptop for hours and yet I'm still paralysed. If I don't start now I'll never do it. Maybe I should leave it to another day? God, why does it haunt me still?

I know I will be forced to dash suddenly to the toilet to throw up. I don't know how often the cold sickness will weaken me but it will come – suddenly and without warning. No matter how exhausted I am when I go to bed tonight, I will not sleep. I will toss and turn and if perchance I do drift off, I will be shocked back to reality by interminable flashbacks. I will smell the sweat mingled with the stale cigarette stink off his breath. The heavy breathing and the horrible over-sized eyes popping out of his big round head will be as real as they always are when I try to outrun the memory.

I will get out of bed and walk around the room in the dark and I will change my soaking pyjamas but I will not sleep. It's not that I'm afraid of the dark. No. It's just that I can defend myself when I'm awake. Sleep, on nights like this, makes me vulnerable to the thoughts and feelings that never go away.

Tomorrow night, or on some other night I can't predict, other memories of a different lunchtime abuse in a classroom eight years earlier will haunt me in a different way.

Maybe that's where I should begin. Because that's where Tommy Tiernan took me when I was one of his 'mystery' guests in the summer of 2019. The chat began with clerical abuse in general and quickly shifted to my experience of abuse at the hands of a brother in Omagh.

'Tell me what the abuse was like,' Tommy asked. It wasn't a nasty question, though it could have been. Tommy trusted me to be honest and I trusted him to understand.

The interview was traumatic – for me, for Tommy and for the audience. The atmosphere spoke louder than words did.

Throughout the summer months of 2019 everywhere I went, North and South, people wanted to talk about the programme. There were some who agreed with Tommy's style and some who didn't. Everyone, though, understood that it was an important and sometimes harrowing interview. It was all that.

However, it did help to bring home the devastating and lasting horror of sex abuse. Men and women of all ages contacted me to reveal their own living hell. Abuse is still a massive problem; we have only scraped the surface. There are thousands of damaged people trying to cope with a secret they've never revealed. How many alcoholics has abuse produced? How many broken relationships? How many suicides?

I didn't sleep much on the night we recorded the Tommy Tiernan show – which was six weeks before it was aired. After the recording I drove from Dublin to Crossgar, seriously worried that I had revealed too much of my vulnerable self. Tommy's first question wasn't the friendliest and I was lucky to be able to think of a quick answer that made the point but didn't betray any anger.

To be honest, I didn't sleep much on the night it was shown either. It unearthed some deep vulnerability within me which I have not been able to deal with properly.

I have a golden rule about interviews, which I have kept for years now. I tell the truth. If I'm asked a personal question I answer it as honestly as I can. It gets me into trouble, but telling lies or trying to be cute or smart would be pathetic. I can handle honesty but living with lies would destroy me.

I have no regrets about being honest. I have no regrets about my life story either.

On the night the show was broadcast I locked myself away in a room by myself to watch it. I needed space to come to terms with my own failures. I feared I would embarrass my family and friends by revealing too much.

Retelling the abuse becomes the same as reliving it.

Tommy rang me the morning after we recorded it to see how I was. I was just as worried about him. Tommy has a unique style of interviewing. He listens, he thinks and he's not afraid of silence. Luckily neither am I.

After the interview social media went berserk and the debate went on for weeks. I am grateful to Tommy and his team for being fair and concerned.

They were compassionate and caring. I appreciate that.

What really surprised me was the number of people who contacted me as a result of what I said and because they recognised that they too are crippled emotionally as a result of being abused as children. Hundreds of messages came in, some looking for help; others grateful that I put words on their feelings; most just thankful that I raised issues that society won't or can't face.

Abuse cannot be dealt with once and for all. As we grow and mature we have to keep confronting the abuse in different manifestations. It affects us all our lives. We never get over it. If we're lucky we learn to manage its cruel effects as best we can to live a reasonably normal life.

Crucially it's never just a matter of signing a cheque and forgetting about the victim. I've discovered I need to deal with new issues every couple of years. It's a life sentence that constantly needs attention.
That's life. I'm grateful to Tommy for asking the awkward questions.

* * *

I was an innocent boy of eleven years of age, away from home and anxious to please everyone. My parents, wanting to give me the best possible start in life, sent me to stay with my aunt in Omagh so that I would know enough to pass the Eleven-plus exams at the Christian Brothers' school.

I was a naive country child, overawed by the 'smarter' townies. Everyone wanted to help me. My aunt and cousins were good and kind to me and my teacher knew how to get me through this exam, which would open the door to the bright future of free education in a grammar school.

Everyone, that is, except that sinister unchristian brother who spotted a lonely, helpless, vulnerable child out of his depth in a town school, away from home and missing the protection of parents and friends.

He knew he could get away with anything because no Catholic would question his reputation in a Catholic town in Northern Ireland in 1956. A respected, though not respectable, elderly brother's word against a poor, insignificant boy from Fermanagh? No contest.

He pretended to take an interest in me, even though he wasn't my teacher. He never taught me. Yet at lunchtime, when the classroom was empty, he took me by the arm and led me away from the schoolyard on the pretext of wanting to help me settle in. Of course I believed him. Of course I felt safe and important.

He wrapped my head between his soft hands. He put a reassuring arm around me. He ran his fingers through my hair. He whispered that I shouldn't be so fearful. He took me up on his knees, while he sat complacently on his teacher's throne. Then he swung me around across his knees until he had me upside down, straddled face down across his groin.

At first he patted my bum and then he drew me in around him. I knew there was something wrong but I had neither the wit nor the words to understand what he was doing. He held me there in silence for a ten-minute eternity.

I didn't understand why he was so excited and I was trembling in fear. I didn't understand what had happened to me but I knew I was no longer an innocent boy from Bellanaleck. In truth, after what he did to me, I have never felt at home anywhere since. He let me go with a dismissive pat on the head when he was finished with me. He went on to teach his class and I was puzzled why my short-legged pants had become so damp so suddenly. I felt dirty and bad and pathetically fearful.

Yet I had done nothing wrong. I had done nothing, period.

I lived in dread that my aunt would find out, or my cousin, who was a teacher in the school. Everyone seemed to submit to this brother; even the other brothers kept out of his way. I couldn't tell anyone because at the time I didn't comprehend what had happened to me. But I knew in the silence of the night that it was wrong. I was consumed by shame and guilt. I knew my innocence, my childhood, was gone forever.

I tried to find comfort in the Sacred Heart Church. I used to visit there going to and coming from school. I went to Mass every morning and tried in my innocent boyish way to be extra good, as if I had to repent for whatever he was doing to me. Yet, when the weekly tap on the shoulder came in the playground, it was back to the empty classroom to become his recreation for another dirty lunchtime. It went on for weeks – though I can't put an accurate number on it. No wonder I was consumed by guilt. I should not have been but I was.

Now I often wonder if there were other boys on the Mondays, Tuesdays, Thursdays and Fridays.

I'll be honest and admit I didn't know I was being abused. I had never even heard of the word. All I know is that there's a day in 1956 when I lost my childhood and never found it again. Since that day there is a lonely empty hole in the pit of my stomach. That's how I picture it, anyway. Ever since I feel I have to make it through life on my own. The vacuum deep down within me has never been filled and never will be. Not in this life anyway. There are no words to describe the damage child sex abuse does. It's a life sentence.

The brother wasn't overpowering or rough or, indeed, obviously sexual. He just cruelly used me for his own gratification. He bullied me with a smiling face, in a sly, cynical way. He abused a naïve country kid just because he could.

To this day, I've an inner longing to be accepted for who I am and not for what I am. If only I could really believe that God accepts me. I long to be understood. I wish I could make up for my stupidity, for not knowing what abuse was, for not being able even to recognise the impurity of a man who constantly talked to us about the need for purity if we wanted to avoid hell.

I still have an irrational desire to do what God wants. It's part of the please-at-all-costs symptom. I continually allow myself to be abused by those in authority who only have to hint I must do as I'm told because it's God's will. I just wish I could grow out of that frozen eleven-year-old abused child.

It won't happen now. I know in my heart that I never will be 'worthy' enough when it comes to religion. I don't fit in and I never will. I may, at times, manage the memory of abuse, but I can never grow out of its clutches.

I thought then and for years after, that I was the only one he messed up. In my earlier memoir, 'a Different journey', I mentioned briefly that the brother abused me. I thought no one would recognise the man I was writing about. However, at a book signing near Omagh, to my amazement at least twenty men told me that everyone knew what he did to some boys. Parents, it seems, warned their children to stay away from him. Yet they did nothing about it and so he was able to groom vulnerable strangers like me. That makes me angry. It drives me on to root out abusers and those who enable their pernicious abuse.

On the other hand I recognise that I have grown stronger in the broken places. Because of what happened to me I am able to tell the clerical Church with utter conviction how cruel they were in not stamping out abuse. Because they deliberately chose to put the alleged good name of their institution ahead of protecting innocent children, no sensible person will ever trust them again. I can never be silent about the abuse of power and the abuse of the vulnerable.

It seems to me that I live out, at one and the same time, a vocation and a curse.

* * *

I'm reluctant to move on through the years to 1963 and to relive another abuse I spoke about earlier.

Despite being repeatedly abused by a brother in Omagh, I did pass the Eleven-plus. I'm forever grateful to my late aunt and her family in Omagh for helping me to do that. Thankfully, neither my aunt nor my parents ever found out about the abuse. Knowing them as I did, they would blame themselves and not the abusers. My life would have taken a different course had I not had a grammar school education, even though the price, being abused in a way that left me marked forever, is inordinately high.

After the Eleven-plus I moved back to my family in Bellanaleck, near Enniskillen. I attended St Michael's Grammar School for five years, after which I entered the Passionist monastery at The Graan in County Fermanagh.

At school I was an average student who successfully plodded my way through. Looking back, it's hard to comprehend why I entered the monastery when I was seventeen going on seven. I didn't realise how naive and immature I was or that I was so marked for life by abuse.

I made my first profession of vows – poverty, chastity and obedience – plus a vow to spend the rest of my life reminding the world of the saving power of the Passion of Jesus, that is that Jesus was a spectacular failure and was at his weakest when he won salvation for all, especially other vulnerable failures like me.

After thirteen months of what amounted to spiritual brainwashing in the novitiate, I moved from The Graan to Mount Argus, in Dublin. Whatever maturity or self-confidence I garnered between the ages of twelve and seventeen was totally demolished after enduring what they called the novitiate.

I began student life in University College Dublin – then located in Earlsfort Terrace, where the National Concert Hall is now. I was little more than a pious youngster dressed up in a black suit, a full clerical collar and large black hat hiding a pimpled face. Mixing with, or even speaking to, 'seculars' – our name for ordinary students - was frowned upon. We were training to be priests and therefore we mustn't become 'contaminated' by young men and women of the world. It was the antithesis of what a university education entails. Needless to say I did mix with other students. It would have been impossible, as well as irresponsible, not to.

Here I go again, living in two different worlds. There was the normal questioning, maturing, broad-minded approach of university life in contrast to the restrictive, oppressive false religious life back in the monastery.

The struggle to be a balanced eighteen-year-old, listening to the Beatles and reading widely, on the one hand, whilst on the other hand, disappearing into the archaic, unrealistic, almost hypocritical world of religious life of the 1960s, was bound to take its toll. I was convinced God wanted me to be a priest who could learn from, and communicate with, a fast-changing world.

Incredibly, everything about my actual clerical training told me the world was an evil place to be despised and avoided. No wonder I was a troubled, gaunt, sickly teenager confused in a monastic wilderness.

It wasn't helped by outrageous penitential practices. There was early morning rising at six. We had to break our sleep to gather in the community chapel at two in the morning to chant the Divine Office. We spent endless hours chanting Latin psalms at each other across a cold, pitched pine choir. We listened to, and read, inane volumes of out-of-date spiritual drivel, knowing that no one could possibly live the kind of life they described.

We made cord whips with our own hands and three times a week I was told to drop my pants and beat my bare backside, all the while chanting, through gritted teeth, Paters, Aves and Glorias. Until a few months earlier this self-flagellation was carried out in community in the choir. We, at least, had the privacy of our cells for this almost pornographic exercise of self-hatred.

Yet, even though I couldn't make sense of this suffocating spirituality, I was racked with scruples. I constantly felt the need to confess my 'sinful' failures every week, with overwhelming guilt. Young and old bought into this depraved vision of the religious life and those who didn't were forced to leave the monastery. I never could accept it, even though the overwhelming desire to be a priest drove me on. I so wanted to be a priest that I was willing to endure abuse, humiliation and brainwashing. How could that be right? Why did I not see then what I see so clearly now?

The outgoing student life of UCD kept me sane.

The hypocrisy of such a life came home to me in shocking circumstances later. I was an over-anxious, jaded, guilt-ridden, immature, confused eighteen-year-old when I was asked by two senior students in the monastery to take on the role of looking after a certain priest in the community who was sick and confined to his cell with flu.

The two senior students came to me in the recreation room after supper. Together they told me the priest specifically asked for me because he knew I was a helpful young student. Because I was the youngest student in the monastery I was also the junior student. They convinced me it was a special privilege to bring him his food and whatever else he required, night and morning.

It's only now I realise they were grooming me on his behalf.

There was a rule that students should not even speak to the priests and brothers. It was strictly forbidden to go to their rooms except when they needed care or we needed confession.

I put everything into caring for that sick priest, who was a well-known preacher with an impeccable reputation. On the second day he said he needed me to massage his 'sore' leg. It was, he said, an old injury and that students who cared for the sick had to learn how to massage him. He would teach me the proper way to do it. I believed him. A priest would not tell a lie, surely? I did as he said – an innocent abroad who was chuffed to be told I was the best student in the monastery.

The next evening when I entered the cell he was out of bed and dressed in the loose black habit of the Passionist order. It all seemed so normal. Obviously my caring skills were working wonders. That's what I chose to believe.
I should have become suspicious when he locked the door of his cell. He now wanted me to massage both legs. He lay on the bed and pulled up his habit. He was naked underneath. He had a supply of towels ready. He ordered me to begin massaging and to move ever closer to his groin. He became angrier and began to speak sharply to me with his overbearing preacher's booming voice.

By now my stomach was churning. He sensed I was reluctant to do his bidding. His demeanour suddenly changed. He got angrier by the second. His mad eyes began to bulge. He told me to do as he said and if I didn't, he would report my 'insubordination' to the director. He would make sure I would be sent home instantly; I would be disgraced and would never become a priest.

He grabbed me and pulled me on top of him. The smell of smoke, whiskey and sickly perfume repulsed me. I tried to get away but he hit me hard with his fist on the back of my head. He attempted to bugger me. I struggled and fell to floor. I don't remember much after that but when he saw me on the floor he was calmness and sweetness personified. He assured me I was a great student and he would never tell anyone what I had done.

What I had done? I did nothing. He assaulted me. He wasn't likely to tell anyone that. But I was too shocked to say anything.

I want to be honest here. I'm not revealing all the details of the abuse because I simply cannot bring myself to put the words on paper and I'm not sure I can justify more detailed description. I am putting some details on paper to ensure we know precisely the damage abuse does. I'll explain the lasting effects of abuse in more detail later. Suffice to say that fifty years on I'm still traumatised.

* * *

I broke away from his clutches but not before he had abused, assaulted and bullied me. I escaped, but not for long. I knew I had to go back into his den later that night to bring him his hot cocoa. Once outside his cell I leaned against the wall and waited for my legs of jelly to settle. He must have heard me sobbing because he came out of his room with his long black habit still hanging loosely. He recognised how upset I was.

Thinking only of himself, he grabbed my arm and tried to drag me back into his cell, pointing his finger and telling me the monks going to pray would see us. I felt unable to move but I was determined I was not going back in. I went to my cold little cell and cried. This time I recognised what abuse was and felt like a sinner that I had allowed myself to get caught in an abuser's web again. Guilt, blame and shame destroyed, not only my peace, but also my ability to judge wisely. I blamed myself for his sins.

I wanted to jump in a bath to wash myself clean but students were allowed to have a bath only once a week. I just washed myself down with a face cloth in the privacy of the student toilets.

Later, the two students who had set me up came to speak to me. They told me the priest was pleased with me and insisted that I must continue to look after him. Years later it dawned on me that they were part of his grooming net. I'm furious with them now – they are no longer around so I will never be able to confront them. They set me up; they were part of his inner circle. I trusted those fellow students and they walked me into his trap. Both of them are now dead. I hope and pray both met God at his most merciful.

My torment did not end that night. During my first year as a student, I was repeatedly approached, groomed, bullied and groped by that priest every time he came back to the monastery between missions and retreats. The pressure nearly drove me over the top. My introduction to religious life that year was hell on earth.

The priest continued to pester me off and on for two years. The pattern was always the same. He would feign sickness and somehow always managed to have me appointed to look after him. I was too scared to take him on or to tell his superiors. Anyway, I wouldn't have been believed. The 'holy' priest's word would have been accepted and I would have been dismissed. It's always easier to get rid of a 'troublesome' student than to face the fact that one of their star preachers was an abuser.

The abuse took many forms. Sometimes it was emotional, occasionally he attempted physical abuse, and on every occasion he threatened me with expulsion from the order. He knew how to control and manipulate me. He knew I was soft-hearted and found it difficult to refuse to help him.

As I got older I made sure he never got away with sexual abuse. However, the psychological abuse, the bullying, lasted for years. On a few occasions he burst into my cell during the night. I knew if I screamed out he would scarper, and on numerous nights that is exactly what I did.

In 1965, just before Second Arts exams at university, I got a call from my family to say my mother was seriously ill. I was allowed to go home to see her. I was utterly shocked to see how ill she was. Sadly, she died twenty-four hours later on Ascension Thursday morning, 27 May 1965.

That was the saddest day of my life, yet in the midst of grief I convinced myself that she died as a punishment for what happened between me and the abuser. I know it doesn't make sense but that is what abuse does to you. You accept blame for everything even though you realise it's utterly irrational.

Today when I visit my parents' grave the guilty thought slips into my subconscious that I was responsible for what happened in a sleazy cell down the side corridor of Mount Argus monastery.

Abuse is permanent; relief is temporary.

Years later the priest's alcoholism was recognised as a problem. He spent time in treatment in different centres and was out of ministry for years.

By then I was the superior of Mount Argus monastery, desperately trying to save it from destruction. It fell to me to head the appeal to raise over £2 million in a restoration fund. That's another story.

The abuser priest was now a pathetic, elderly, wreck. I visited him in hospital as anyone would. One day when we were alone he admitted he was nearing the end of his life. He wanted to have a serious talk with me. Naturally, I promised I would do as much as I possibly could to make his passing easier and as peaceful as possible.

I honestly believed he was about to admit that what he had done to me (and certainly to others) was wrong. I psyched myself up to say I forgave him as soon as he apologised. He raised himself up from the pillow and in an audible whisper assured me that he had chosen me to be the preacher at his funeral Mass. There was no apology; no repentance.

In the end he died suddenly and I delivered the homily at his funeral Mass just as he had arranged. He knew he could manipulate me in life and in death. The small congregation present could not have realised how stressful it was. 'You had him to a tee,' a relative said. 'Nobody could have done it better.'

If only they knew.

CHAPTER 33

WOMEN IN THE CHURCH

I know from experience that to speak in favour of ordaining women priests in the Catholic Church is the ultimate taboo. As far as I can tell, it was one of the reasons the CDF censored me in 2011.

As the years go by I am more convinced than ever that we must give serious consideration, not only to whether women can be ordained, but to how women are respected, understood or even tolerated, in the Catholic Church. I have had an interest in equality from my earliest days in the priesthood. I am convinced that a male-dominated Church is not what Christ wants.

Even when I was Editor of The Cross magazine, I handed over one issue to a panel of influential women who compiled articles for women and by women. That was in the early 70's.

In practical terms, women are central to everything that goes on in the Church. It is not an exaggeration to say that without women, there is no Church, in theory or in practise.

When I went to study in America in the late 1980s I immersed myself in study about the role and position of women in the Church through the ages.

I lived in a community with two of the leading scripture scholars in the world. Privately, they undertook, with other scripture scholars across America, an investigation into whether the early Church ordained women deacons. Furthermore, they researched scripture and theology to discover if there is an inherent impossibility within Catholic theology legislating that women can never be ordained.

Naturally, we had many conversations on the topic. My own intelligence simply would not allow me to understand the full implications of whether women can or should be ordained.

What I can say is that those two experts, with their team of researchers, found that (1) scholarship indicates that there were women deacons in different periods of the early Church; (2) there is no conclusive evidence from theology or scripture, which of itself would prohibit the ordination to the priesthood of women in in the Catholic Church.

They could not conclude that women should be ordained. But they could find no evidence that would prohibit the ordination of women. Their research was later published widely.

Let me take the discussion to a different level. I'm now convinced that it cannot be just about women's ordination. The conversation must go above and beyond the ordination of women to look at how women's gifts are used in building up the Church. If we restrict the conversation to ordination, it means that we are willing to perpetuate the present structures within the Catholic Church so that clerical domination of the laity will persist. Whether the laity is oppressed by men or women clerics is irrelevant. We need to institutionalise equality within the community. It's a new model we seek, not more of the same. We need a more inclusive arrangement where the gifts and talents of all will be respected, encouraged and used fully.

It's hard to credit that Pope Paul VI was the first pope in history to proclaim two female doctors of the Church. Until then no women were part of the Church's teaching body, the Magisterium. It is only in recent times that we have begun to realise that what Pope Paul did should have changed everything. It didn't. The male establishment dismissed it as little more than an honour to the women saints. However, a doctor of the Church becomes an essential element in Church teaching. We needed to examine what those women taught us.

Sadly, the Second Vatican Council failed to provide a theology of priesthood. It left a vacuum which has in many ways, been responsible for the rejection of the council's insights for fifty years.

We have to admit that the contribution of women to the Church has been quietly airbrushed out of history. Worse still, we are now aware they have been airbrushed out of scripture, liturgy, theology, structures and even Church language, which is entirely male.

Scandalously, when the Catechism of the Catholic Church was first published it was held up, revised and rewritten to delete inclusive language from the text. A revisionist team was appointed to reinsert male pronouns and delete female and inclusive pronouns. It was a clear statement that men rule the Church and that women don't matter.

Because of the culture of the time the Second Vatican Council was a male dominated council. Historians tell us that when scholars went back to study the sources of scripture and tradition they considered male sources only, because, let's face it, throughout the history of the Church women were subservient.

Many theologians now realise that in the early Church, i.e. before AD 55, women were central to Church structures. It was women who comforted Christ at his crucifixion. Women were the apostles of the resurrection. Women established and kept alive the faith in the resurrected Jesus.

Yet, after those earliest times, women in the Church have been treated as second-class citizens. Now that women are studying theology and teaching in seminaries, they are discovering for themselves how women have been demeaned within the Church throughout history. For example, scholarship proves that those who compiled the readings for the Sunday liturgy cycle of the Lectionary have excluded passages from the scripture read at Mass which tell of the central role of women in the early Church. That's why it isn't just about the ordination of women; we have to accept a new vision where women's role is radically different. Their role is not just to complement men. We can no longer accept male theology as the norm.

To put it at its simplest, what other major institution would be allowed, or could afford to, permanently exclude women from leadership? Why then do we accept it from the Catholic Church?

Other religions exclude women from leadership too, but I confine myself to the church I know and love, the Catholic Church. I have worked all my life with inspirational women and I have learned emotional intelligence and much more from them. Seeing the world through a male lens only can never be healthy or balanced. Think of what would happen if men were excluded from participating in Church leadership.

I got a letter to The Sunday World recently from an articulate and concerned Catholic woman who concluded her letter with this memorable phrase: 'I no longer see it as my duty to try to save the mess that is this male Church.'

Another relevant area that needs attention is: Who exactly did Jesus formally ordain? That would help to clarify what it means when the male clerical club insists that women cannot be ordained, because Jesus didn't ordain women. That may be true, but if it is, what reason did he give for not ordaining women; does it mean women can never be ordained? Because times change, could the rules change too? Those questions must be addressed in an adult academic way. The attitude which insists an opinion is true because "I say so" is utterly outdated now.

Deep down I believe men in the Church are afraid of the special gifts women will insist on; they will bring deeper and different insights; it will become a church of the heart and not just the head. Compassion, understanding and a more holistic church will emerge. They will lead us to the heart of the Gospel.

The two scripture scholars I spoke with were convinced that in the early Church women were not just followers but disciples of Christ. Women were martyrs for their faith, lived active missionary lives, were leaders of small communities and preached the Word of God just as men did.

As I come to the end of my life, I rarely regret the times I have spoken out about clerical sex abuse within the Church, even though that's what got me into trouble; what haunts me is the number of times I've been utterly silent about injustices within the Church. The Church's disregard for the gift of womanhood is the greatest of those injustices. Deep within me I don't know if I can be, or even should be, forgiven for accepting this exclusively male version of Christ's message.

As with so many other aspects of modern living, I no longer accept that fine words or dramatic gestures suffice. You would think that the Church which promotes such a strong devotion to Mary, the mother of God, would understand and promote the unique values that women offer us. Instead we distort the role of Mary by minimising her heroism in following God's will and instead canonise her subservience.

I believe that if women were encouraged to play a critical role in the Church, we would have a healthier, more realistic, more affirming theology of sexuality. There is more to sexuality than genital activity. The narrow vision of sexuality we now have may be central to why the Church is becoming more and more irrelevant in people's lives. We need to learn from the values women hold dear.

The wider world is beginning to cherish the dignity of sexuality. That enlightenment has not come from the churches but from women who have been given a voice. The sheer authenticity of their voice is more effective than the combined teaching of all churches. It is a hard lesson to accept, but is a gift we should treasure.

I am only too aware that I, as an ageing male celibate priest, may be missing the point. But until I express it, how can anyone know?

Living in denial is no longer a healthy option. If I've learned anything it is that we're in this mess for a reason. Until we accept our inability to solve it, we condemn ourselves to remain forever in a confusion of our own making. The Spirit works when we stop, reflect and be patient.

There is a purpose for us being in this place at this time. We shouldn't become frustrated; we should just be humble enough to learn that there is something that must change in us before we can be part of even greater change in the future. Thomas Merton used to say that the spiritual life invites us to have hope, to endure and never to grow weary.

The Benedictine nun Joan Chittister puts it prophetically: 'Success really lies in learning to stay at the task so that generations to come are not left to begin again what we failed to pursue with patience.'

CHAPTER 34

DISCOVERING GOD'S CALL

Working in the North makes ecumenism a real priority. I have been blessed to have worked closely with many exemplary men and women from many different religions and faiths. Dr Bert Tosh in the BBC religion department in Belfast is a close friend with whom I have much in common.

My near neighbours and very close friends Archdeacon Cecil Pringle and his wife, Hilary, were responsible for one of the most genuinely deep religious experiences of my life. Cecil, as rector of Rossorry Church of Ireland, invited me as rector of The Graan to preach in his church in January 2004. It is less than a mile from our monastery to his church but it took ninety-five years for us to share our pulpits. When I preached in Rossorry, I realised my family background had prepared me well.

Bellanaleck was a country village of forty houses when I was growing up. Neither my mother nor my father would have been able to spell ecumenism, but they lived it. In our humble house by the side of the road, Mrs Moore was as welcome to a cup of tea as was Mrs Murphy. My mother's motto all her life was, 'It doesn't matter which church you go to on Sunday as long as you go to some church.'

When her neighbours were sick, she often took their children into our house. We hadn't much but we shared what we had. And I was always aware that the clear spring water we got by the bucket from Thornton's well was given to us freely and generously. Even a cup of water given graciously is one of the keys for a Christian to enter heaven.

On my father's birthday, our house was usually full of children. My father's birthday was on 12 July and my mother looked after our neighbours children while their parents went to march.

The journey from The Graan to Rossorry was, literally and metaphorically, an uphill one. Some Protestant people could not see their way to be present at the prayer service. I respected their integrity. I don't regard such principled people as enemies; far from it. I see them as friends and in that friendship, God's spirit is present, leading us down roads we cannot predict. A few fundamentalists held a protest and others wrote to the papers objecting, but the vast majority welcomed the opportunity to move on.

To me the real scandal is that our various Churches don't nurture goodness. Instead we emphasise our differences. I believe we should appreciate some simple truths:

All of us, whatever our differences, believe in the same God.

That same God loves us, saves us, died for us and lives again as the source of all our hope.

It will be the same God we all meet when we leave this world. He is the maker who will judge us justly, mercifully and compassionately when we die.

The same God recognises the hurts we have, the love we have for our families, and he cries with us in our times of sadness and sickness.

That same God has blessed us with many gifts. At the end of our days, a patch of earth six feet by three feet will do us, unless, of course, we are cremated, in which case a decent-sized matchbox will do.

That's the countryman's ecumenism, the kind that begins with good neighbourliness. It was bred in me as I grew up going to school on a bus with my Protestant neighbours and friends. And although we went to different schools, we lived side by side when we came home from school. Integrated education is helpful, but sectarian ghettos are the real problem.

It was practical ecumenism that allowed me to visit my sick neighbours when I came back to Enniskillen as a priest years later.

There was one woman, Mrs Black, who was gravely ill in her old age. I sat with her in hospital and prayed with her. The next day, I was visiting again when I met her Church of Ireland minister on his way out from visiting her.

'It's only a waste of time my going in there,' the minister said. 'I went in to Mrs Black and I prayed with her for twenty minutes and at the end I said, "Do you know who I am?" And she said, "I do indeed, you're Father Brian, that's who you are." So,' he joked, 'there's no point in me coming here at all. You get the credit.'

Today all our churches are in danger of being relegated to being relics of the past. It is my experience that people, and particularly younger people, have grown tired of the clichéd rhetoric of 'the two communities'. Isn't it petulant of us to think that when we speak of two communities we mean Protestant and Catholic? If we were really Christian, would we not divide communities into rich/poor or believers/non-believers?

Soon we will be grateful that people are believers. What particular brand of Christianity will be of little importance. I look forward to that day.

CHAPTER 35

UNIVERSITY OF ULSTER HONORARY DEGREE

I doubt if there's a single person who hasn't a story to tell about how they achieved success in life that others thought was beyond them. It happened to me on 30 June 2009 on the University of Ulster campus at Coleraine when I was awarded an honorary doctorate of literature.

Another higher education establishment had contacted me suggesting they were considering me for a similar honour. I was grateful to them, but decided that while one honour per year is acceptable, two might be embarrassing – for them and for me.

The University of Ulster kindly asked me to accept a doctorate in recognition of forty years' building bridges between communities in Northern Ireland. They explained the ceremonial involved, especially the address the honorary graduate is expected to deliver on behalf of all the other graduates.

My fellow Enniskillen man, actor, writer and musician Adrian Dunbar, of Line of Duty fame, was also honoured at a different graduation ceremony in the afternoon. Both of us were delighted to accept.

The irony is that my family had to send me to an aunt in Omagh to make sure I'd pass the Eleven-plus. My cousin Donal Donnelly, who worked so hard to get me through the exam, had a good laugh when his 'slow learner' became a doctor.

My family was present in the unfamiliar surroundings of a university campus and were more nervous than I was as I stepped up to the podium to address the vice-chancellor, distinguished guests, ladies and gentlemen.

In the talk I encouraged the young graduates to enjoy their day before launching into a whole new world of business and academia.

'I hope it will be the beginning of a new and exciting part of your lives,' I told them.

'The world needs educated, enthusiastic young people at this time. You will find your niche. You have worked hard to achieve your goals; you have earned the right to be proud and to celebrate.'

I wasn't joking when I told them I felt the most unworthy person present. Dr Gerry Burns, the chancellor, had given a most uplifting talk, explaining why I was being honoured. He listed all kinds of activities, including journalism, broadcasting, cross-community initiatives. I was particularly delighted to hear my work with showbands and entertainers was included.

It was good to hear one's own eulogy without having to die first.

Everyone likes to quote Oscar Wilde. But since he went to school in Fermanagh I felt safe borrowing one of his pearls of wisdom. He once said, 'A sermon should have a good beginning and a good end. And the closer both are together, the better.' I dedicated the occasion to my late parents, both of whom made huge sacrifices to ensure all of my family got the best education available.

When I was a small child, walking an Irish mile to school and back every day, sometimes in bare feet, 'university' and 'degree' were never imaginable.

If I can receive an honorary degree from an academic institution like the University of Ulster, then anything is possible even for the slowest of slow learners.

The honour came at an opportune time. The Graan was celebrating the centenary of its existence the same year. We tried to make a contribution to the life, the community spirit and the spiritual well-being of all those in our area – rich or poor, whatever their belief.

But I had to admit all was not well in the day job.

'The Catholic Church has been rocked by scandals and quite rightly too. There is no excuse or justification. It has not been easy, but unless we build our lives on solid foundations nothing will survive, nor should it survive. Truth, honesty, integrity, sincerity and, most of all, compassion must be the foundation stones on which education, life and churches are built.

'Northern Ireland has been to hell and back, enduring forty years of violence and turmoil. Thankfully, the integrity of good people, working together, overcame the evils of violence, bitterness and bigotry. In life we have to embrace the hand we're dealt.

'As a priest, as a journalist, as a broadcaster and as one who has been privileged to be a leader of communities, I have learned that humility is the most precious gift of all. After the University of Ulster, the University of Life will be your great educator. We must be humble enough to learn from our experiences.

'The world changes, life changes, and we, if we are to be useful, must change too. As that inspirer of university education, John Henry Newman, philosophised: "To grow is to change; to be perfect is to change often."

'I gave the students a potted history of my life, specifically to highlight the wisdom to be gleaned from the university of life.

'I joined the priesthood when two very important events happened in the history of the world and in the Church. The first was the Second Vatican Council, which allowed people like me to be ordained. Before it I wouldn't have had a snowball's chance in hell.

'The second was the arrival of the Beatles. They were the icons of the sixties revolution. They allowed us to shake off the burden of post-war conservatism.

In the University of Life, one learns humbly from the ordinary as well as the extraordinary.

I was interested in pop music. That was enough to convince my parents that I was a ne'er-do-well in the making. Yet, through pop music I got into a career in journalism, through an accidental meeting with a man in show business who insisted I write a weekly column for his paper. That was in 1967, and I've written each week for some publication since that date.

That man was the former Taoiseach Albert Reynolds. The University of Life is full of odd coincidences. You should make the best of them.

In 1981 when I studied at Berkeley University in San Francisco I had my first encounter with AIDS sufferers. AIDS was recognised there in the early 1980s. The blessing for me was that I instantly overcame any prejudices against AIDS sufferers. For me it was not a plague to be feared but a person needing healing, care and love.

When I came back to Dublin I presided at the funeral of a young man who died from an AIDS-related illnesses. In those dark days AIDS victims were buried quietly in plastic bags; they were considered a health risk. My San Francisco experience allowed me to bring common sense and dignity to their funerals. That's the University of Life in action.'

I reminded them that so far they had learned from books, but life would be a better teacher.

I was in South Africa in 1988 when apartheid was at its worst. I was the only white person allowed to visit or hold services in that black township. The people lived in little tin shacks and were treated abominably. The white people, many of whom were devout Christians, lived five miles away, largely oblivious to the plight of their black neighbours.

The guard dog in the presbytery was trained to attack black people because of their scent, yet lick the faces of white robbers. I saw three young black men shot dead because they stole chickens from a white farmer. The white farmer was commended, not convicted by the judge for doing so. Six chickens were considered more valuable than three black youths. It seemed that evil would triumph; there was no hope at all.

Six years later I went back to South Africa and shook the hand of the country's first black president, Nelson Mandela. I asked him if he saw himself as a saint as most of the world considered him to be. His answer was enlightening. "I am told that a saint is a sinner who tries harder. And if that is so then I am proud to be called a saint." And I saw power and humility come together in one man to set his people free.

So as the oldest graduate on view today,' I concluded, 'I would like to remind you that life is for living. Nothing is impossible. You can achieve; you can change the world. Be brave, be different. Don't always settle for the obvious. Use your gifts. Make your contribution. Give something back to your family, your community, your university, and you will not have lived in vain.

People will criticise you and condemn you if you do good but do good anyway.

Cross boundaries, live enlightened lives, don't let religion or prejudice or politics fence you in. Nothing is impossible when good people do good.

As Ralph Waldo Emerson wrote: "Do not go where the path may lead; go instead where there is no path – and leave a trail".

The University of Ulster believes in humanity; in treating human beings holistically. It's a university which honours the contribution of the small and the great alike. That is why I am proud to be part of their family.

So, on behalf of all people who have learned their wisdom from the University of Life I willingly and humbly accept this undeserved honour from the University of Ulster.

CHAPTER 36

VISIT TO QUEEN ELIZABETH

I find others are more interested in the famous people I had the privilege of meeting than I am. I'm often asked who the most impressive person I've met was. The answer is not a famous person at all, but that's another story.

I have to admit that on the half a dozen times I've met Queen Elizabeth II, she made a deep impression on me because of her dignity, her sense of presence and her humility. I've met her three times in my native county and once in Belfast. But being a guest at both Windsor Castle and Buckingham Palace have been the most memorable.

I was honoured to be invited to a reception in Windsor Castle and to the gathering in the Royal Albert Hall on the occasion of the state visit of President Higgins in 2014. Both events can be best appreciated only by those who were lucky enough to be present.

I have been to England hundreds of times, mainly to broadcast for the BBC for whom I've worked for thirty years. Being a priest has never been an obstacle; being an Irishman was never even mentioned. I've never encountered prejudices in England like I have here in Ireland.

When I arrived at Windsor on a blustery afternoon I was taken aback by the sheer magnitude and number of Union flags and tricolours. They were beautifully arranged on alternate flagpoles for miles around the castle.

I immediately thought of a Friday evening in Belfast some months previously when I was caught in an agonising traffic jam because a small group of people held a protest about flags near the M1 motorway. Small-minded politicians had voted to remove the Union flag from Government Buildings, prompting other ghetto-minded people to protest by disrupting the lives of those who had no hand, act or part in this bigotry.

There in Windsor, though, outside Her Majesty's home, both the union flag and the tricolour flew respectfully and beautifully beside each other.

Inside Windsor Castle I marvelled at how people from different backgrounds mingled freely and proudly together. Representatives of the churches, sporting bodies including the GAA, all political parties, amongst them the late Martin McGuinness, mingled freely. Her Majesty and Martin McGuinness had a most friendly conversation. It took courage on both their parts.

At eighty-eight years of age, as she was then, she stood beside President Higgins and his wife Sabina, along with the Duke of Edinburgh, whilst 195 people individually shook her hand. She remained friendly and alert.

I was in the queue along with Pat Jennings, the famous international goalkeeper, and his wife Eleanor, whom I've known from her days with the Hilton Showband. We agreed that it was unfair on the Queen and Duke having to shake hands with people she never heard of and was never likely to meet again. Surely a general walk around would be suitable for a person her age. All those waiting in line concurred.

The names of the guests were solemnly announced by one of the attendants standing beside her. We were advised she might shake hands, that we should bow and move on along the line to meet the other three dignitaries, and we should not make any conversation unless she asked a question.

We noticed that she was meticulously bowing to each guest, but rarely engaged them in conversation.

Pat and Eleanor and I arrived at the greeting table together. The gentleman announced Father Brian D'Arcy. I bowed and made to move on as instructed.

Queen Elizabeth looked at me. 'Oh I'm so glad to see you here. I know you've been ill. I hope you are well now. When will you be back on Pause for Thought on radio? We like what you tell us. We've missed you.'

I was speechless, and the conversation with Pat and Eleanor came back to haunt me. She really was interested in her guests. She was fully attentive to each person, alert and listening to their names.

I thanked her and assured her I'd be back on radio on the following Monday morning.

'We look forward to hearing you,' she whispered.

President Higgins and Sabrina also had a little conversation, and when I reached the Duke he looked at me and smiled: 'And who are you, anyway, they all want to chat to you?'

I didn't even attempt an answer. I just burst out laughing.

When we reached the next room we all were suitably embarrassed by our total misreading of Queen Elizabeth's awareness. Talk about being with it? She knew far more than we realised. Served us right to be caught out.

Everyone there recognised the occasion as a wonderful time of hope. Many of us had lived through repeated tragedies in our country, especially in the North. We could never have imagined that such a coming together would take place in our lifetime.

As a young boy, when 'God Save the Queen' was played in cinemas, I, and all other young Catholics, made a point of walking out.

It was a criminal offence to display a tricolour anywhere. Now the flags hung side by side and both national anthems rang out over the entire village of Windsor.

I thought of the killings in Enniskillen and the slaughter in Omagh. I remembered the leadership of Gordon Wilson and the hostility he had to endure because he spoke of reconciliation and not retribution. I wish he could have been in Windsor Castle to finally be reassured that people like him were right all along. The suffering of good people is never wasted.

In my lifetime the impossible has happened repeatedly. We journeyed from war and hostility to friendship and tolerance. The Queen visited Ireland and spoke magnificently of a better future. Two Presidents of Ireland have visited her.

I hope those days of hostility are over forever because, as Eleanor Roosevelt famously said, 'We have to face the fact that either all of us are going to die together or we are going to learn to live together, and if we are to live together we have to talk.'

CHAPTER 37

LUNCH WITH THE QUEEN

One beautiful summer's evening I was travelling in a car driven (unusually for me) by Peter Quinn, former president of Cumann Lúthchleas Gael (GAA). We were heading to County Down on a mission.

The phone in my breast pocket rang. Since I wasn't driving I answered it. An exceptionally posh-sounding man asked if he could speak to Father Brian D'Arcy and if this was a convenient time to talk. I was certain it was someone having me on and told him so. He assured me it was a serious call and that he had got my mobile number from Viscount Alan Brookeborough. If I wished I could check with Lord Brookeborough.

That was good enough for me. Alan and Janet call me regularly.

He explained he was phoning on behalf of Her Majesty Queen Elizabeth. Each year she hosts a special lunch at Buckingham Palace to which she invites one person from England, Wales, Scotland and Northern Ireland with whom she would like to converse informally over lunch. He wondered if I would be open to an invitation. I replied I wasn't in a position to speak because I was travelling and I wondered if I could ring him at a convenient time next day. We agreed that would work.

Peter and I had a discussion and laughed that someone from the Queen's office would contact either of us. I still wasn't sure it was an authentic call, but we thought it highly unlikely the Queen would host such an intimate lunch at this time of her life. We forgot about the call and went back to talking football.

Early next day another call came. I was more comfortable this time and agreed that if such an invitation should come I would be delighted to accept. In no time at all a gold-rimmed invitation arrived inviting me to a lunch in Buckingham Palace on 29 October 2017.

In time I got detailed arrangements how to get there, what the protocol was and what was needed for security. There was nothing about the agenda other than it was the Queen's informal way of consulting ordinary people. Her Majesty, who would be accompanied by the Duke of Edinburgh, wanted to hear what her guests had to say about society.

I was told not to feel nervous about it. She wanted to encourage as well as to listen; it would be an enjoyable experience. The man who made all the arrangements, through Lord Brookeborough, was Lieutenant Colonel Charles Richards, Deputy Master of the Household.

And so it came about that I hailed a taxi in Russell Square and asked the driver to take me to Buckingham Palace. 'Is there something happening there today? Bloody hell, the traffic is bad enough without all that jazz going on!' Not much of an impression there until I handed him a security pass for his dashboard which allowed him to skip queues and drive unhindered through security. 'You must be an important bloke,' he muttered. I told him that if I were important I wouldn't be using a taxi!

Once in, after routine security checks, I got a warm, personal welcome from all the attendants. They were efficient but very reassuring. In the waiting room I met the other guests, all three of whom were as nervous as I was. We moved across the immaculately groomed gravel yard to enter the palace, where we were offered drinks in crystal glasses with the royal insignia – and yes, they had water, for freaks like me.

I was thrilled when the lady-in-waiting came into the room. She was Lady Elton, wife of Marmaduke Hussey, former chairman of the BBC. We had met on a few occasions as she and her husband were close friends of the Wogan family. We had a lovely chat about the dear departed Sir Terry, and Lady Helen too. I felt much more at home now because every person in the room wanted to talk about Terry and how much they missed him from Radio 2.

Then the Queen and the Duke entered and were introduced to each of us in turn.

'It's nice to see you again,' Her Majesty said as we shook hands ever so gently. She once again not only looked interested but made us all completely relaxed, so much so that all the protocol went unnoticed.

When the Duke came around he stopped for a chat. He asked questions about all sorts of surprising issues. He was totally on the ball.

'You're looking marvellous, sir' I ventured. 'Do you think so?' he asked. 'When was the last time you visited Specsavers?' He burst out laughing. 'Someone asked me recently why I have stood down from public duties? I told them I stood down because I can't bloody well stand up!'

He loves being mischievous, the Queen told me afterwards.

The Queen laughed too. 'It serves you right, Father. You should not give him a compliment. He does that all the time.'

That year, incredibly, they were celebrating seventy years of marriage. She was just twenty-one and he was twenty-six when they got married. We continued to talk about their longevity over lunch, which lasted just over two hours.

The seating plan for the four guests, plus attendants, had me at the Queen's right hand during the lunch. We had the most inspiring conversation. She had just been speaking to the leader of the Virgin Islands, which had lost everything in hurricane Irma. She was visibly upset to learn of the devastation.

It was the easiest conversation I ever had. She served herself from the dish of chicken and bowls of vegetables. She took small portions and clearly enjoyed what was on offer.

Of course I will not divulge what we said but she was anxious to talk about religion, ethics and the growing apathy towards religion in the First World.

She talked at length and had much to offer on family life and how important the family will be if society is to survive. Parents should take responsibility for their children; respect for God allied with the centrality of hope should be central in all our messages, especially at Christmas.

We talked about spirituality. She knew who talked sense and recalled holy people she was privileged to meet. One Catholic churchman in particular left a lasting impression on her, especially during his final illness. She could quote almost everything he said at their last emotional meeting.

She was fully aware of the difficulties young people have to face in the modern world. Technology can be a mixed blessing. On and on it went; I learned so much from her that the time just slipped by.

'You have a wonderful ability to speak about the most serious issues in a compelling way,' she told me, and wanted to know how much time I invested in my talks and broadcasts.

She herself has become a superb communicator; her Christmas day messages tower above those of leading churchmen and women. She has reflected well over her long life and it shows.

As lunch ended, we were ushered into another room for coffee. Everyone stood around and once more both the Queen and the Duke moved around the guests without a hint of tiredness. Two people in their nineties stood for the duration, spoke enthusiastically about the future, the horses she owns and the pleasures of pony riding – 'It's easier on my knees,' she told us.

She thanked us for coming to visit her at Buckingham Palace. 'I hope you all have a safe and pleasant journey home. Perhaps we may meet again,' Her

Majesty assured us as she moved towards the door with her lady-in-waiting.

'I'm sure we will,' said the Duke, 'They all look reasonably healthy to me.'

* * *

It's impossible for a Nationalist from a village in Fermanagh in Northern Ireland to realise how anything they achieved in life would impress anyone in high places. Receiving an OBE from Queen Elizabeth is therefore beyond imagining. However, strange as it may be, I was one of four people in Northern Ireland who were awarded an OBE in the Queen's Birthday List in June 2019.

There had been rumblings over the years but I always insisted I should not be honoured for doing what any Christian, never mind any priest, should do daily. The honour was given for a lifetime of cross-community activity in Northern Ireland and Britain.

I was made aware later that a number of influential people had nominated me. I knew nothing about it as the process is confidential.

Friends, whose opinions I respect, told me that the award was being considered, and since it was for cross-community initiatives, I was not in a position to refuse it. It would encourage others to cross boundaries and it would affirm all the people I worked with over the years.

I agreed that it would be churlish to refuse such an honour and I wouldn't dream of doing so anyway. We must stop living in bigoted, cave-like ghettoes. A person in a position of leadership must have a broader agenda and be prepared to show others the way forward; accepting this honour from Queen Elizabeth was not just the right thing to do; it was the only thing to do.

I was pleasantly surprised that so many people expressed their delight when the announcement was made public. Letters, cards, emails and texts poured in for weeks afterwards. As I write now there are hundreds of letters I haven't been able to read. People, North and South, were fully behind the award. Naturally, those in Britain who have listened to me on radio and television for more than thirty years thought it should have happened years ago. Many senior politicians wrote personal letters of congratulations, including the then Secretary of State for Northern Ireland, Rt Hon. Karen Bradley, MP.

I was particularly moved when the superior general of the Passionist Congregation sent a personal message telling me how proud he was that a member of our order should be so honoured. That meant the world to me.

Most of my Passionist brothers in Ireland and Scotland sent personal messages of congratulations. It was universally accepted that it was a sign of the times we live in.

President Higgins and President McAleese visited Queen Elizabeth, and who can forget when the Queen came to Ireland? Their leadership has made it possible for us to move on. We can only hope that those still imprisoned in their prejudiced little worlds will soon follow.

For me it was acknowledgement that I should continue to work, as I always have, for respect and understanding among people of good will.

My family and friends were genuinely thrilled, and that is all that mattered to me.

CHAPTER 38

VOCATIONS DAY - What's It All About?

I reluctantly went to a boy's grammar school in Northern Ireland for a Vocations Day seminar in the recent past. There were 110 bright young adults broken into small groups.

The group I joined asked me why I became a priest. I told them it started in a confessional over fifty years ago when the priest asked if I had given any thought to the possibility that I might have a vocation. I said no and he said you should think about it. So I opened my mind and my life to the possibility. over fifty years later here I am. I have no idea how I arrived at this point, but I know that's where it started. I explained all that to the pupils and they asked what it was like to be a priest.

I said some days it is so uplifting that nothing on earth compares. Helping a person in despair to see a way through; encouraging a dying person to be at peace are regular miracles I do not take for granted.

At other times it's miserable. I live in a world where as soon as you say the word 'priest' people immediately think 'abuse'. The lonely days become more unbearable as I grow older, realising that despite my best efforts, fewer and fewer show any interest in religion.

I explained that everyone has to find a path in life; no one can be everything. Choices must be free; it's only right that I should share the gifts I have received.

I added some 'Don'ts.' Don't come if you're not enthusiastic. Don't think celibacy is easy, but realise marriage has even more sacrifices. Don't fall into the trap of loving nobody. Some men I've lived with think they love God because they love nobody. Don't think you'll convert the world. Don't have a grudge against anyone who doesn't think the way you do. Don't come if you're running away from the world; priesthood is only for those who want to be involved. Don't come if you're looking for status and power. Don't come if you're a yes man; priesthood needs rebels.

We had a great discussion about it. I asked them what they thought of priests. They knew that:

1. Priests worked very hard.

2. That they are getting older all the time.

3. That often they kept too much control of things in the parish. They are afraid of anything new.

4. They are out of touch with the lives of young people and indeed most priests were so old they were out of touch with their parents' lives too.

5. They were against celibacy. One of the boys couldn't think of the word. So he said, what's that thing where you can't marry? Another said it was a blessing. I suggested the word was celibacy. They didn't see any sense at all in that. One said it must be for gay people.

6. They didn't see why we should be priests for life. They said they'd be willing to give a few years of their life, the same as they do when going abroad with Concern or Trócaire. But they said there is no job for life now, so why should being a priest be for life?

I enjoyed the chat. There was no hostility. I thought they were terrific. They had a real sense of where the Church is going. There was no anger. It was just a genuine realisation that religion as we present it is out of touch with their experiences.

I went into it reluctantly but came out of it enthused. I'd love to be starting off again because I think the Church of the future will be better, healthier and freer. I'd feel more at home in it than in the Church of the past or the present.

Maya Angelou says it all:

People will forget what you said, people will forget what you did, but people will never forget how you made them feel.

That's vocation!

CHAPTER 39

WHAT KIND OF AN EEJIT ARE YOU?

Six years ago, just when I genuinely thought I would have to leave the active ministry altogether, I sat at my laptop and, with barely concealed anger, thumped out a diary of that week's engagements. Every story is true, and believe me this was not the half of what I was involved in that week. When I finished writing I went for a walk. This is part of what convinced me my life as a priest was too precious to walk away from.

'It's been a busy week. Far too busy,' I wrote at the beginning of 'a week in the life of … ' After a long interview on the radio I felt so exhausted that I was weepy and far too emotional. So much so that Marian Finucane, the interviewer, rang that evening to check I was okay. She thought I should be careful because I was near the edge. It was time to do a bit of thinking.

As usual I went into Enniskillen hospital to do a few visits and then came back and began to look through some of the events I'd been part of. I tried to learn something from them and asked myself the one essential question: Where is God in all of this?

Maybe a better question was that old one which we were forced to ask when we messed up at playing football as youngsters – "What kind of an eejit are you?"

At my age, when I should have my two feet up spending my life in retirement and only doing what I have to do, or want to do, I really do have to ask myself after the week I've had, what kind of an eejit am I? I am not sure I will discover what kind of an eejit I am, but just come with me for part of the week anyway.

My destination on Monday was Austria, but on Sunday evening I attended a rally in support of a neighbouring family in Ballyconnell (the Quinns). It seemed to me to be an ordinary, insignificant thing to do. But as you now know it's all the press has had to talk about since. I learned the hard way that the old values are gone in Ireland. I never thought as a priest I would have to defend walking with neighbours when they are in trouble.

I did it when I was barely a year ordained in 1970, for a civil rights march. People asked me then what was a priest doing marching for civil rights? I knew then what I know now, that I have to be strong in standing up for what a priest should be. Don't be your typical overly political clerical who plays cute and call it prudence. And that was why I explained on the radio that we are still, in this part of the world, able to love the sinner without condoning the sin. Whether people are right or wrong we still help them when they're in need.

Then I drove to Dublin, had an hour-long meeting, got to bed for a couple of hours, got up in the middle of the night, was at the airport before 5 a.m., got on a plane, went to Austria and landed there at half past ten their time. At half past eleven we began filming and we finished filming just after 7 o'clock in the evening. We had a quick bite to eat, went to bed and rose again at 6 o'clock the next morning to fly home and be ready for visiting the hospital and to say Mass in Enniskillen on Tuesday evening.

What did I learn in Austria? Four hundred priests there have publicly said they will disobey the Vatican's orders on certain disciplines of the Church. They will talk and ask about women priests. They will talk publicly about the need for married priests. They are refusing to run five or six parishes because they recognise there are plenty of lay people in those parishes who could run them. They are refusing to say more than one Mass on a Sunday. If they continue saying multiple Masses nobody will address the real issues.

They will give communion to people in second relationships if the people show themselves to be committed to each other and committed to their faith.

But they are staying united as four hundred priests and not one of them has been silenced or censored yet. I wanted to know why, and the main reason, the priests told me, is that much of the money which keeps the Vatican going comes from Austria and Germany. That made me more cynical than before.

* * *

When I came home I discovered that Maeve Binchy had died. Maeve was a lady I met often and I had a few unforgettable lunches with her. She interviewed me and I interviewed her. Both of us told stories – hers were always better. There are many stories about Maeve but the one I like best happened when she was a young editor of the women's page in The Irish Times. Each Saturday she had a cooking column by Theodora Fitzgibbon. Theodora was a precise lady and each week would leave in an article of precisely 650 words. Since her husband was a photographer there was usually a special picture left in too.

One Friday evening when Maeve was in a rush, Theodora left in her copy but there was no photograph. Maeve looked at the copy, read it through, passed it and then went to look for a photograph to go with the description of the meat dish that Theodora had described. As she looked through her files she saw an attractive picture which had just landed on her desk. It was a close-up picture of a beautiful slice of raw meat. She thought it was perfect for Theodora's recipe; she sent it to the printers and went home.

That evening she was sitting at home with her father watching the nine o'clock news. The very first heart transplant by Professor Christiaan Barnard had taken place that day. The picture of the operation flashed up and to her horror Maeve recognised the picture. Instead of a nice piece of raw meat with a knife and fork, what she had put in the cookery column was the picture of the heart transplant with a scalpel and grip.

After a moment of panic she asked her father, who was a judge, what she should do. She went out on the street, but couldn't find a taxi to take her from Dalkey to the centre of Dublin. She stopped a car and breathlessly told him she needed to get in to take a picture of a heart transplant out of a cookery column. 'Are you going to the centre of Dublin?' she asked. He said he wasn't but he would now. He brought her there and by now The Irish Times had to be held back from printing – the ultimate mortal sin for a journalist. Maeve eventually found a harmless picture of a Wedgewood egg cup. She put that in with the lines, 'precious food should always be eaten on Wedgewood'.

As she tried to go home, exhausted, the editor called her into his office and gave her a severe telling off ending with the words, "We could have become the first paper in the world to be sued for cannibalism."

There was always redemption in Maeve's wonderful stories.

* * *

When I opened my letters I found one from a man in Wicklow who enclosed €40 asking me to offer Mass for Marilyn Monroe because she would be fifty years dead on this day. He said he knew of no other priest in Ireland who would do it. In fact most of them would laugh at him. But he knew I was the kind of guy who wouldn't mind offering a Mass for Marilyn Monroe and of course he was right.

Marilyn Monroe was no dumb blonde. She was the one who said, "I don't think women should try to be equal to men – they should aim for something higher than that."

* * *

Next day I was off to do some more interviews for the documentary I was making for the BBC. One was with Mickey Harte. I asked him how his faith helped him through his difficulties. He began by telling me from whom he got his faith. The Hartes lived next door to their parish church. The family took turns to look after the chapel. They were altar servers and they opened and closed the church each day. When he got up each morning and looked out his window he saw a graveyard, so he was never afraid of death.

He knew all the prayers in Latin and in English. Each evening all the Harte family gathered into the kitchen where they leaned on wooden chairs and said the Rosary. The family never questioned it, they just did it. And he said one of his most comforting moments ever was the evening his father allowed him to sit on the chair he was leaning on. He put his arms around him and his rosary beads dangled in front of him. He could feel the warm air of his father's breath as he led the Rosary. Mickey says that was the most secure, godlike, safe moment of his life.

He in turn taught his children to say the Rosary and they always said it in the back of the car while they were travelling. Michaela, who was so cruelly murdered in Mauritius whilst on honeymoon, said the Rosary on her way to and from work each day. It was her precious time, to think about God, and to offer the good and bad things of the day to God. Mickey said that without faith, he would never have got through the murder of their daughter.

His father taught him that prayer itself isn't enough. You have to love your neighbours, be kind to them and help them to achieve their potential. A real practical form of daily living from Mickey Harte.

* * *

Another old friend, Con Houlihan, died. Con was a wonderful journalist. He was a caring man who lived in Dublin all his life and he used to say: "Kerry is my wife, but Dublin is my mistress." He stood on terraces at matches and wrote the most beautiful prose. He had a first-class honours degree and was a doctor of the classics in Greek and Latin. He could quote any conceivable author in a report of a dull match. He wrote about the 'game of life' and used the game of football to illustrate it.

His articles were written in large handwriting that could barely fit two paragraphs on the same page. But it was pure gold when it was transferred to print. Con and I often walked to matches in Croke Park. He'd wait for me in Mountjoy Square and we'd chat on the way. He had a Kerry accent which was difficult to understand. He asked me one day, "Did you come down through Cavan?" I said I did. He said, "Did you hear about the Cavan man who had a hip operation – he brought the bone home for the dog." On another day he said, "I bought a pair of shoes in Cavan last week, but they are very tight.

We were together in Las Vegas in 1986 for Barry McGuigan's big fight against Stevie Cruz. It was 110 degrees and I was hardly able to walk in a shirt and trousers. But Con was there with a top coat, scarf, jacket, pullover, vest and God knows what else. He said when we came out of the hotel one day: "There's a great bit of heat today Brian. We should be at home winning the hay." Con showed me that you can be yourself and still be a genius.

* * *

I also went to three wakes and two funerals. I visited the hospital four times and had a meeting with a group preparing for a year of culture. There I got a clue of how to put it all together. In a handwritten note from Seamus Heaney on a piece of paper I read:

So hope for a great sea change.

On the far side of revenge.

Believe that a farther shore

Is reachable from here.

Believe in miracles

And cures and healing wells.

And really isn't that what Jesus said in the Gospel: "I am the bread of life. He who comes to me will never be hungry. He who believes in me will never thirst."

So at the end of all of that I don't really know what kind of an eejit I am. But I am going to remain an ordained one. My connection with good people is too strong to leave behind. People are my vocation; people are and always will be the reason for me being a priest.

That's how I thought then and still do today.

Chapter 40

TIME TO LISTEN

Fr Donald Cozzens is an American priest who has bravely spoken out about abuse within the priesthood. He is a pastoral priest who knows what's happening in parishes. He has many things in his favour. He has been a teacher, a psychologist, a rector of a seminary and the man who dealt with many of the abusing priests in his diocese. More significantly, he dealt with the families of the abused too.

In his book, Sacred Silence, (3) he pinpoints many of the issues destroying the institutional Church, but which nobody talks about. In one glorious passage, he highlights the type of schizophrenia that exists in Church circles.

He talks about moving towards Christian unity, and then issuing a document saying our Christian Churches are not real Churches at all.

We talk about the important role the laity play and then exclude confident men and women from any meaningful leadership in the Church. We recognise there is a shortage of priests and then refuse to allow a discussion about celibacy as a cause of it. We deplore the abuse of children by clergy and then exclude parents and adult victims from any meaningful role in shaping the policy that might prevent it in the future. We insist that the Eucharist and the Sacraments are central to the lives of believers, and ignore the fact that half the world's parishes don't have a resident priest.

We speak with authority about human sexuality without listening to the lived experiences of married, single, celibate, gay and lesbian Catholics … And perhaps saddest of all we acclaim the quality and dignity of women yet insist they maintain their distance – and their silence.

The problem according to Cozzens is that any priest who attempts to speak the truth is ostracised.

Personal experience as well as our collective memory make it clear that to speak the truth as one sees it, no matter that it is spoken in love, runs the risk of being perceived as disloyal. And those who are judged disloyal are well and truly isolated.

The only hope, according to Cozzens, is that all Church people, and especially those in leadership, learn to listen. And he describes the process of real listening which leads to converted hearts and converted lives.

I can do no better than to repeat one of my favourite prayers written by Thomas Merton, and quoted with approval by the author. The doubt and the hope of all are summed up perfectly here:

My Lord God, I have no idea where I am going. I do not see the road ahead of me. I cannot know for certain where it will end. Nor do I really know myself, and the fact that I think I am following Your will does not mean that I am actually doing so. But I believe that the desire to please You does in fact please You. And I hope that I have that desire in all that I am doing. I hope that I will never do anything apart from that desire. And I know that, if I do this You will lead me by the right road, though I may know nothing about it. Therefore I will trust You always though I may seem to be lost and in the shadow of death. I will not fear, for You are ever with me and You will never leave me to face my perils alone.

CHAPTER 41

HERMAN'S PRAYER FOR THE CRACKED AND OTHER 'TAILS'!

When Father Ted first came on television, it was hard to handle because it helped people to laugh at priests at a time when we priests found it hard to laugh at ourselves. I knew Dermot Morgan well, as his first venture into 'holy' comedy was as Father Brian Trendy. I was the Brian in Trendy.

Now I realise how innocent Father Ted was. Wouldn't it be wonderful to have people laughing at such innocent events in priests' lives today?

In truth real life in presbyteries and monasteries was often more ridiculous than any scriptwriter could conjure up. Mad things happened. Frank Kelly loosely based his Father Jack on two monks well known to me and to him.

Niall Tóibín observed two monks in Mount Argus to base a few of his priest characters on as well, but Niall was always kinder and funnier than they were.

The older monks I lived with used to tell me about a former member of our community who was fond of the drink. After some public display of drunkenness back in the 1940s, the unfortunate priest was confined to barracks – three storeys up at the back of the monastery. He was well away from harm, they thought. One morning he turned up for prayer full to gills. The rector was astounded. Where did he get the drink? Eventually they discovered he had a friend outside who brought the booze to the back of the monastery under cover of darkness. The priest lowered a basket on a rope from his window. The whiskey was placed in the basket and he pulled it up to his room and drank to his heart's content.

There is another tale about the same man, which became legendary. There was a small farm attached to Mount Argus back then, which was used to grow crops for the monks to survive on. We owned a strong white horse for tilling the land.

One day the monks saw the white horse galloping furiously around the fields. Then they discovered why. The drunken priest, fully dressed in his black robes, was up on the horse's back, except that he was facing the wrong way. He had the horse's tail, not his mane, in his hands, and he was holding on for dear life – the horse galloping forward and the monk looking backwards. Either way, he was 'heading' in the wrong direction for his own good. When the people from the Kimmage Road got him stopped they couldn't decide who was the more confused – the exhausted white horse or the drunken monk in black.

That would have fitted well into the 'Oh, What a Lovely Horse' episode of Father Ted.

There were always 'characters' in every community. I lived with many such men over the years. In fact the men who retained their individuality were heroes to me.

One saintly hero was Father Herman. John Nolan was his baptismal name. In his younger days he was an accomplished middle-distance runner who worked for T & C Martin's builder's providers – the same firm that gave occasional employment to the saintly Matt Talbot.

The custom in religious congregations then was to get rid of your baptismal name and be given a saint's name to signify a new, more perfect life. John was landed with the name Herman. In a strange way he grew into the name – it seemed to fit better than the very ordinary John did.

Father Herman was no ordinary man and became, in time, an extraordinary priest. He was a cradle Republican who idolised Pádraig Pearse and revered the poems of Joseph Mary Plunkett and Gerard Manley Hopkins and the theology of a sacrificial death – especially for a higher cause like Irish unity. 'I Saw His Blood Upon the Rose' was one of his party pieces. He spoke Irish as often as he could, Latin when it suited, Polish badly and English only when he had to. He suffered all his life. He was crucified by migraine and scruples.

In a run-down house like Mount Argus, dripping taps were the norm. Dripping taps to Herman, though, were an absolute nightmare because of his migraine. On countless nights I helped him stuff carbolic soap into dripping taps just to silence the hissing for a few hours of peaceful sleep.
Herman was a free spirit who had a unique set of apostolates.

He was a close friend of Frank Duff, the layman who founded the Legion of Mary. They both went on cycling holidays around Ireland most summers. Herman spent many hours every week in the Legion of Mary hostel for women who had fallen on hard times, some of whom still laboured in prostitution. Caring for them was demanding work that required great patience and endless compassion.

On occasion he gave talks and spiritual help to the women. Later, when I was responsible for Mount Argus, he arranged for me to give retreats to other prostitutes. It became a privilege to do so because they were, at heart, good women, who put me in touch with the understanding, loving God they depended on.

Through all their suffering, God was the only one they could trust to love them unconditionally. The talks I shared with them were always inspirational and uplifting occasions for me. Those women taught me about real compassion, because they were in touch with raw human nature. They relied on mercy and forgiveness.

The vast majority walked the streets to earn money so that they could give their children the essentials of life. First Communions were expensive and had to be paid for. So were Confirmations and back-to-school uniforms. The only sinners I met were the people who judged these heroic women harshly.

Herman and I shared common interests because I too had a unique apostolate to entertainers; almost every night I could be found visiting the nine ballrooms in the centre of Dublin. Not too many understood that ministry, either. We both chatted about the people, the problems and the saints we met. I respected Herman and what he did. Contemplative, monastic life did not suit either of us. We needed to be where people were – outside the cloister.

Herman simply had to break out into the open spaces of the Wicklow hills on his trusty bicycle at every given opportunity. He kept his bicycle in his cell high up on the third floor of Mount Argus. The corridors were long and bleak, so the ever-practical Herman rode his bike along the pitch-pine floored corridors.

I lived around the corner from him. Coming out of my cell, I observed the green cross code, looking left and right to make sure I wasn't knocked down by Herman as he pedalled along the corridor. To be fair, he'd ring his bell to warn me. It sounds utterly insane now. And so it was.

It was even madder inside his cell. Mount Argus was built on the Roman model. The floor space was pathetically limited but the ceilings were incredibly high. If we could have turned the building on its side we would have had sensible rooms with ample space.

Herman was determined to fill the wasted space above his head. He hung two hooks from the ceiling. When Frank Duff's bicycle was not touring Ireland it hung by its wheels from the hooks above Herman's bed. How he could sleep, knowing the heavy Raleigh relic was perilously perched three feet above his pillow, was beyond me.

From his earliest days he expressed his inner genius through the arts. He wrote poetry full of puns, rhymes, alliterations and thundering onomatopoeia. He used to come out with prayers like 'The Lord is My Shepherd and you shall not pull the wool over His eyes.'

He carved marvellous wooden likenesses of Mary the Mother of God and St Patrick, and shocking crucifixes with a writhing Christ frozen in suffering, borne out of love for sinners like us. It is only now I fully realise that Herman's crucifixes did not glorify suffering for suffering's sake. The pitiful image depicted pure love for the suffering and the sinner. Herman's insight into the Passion escaped me then but makes perfect sense now. His life eventually taught me what I didn't realise I had to learn.

During the 1980s, Mount Argus became riddled with dry rot and decay. The massive building was about to collapse in a heap of rubble. I was the man in charge and had to raise over two million punts by begging from ordinary people all over the country. Thanks to those generous people we raised the money and completed the work.

The monastery and church was a building site for five years. A larger-than-life crucifix dominated an end wall of an eighty-metre corridor on the ground floor of Mount Argus. It hung on that wall for 100 years, reminding the monks on our way to prayer that we are Passionists; we must experience the Passion of Christ in our lives before we dare preach to others. One day a careless worker swung a large plank of wood he was carrying, caught the arm of the crucifix and broke the figure of Christ at the shoulder, leaving a pathetic looking Christ hanging from his cross by one fragile arm.

I knew Herman loved working with plaster and paint so I asked him to try his best to put the broken Jesus together again. He was delighted. He ran upstairs, put on his dirty overalls, pulled his navy beret over his ears and got to work. He climbed the ladder and lifted the broken shoulder. He mixed plaster as skilfully as a consultant in A&E. His tiny trowel shaped the shoulder with wonderful precision.

Every ten minutes he descended the ladder to look up at his work. The figure had to look exactly as it had for a century, with arms, nails, the crown of thorns and pained, bearded face in perfect symmetry. It took Herman two days, shaping and reshaping the plaster body, whilst waiting for wet plaster to dry and all the while keeping the broken shoulder clamped in place. When he was satisfied all was secure, he mixed shades of grey, yellow and white until it matched the rest of the corpus. Then he climbed his ladder and washed the wooden cross and the mended figure from top to bottom. He asked me to look at his handiwork. It was perfect in every way; there wasn't a sign of where the break was. It was, if anything, better than ever. I climbed the ladder to get a closer look.

I told him honestly what a great job he had done. I was a little overcome because I knew his repair work was heartfelt. His life as a Passionist priest was expressed practically by putting the broken Christ together again.

So I said, 'Herman, you've done a magnificent job. Now that the crucifix is fixed maybe we should offer a little prayer of Thanksgiving.'

Herman stood beside me looking up at the cross. He whipped off his beret, took a deep breath and prayed. 'Jesus, like myself you're cracked, but hang on!'

A tear trickled down my cheek. Herman stuffed his beret in his dirty dungarees; we hugged; he picked up his ladder and I stayed on to contemplate the best sermon on the Passion I ever heard.

'Jesus, like myself you're cracked. But hang on!'

Chapter 42

THE FRANCIS EFFECT

In the Spring of 2013, Pope Benedict XVI's resignation was the equivalent of an ecclesiastical earthquake. He was the first pope in 600 years to resign and, one would have thought, the least likely Pope to do so.

I personally spent days in quiet prayer repenting for the despair I had felt, whilst hoping the guidance of the Holy Spirit would be welcomed again in the election of the new pope.

For a decade or more I was convinced that the Jesus I had come to know in the Gospels was redundant because he was rarely mentioned in Vatican statements. It was obvious at the time that the leadership in Rome wished to impose a regime from a past age on the universal Church. Fundamentalism is in essence a decision not to change, a decision to die, and I couldn't be part of a meaningless death.

I wasn't hopeful that a new pope would be radically different from John Paul II or Benedict XVI. The College of Cardinals was carefully chosen by them because they were compliant and safe. How could they possibly choose a pope radically different from what had gone before?

Thank God I was wrong once again.

On 13 March 2013 Jorge Mario Bergoglio became the 265th successor of St Peter. He was the first pope from South America, the first Jesuit to be elected Pope, and the first pope to take the name Francis. From the moment he stepped onto the balcony asking for prayers I knew he was different. By taking the name Francis he was making the poor, as well as simple living, central to his mission.

The atmosphere throughout the Church changed instantly. The Cardinals who elected him were filled with the Holy Spirit, and I relived the excitement I experienced when Pope John XXIII first appeared – a light dispelling the darkness and heralding a new spring for believers in a new world.

'Now let's begin this journey, bishop and people, this journey of the Church of Rome, which is the one that presides over all the churches – a journey of brotherhood, love and trust among us,' the newly elected Francis began.

A rising tide lifts all boats, and since Francis came to the barque of Peter, for the first time in twenty years I have hope for the future and I am able to feel at home in the priesthood again.

Without wanting to labour the issue, the previous administration's attempt to silence me left me in tatters. Had Benedict not resigned, and had a pope like Francis not been elected, I would not be a priest today and possibly not even a member of the Catholic Church. I would have been forced out. To leave seemed the only choice available to me because I knew I had to continue speaking the truth. The accusation that I was causing scandal to the faithful hurt me most. It was plainly not true. The faithful were being scandalised, not by me, but by the leadership that was now trying to 'silence' me.

For almost two years I sank into a deep depression. I lost confidence in the Church to which I had given my life. Thankfully, though, I never lost faith in a merciful God. Underlying it all was a deep, unhealthy suspicion. I knew I had been reported to Rome by someone within the Irish Church. The fact that clerical colleagues had been responsible for persuading Rome that my writings in The Sunday World were causing grave scandal left me angry and resentful. It was the lowest point in my life. I knew that the opinions I expressed were in fact what 80 per cent of the people, including many priests, believed too.

That's where I was when I went into hospital for an operation early in 2013.

Whilst recuperating from the operation, out of the ether news came that Pope Benedict had resigned. It's no exaggeration to say that I felt like a complete stranger in the Church to which I had given my life. Recuperating gave me precious time to pray, reflect and plan my future.

That someone like Pope Francis could be elected as Benedict's successor seemed to me to be miraculous. It immediately became clear that his model of Church and his modus operandi were vastly different from Benedict's. He is clear about the need for reform; he named clericalism and careerism as a major problem. He has, by word and action, clarified the mandate given to him by the other Cardinals during the conclave.

Firstly, despite the protestations of the extreme right, it is clear Pope Francis is determined to have a more compassionate Church. In interviews he insisted those who drag the Church back in time are wrong and must be resisted.

Secondly, he wants a Church that lives the values of the Gospel. Mere words are not enough.

Thirdly, he is convinced the conservative College of Cardinals, who gathered at the conclave in March 2013, gave him a mandate to purge the Church of careerist clerics, corrupt institutions, and the cynical politics which worked to undo the principles of the Second Vatican Council.

Most of all he wishes to proclaim the primacy of the Gospel with its core message that Jesus Christ died to save everyone, and not just a select few. He died for all and not just for the many.

Pope Francis admits he's a sinner in need of redemption, 'I am a sinner whom the Lord has looked upon. He who does not sin is not human ... we need to recognise our weakness,' he told religious superiors recently.

Pope Francis learned from his failures, as all of us should. As pope, discernment is central to his governance. He believes in the motto of John XXIII, 'See everything; turn a blind eye to much; correct a little.'

Discernment cannot be rushed: 'Many think that changes and reforms can take place in a short time. I believe that we always need time to lay the foundation for real effective change and this is the time for discernment. Discernment is always done in the presence of the Lord, looking at the signs, listening to the things that happen, and to the feelings of the people, especially the poor.'

Doubt is necessary for faith to mature. 'If a person says that he met God with total certainty, and is not touched by a margin of uncertainty, then that is not good ... If one has answers to all the questions – that is the proof that God is not with him. It means that he is a false prophet using religion for himself ...

'The Church is the people of God on a journey through history with joys and sorrows ... we should not even think therefore that 'thinking with the Church' means only thinking with the hierarchy of the Church ... '.

'Those who today always look for disciplinarian solutions, those who long for an exaggerated doctrinal "security", those who stubbornly try to recover a past that no longer exists – have a static and inward-directed view of things.'

Pope Francis believes that if the Church doesn't change it will collapse like a house of cards. You have no idea how affirming it is to hear the pope preach the very principles that the previous regime silenced me for suggesting.

The Francis factor is changing the perception of the Church. People are attracted by his openness, his simplicity and the depth of his spirituality. Explaining the central message of Christmas in an interview he said, 'When God meets us he tells us two things. The first thing he says is: Have hope. God always opens doors. He never closes them ... when Christians forget about hope they become a cold Church.'

Pope Francis aligns himself with Pope John XXIII when he takes on the prophets of doom. Pope John referred to the Curia officials as prophets of gloom, always forecasting disasters instead of helping people 'to look to the future without fear ... Positive faith is one thing ... the way it is expressed is another,' he added.

Both believe in 'the medicine of mercy'. If the Church doesn't move forward we become mere onlookers while the faith stagnates. Francis is not a revolutionary pope but one who is faithful to the infallible teaching of the Second Vatican Council.

Whilst Pope Francis is vehemently opposed to abortion, he acknowledges that we 'have done little to accompany women adequately in very difficult situations where abortion appears as a quick solution to their profound anguish, especially when the life developing within them is a result of rape or a situation of extreme poverty'.

The pope understands that risks need to be taken for the good of the Gospel message. 'I prefer a Church which is bruised, hurting and dirty because it has been out on the streets, rather than a Church which is unhealthy from being confined and from clinging to its own security.' (Evangelii Gaudium, n. 49)

Francis has told priests and bishops that they themselves must come as pilgrims on this journey of discovery. Ignatian spirituality holds that, 'Who so ever accompanies a pilgrim ... should go at the pilgrim's pace, neither too far in front nor too far behind.'

At the root of reform within the Church will be collegial governance and collaborative ministry.

Ultimately the Francis effect will be judged on how radically he reforms the governance of the Church. A constant theme of reports into clerical sexual abuse across the world is a systemic failure within the Church, making it incapable of hearing what the people want or need.

Finally, showing women respect and acknowledging their enormous contribution to the life of the Church will be one of his most crucial tasks in the immediate future. Women are holding this fragile structure together – just about.

The task ahead is difficult but he is so obviously being guided by the Holy Spirit that we must presume God will continue to inspire him and strengthen him for the journey ahead.

That is why I thank God for sending us Pope Francis and why I pray for him every day.

CHAPTER 43

THE MOST IMPRESSIVE PERSON

Because I've been around so long and met so many high-achieving, famous people, many of whom were so-called celebrities, I'm often asked: Who was the most impressive person you've met?

I don't even have to think for a second. The person I'm going to introduce to you now left an indelible impression on me. She inspired me to donate everything I get to the poor at home and abroad and for thirty years she became the conscience of The Sunday World.

During the five decades I've written for The Sunday World, I've been privileged, not only to highlight the plight of the poor, but to help them in a practical way. I did it through the Helping Hand Fund, which became an essential part of the paper for years.

It began in December 1977 in tragic circumstances. I wrote an article, based on a true story, outlining what happened to a young mother and her children. I began: 'There are times as a priest when my faith in God is put to the test. This is especially true when little babies have to suffer.' And then I took the readers through, from memory, a few meetings I'd had with a girl I called Marie, which wasn't her real name.

Marie's life story went from bad to worse. As I remember it, she was one of ten children whose mother died giving birth to the youngest of those children. Her father did a fine job rearing the children, but money was scarce and there wasn't much time for normal family love and attention.

Marie had to leave school as soon as the law would allow and go out to work.

It often happens that someone who missed out on personal affection will become overly attached to the first person who shows them kindness, real or imagined. So, at eighteen she met a Dublin boy who was six years older and gave her the special attention she craved. In the early days he was the perfect boyfriend with charm, good looks, and, as far as Marie was concerned, a deep love for her. She was not from Dublin but he came down to visit her home town almost every weekend.

Travelling didn't suit either of them so Marie moved to Dublin. She fell for his charm and wit and powers of persuasion and after she came to Dublin, he soon persuaded her that in the big city two could live as cheaply as one. In those days it was not the norm for couples to live together so soon.

Marie got pregnant, which didn't go down well with her family, either. They got married and he was good to her during that pregnancy, but soon the bachelor life was more attractive than life with Marie. Marie made all the excuses that women usually do, blaming bad company, her own inability to be an attractive person, the arrival of the child, everything except her husband.

By the time they were two years married he had lost all interest in her and, as she put it, it was 'just the time when I needed him most because I was pregnant again'. She pleaded with him to stay in with her, even one night a week. But he wouldn't. He went out every night drinking with the boys and, furthermore, drank every penny he earned. There were many nights when Marie sat at home, sick and pregnant and without a slice of bread in the house.

'We had rows every night because he'd come home footless drunk at four or five in the morning.' He frequently brought all his drinking pals with him and then would drag Marie and the baby out of bed so that he and his drunken pals could sleep off their drunkenness before heading out again. Obviously she had no family of her own to turn to, but his mother took her in. He inveigled her away from there with the usual promise that he would mend his ways.

It was then that Marie really suffered horrendous treatment at the hands of the man who once declared his undying love for her.

'One night he and two of his mates came home at three in the morning. He ordered me out of bed but because I was pregnant I was slow getting up. He dragged me out of the bed and after he had given me a few punches in the back, he made me cook food for him and his friends. There was very little in the house but I gave them everything that was there. As soon as I gave him the coffee, he lifted the mug and poured it over my head and face.

'He said I had brought him bad luck because he had lost twenty pounds on a horse that day. There I was, pregnant and trying to look after a young child without a penny in the flat, and he was gambling twenty pounds on a horse.

'Then he said to his mates that he was going to show them what he thought of his wife and child. He pulled me across the room by my hair and tied me to a chair and began beating me. He took the stockings from the little baby's foot and lit a cigarette and after every drag of the cigarette, he and his mates thought it was funny to touch the little baby's feet with the lit cigarette. He kept beating me and invited his friends to do the same.'

Marie's screams were piercing and, luckily for her, disturbed three men who lived in nearby flats. They came in and rescued her and held the husband and his friends until the Gardaí arrived and arrested them. By now the little child was screaming in agony from the burns on her foot. That little baby was in hospital for fifteen weeks because of the abuse her father and his friends had inflicted on her. Luckily Marie's husband was sent to prison.

At that time Marie had come to me in Mount Argus looking for help. She knew me from The Sunday World and had travelled quite a distance across the city. I gave her whatever money I had, which wasn't a lot, to keep her going through her pregnancy and arranged for the St Vincent de Paul Society to help her.

She came back to me again when she was eight months pregnant. On that occasion she had been put out of her flat by the landlord because she couldn't pay the rent. Again I was able to help her in a small way and she got another flat. But sometimes the hand of fate is indefensibly cruel. Her flat was broken into and she was attacked again, this time by three robbers, even though she had nothing in the house to give them.

These people assaulted Marie. They beat her, kicked her, and left her hysterical. One of them even stabbed her in the back and she had to get nineteen stitches in the wound. That night she was taken to hospital and the baby was induced. And this was the bit that broke my heart. The little baby's legs were fractured because of the numerous beatings Marie had received during the pregnancy –including beatings from her husband – the father of their baby.

That was the story I wrote at the end of November. My main task was to find a place for Marie and her two babies to live where she would be safe and where she and her children could have time to heal from the attacks. I wrote about it in The Sunday World, not because I was looking for money, which I wasn't, but merely to expose the kind of scandal which was rarely reported.

The reaction was amazing. The following week so much post came to The Sunday World that two of the staff in the offices in Terenure, where The Sunday World was based at that time, had to work full time, opening and trying to acknowledge the letters. I can still remember Sophie Hunt, who was secretary to the managing director, opening sacks of mail with me on the floor in her office.

Thousands of letters came in. When all the money was counted over seven thousand pounds was received; that was the beginning of the Helping Hand Fund, which we continued for years and which was administered and supported by Bryan Kelly and Micheline McCormack.

Many of those who sought help wrote to me in confidence. The Sunday World set up a trust fund for Marie and she received a regular income for as long as the money lasted. Marie still lived in fear. She dreaded the return of the people who beat her up, but because of our fund she had security.

One interesting footnote to it all was that the late Hugh McLoughlin, Manging Director of The Sunday World, really hadn't much time for anything in the paper that didn't produce money. Initially, he was of the opinion that 'A Little Bit of Religion' was a waste of advertising space. He could never see how it would sell papers.

His attitude changed completely the day he came in and saw a thousand letters bulging with money scattered across the floor of his office with Sophie Hunt and me on our knees counting the notes. His eyes bulged like gobstoppers and, as I looked up at him, he confessed: 'I'll admit I was wrong. I didn't think there was that much money in religion.'

Out of all the personalities I've met – and I've met everyone I wanted to except Elvis Presley – Marie and her babies impressed me most.

CHAPTER 44

THERE'S A REASON FOR EVERYTHING

By the grace of God I've lived in an extraordinary period of radical change. It is frightening to reflect on those changes. Frightening but rewarding. It gives me an unshakeable hope to do so because I've had to discover there is a reason for everything.

My life stretches from the end of the Second World War, in the mid-1940s, through the 1950s and into the revolutionary 1960s. My fifty years in the priesthood began at the end of 1969 and the start of the 1970s. I learned more in that decade than any other before or since. It's not an exaggeration to say I finally grew up in those years because the people I met and worked with changed my views on every central aspect of life.

They prepared me well for the trials I had to face in the hungry 1980s, followed by the devastating 1990s, when the Church we believed to be impregnable began to fall apart before our eyes.

The turn of the millennium was supposed to bring new hope, new life and new directions. The 'noughties' probably brought all of those things – but not in the way people of my age expected.

I have now arrived at the beginning of the third decade of the third millennium and even though 2020 represents perfect vision, I have to admit I have no idea of what the future holds.

To put my topsy-turvy journey in perspective, my life went from a time of natural darkness to artificial light; meaning that while my childhood was filled with paraffin oil and Tilley lamps, my old age is blinded by the glare of unnaturally bright LED lights. The tragedy is that we have more light but less clarity.

In my life I have cooked meals over blazing open fires fuelled by turf we dug and won in a backyard bog. As a child, then, it was like a miracle to experience electric rings and fast-boiling kettles; now the microwave oven is my best friend, providing instant, tasteless food.

I've travelled on foot, on the back of a donkey, a bicycle, a Honda 50, in motor cars and numerous jet planes. I'm writing this waiting on a plane to take me from Boston to Dublin and I am just realising that neither my father nor my mother ever set foot on a plane. My mother never left Ireland and my father got to see his brothers in London only once in his lifetime, but he travelled by boat.

I have lived in a country where Catholicism was not only respected but for many years was the only religion imaginable to most of us. But I couldn't imagine the shock it has been to observe a once all-powerful church disgraced by its own sinfulness. After fifty years of a life dedicated fully to being the best priest I could be, I live in a country where overpowering religion has given way to a devastating cynicism.

I have enjoyed peaceful times where neighbours respected and helped one another. But in all honesty, bigotry and prejudice were never far from the surface. So for the greater part of my life I have lived with murder, violence, hatred and division. Such barbarity has left an indelible mark on us which continues to paralyse us more than we realise or admit.

When I thought the killing would never end, common sense mysteriously prevailed and a kind of normality was restored when I least expected it.

Now we wrongly believe that the absence of war is the same as peace itself. This means that for the vast majority of people on this island true peace is no more achievable than real religion is.

We are incapable of taking what is valuable from the past in a healthy, transforming way. We either attempt to live stubbornly in the past or to flirt with the glamorous new, pretending the past never happened. The result is that we are uncomfortable in the present. Yet the present moment is the only one we can change, choose or enjoy. We cannot change the past and we cannot predict or even presume the future.

For example, all my life I have felt that in the Catholic Church's view, sex is the greatest sin and sometimes the only sin. Now, however, society tells me that sex is our greatest gift, to be used principally as recreation; everyone who wishes to indulge has a right to do so even if there is neither commitment nor love involved.

What is in our DNA that prevents us from recognising a more holistic vision worthy of redeemed human beings?

In real life I have to accept the past is gone forever. Did the good old days ever really exist? I have few regrets about the past slipping away so quickly. Yet not all the values of the past were harmful. Respect for people, for customs and for principles learned and handed down has, sadly, in my view, disappeared.

I believe there is a reason for everything if we keep searching faithfully for it. There is a kind of national dementia about what was good in former times. Any wise society would have enough pride to discern what was useful and to use it as a foundation for the future.

* * *

I have always believed in the value of analysing my dreams because dreams can help reveal the subconscious. Yet I find I am becoming less and less aware of my dreams. Instead I sleep fitfully; every few hours I lie awake and pray. It's nothing forced or formal. I wake up and automatically spend ten to fifteen minutes thanking God that I am still alive. I often ask for strength, courage and guidance to make some valuable contribution with what's left of my life. Afterwards I am able to go back to sleep for another couple of hours.

I am not as disturbed as I used to be about what's happening all around me. Firstly, I gave up thinking I have to be God decades ago, so there's not much I can change all on my own. Secondly, whatever is happening, God is in it, and it's up to me to discern what's from God and what's not. Thirdly, worrying achieves even less than burying my head in the sand does.

What genuinely perturbs me is that so few of the good people I deal with have any belief or respect for God, religion, faith or indeed anything beyond this world's values. That disappoints me because I know we need a vision that takes us beyond ourselves and the finiteness of things here.

I thank God daily that I was born when I was born and lived my life from the 1940s to the 2020s. I know I don't have long more to live. I am an old man even though I still think like a younger man. But I want to use the unique experiences I've had to encourage struggling people never to lose touch with the God of love and compassion. That's what 'It Has to be Said' is attempting to do.

It is important not to let anger with the Church rob us of God's guidance, compassion and strength. It is important to be aware of the gifts I have, and even more important to know the limitations which make me the person I am.

It's time to put my thoughts out there. People are wise enough to take what's useful and to discard what's not – just as I have done with what others shared with me. I have an unshakeable hope that this time of change will reveal the goodness of God just as every other time of turmoil has for those with eyes to see and ears to hear.

Fifty years in the priesthood seems to be the proper time to be brave and be free. I've earned the right to have an opinion!

I am aware that churchmen and women like to impart wisdom only when they leave office. I have mentioned Cardinal Martini before. When he was alive he was afraid to express what he really thought about the need for Church reform. He wrote wonderful inspirational words to be published after his death. I respect the cardinal but am disappointed he chose that option.

On many occasions here in Ireland bishops express pastoral views after they retire. They would have gained more respect and more credibility if they had spoken out whilst they were still in office. They lost a God-given opportunity to be real shepherds to their flock.

In recent times one bishop whom I respect, says that the penal Visitation on the Irish Church, ordered by Pope Benedict, was wasteful, unfair and damaging. I just wish he, and others who felt the same way, had spoken out courageously at the time of the Visitation. That would have been true leadership. If they had spoken honestly and publicly to those who were carrying out the Visitation, they would have been seen to defend the committed Catholics who were needlessly humiliated by Rome at a time when Rome itself should have been in the dock.

Some of us did say the Visitation was unjust and a waste of valuable time and energy because we knew they would wrongly attack the easy targets, which is exactly how it turned out. I don't remember any bishop objecting to the Visitation publicly at the time. I wish they had. Telling us now that it was a disaster is too little too late. Believers lost trust in Church leadership a long time ago precisely because bishops heeded Rome more than their own people. The faithful discovered their own way to live peacefully because they had to.

Perhaps one of the reasons we now have an anonymous hierarchy is that we priests have also given up on speaking truth to power. We have contributed to our own irrelevance.

I received a long letter from a concerned laywoman, who is trained in theology well beyond the level most priests are. She attended the 2019 Easter Triduum in her community church. She complained about the priest who presided at two of the ceremonies causing untold frustration to many of the congregation.

'He gave us a cheap imitation of a stand-up comedian,' she wrote. 'The stories and the jokes were all tired, inappropriate, and unhelpful and displayed his culpable lack of knowledge about what Good Friday and Easter Sunday mean in Christian theology. He told us three times that he was not into celebrity, yet his whole attitude smacked of cheap celebrity. He threw out snide remarks about others, some of whom were in the congregation. He repeated his pet phrases, left sentences hanging unfinished; one got the impression he gathered up stories which went down well on other occasions and dished them out to us like a pop star doing a medley of his greatest hits.'

This woman's central point is that Catholics, particularly Catholic women, are finding it increasingly difficult to find food for the soul in church. Too many Masses and too many liturgies are tired and suffer greatly from the lack of any input from women. It is not for me to agree or disagree because I honestly don't know. But I do recognise the symptoms she is highlighting. For many the more recently ordained are the worst offenders.

The institution of the Catholic Church is in tatters not just because of the sexual abuse of minors, or the exploitation of women religious, or the exclusion of women from positions of authority within the Church, or denying women the full use of their many gifts. It is ALL of the above.

As a priest it has become increasingly painful to me to see how women are deliberately excluded, not only from the liturgy, but from every meaningful part of the Church's ministry. In the past year I've attended liturgies that included the ordination of a bishop, the Chrism Mass in Holy Week, the services of Holy Thursday, Good Friday and the Easter Vigil. Women played no part at all in most of the services. In others their role was so minimal that it actually highlighted the all-male, greying priesthood stubbornly controlling their clerical club – which we wrongly call 'the Church'.

Many women I know continue to be outraged while others seem browbeaten into a passive resignation. Neither attitude is healthy for their own well-being or the future of the Church. Women, if they speak at all, resort to quiet whispers. They know they're not accepted and as long as an all-male civil service exists, they never will be accepted. Intelligent women no longer waste either time or energy explaining their position to those in authority. What's the point of a dialogue with the deaf?

I read an article recently by Cecilia Gonzales ('Why Do Women Catholics Stay?') where she wrote: 'One of my students recently introduced me to a new term: the "DONES". Thinking I had misheard her I asked: 'Do you mean the "NONES", that is people who don't identify as belonging to any religious tradition?'

'No, I mean the "DONES", she said, 'like, in, I am actually done with the Catholic Church'.

To be a 'NONE' implies disaffection and boredom. Being a 'DONE' signifies betrayal and disillusionment.

Some argue we need the equivalent of a Catholic Church #Me Too Movement. I am not convinced. That could pit men against women, which is not the way it is. It is the clerical club against the rest of us. We all need to work together. We need dialogue, conversation, openness, a willingness to listen, to hear and to change.

The clerical Church needs to understand that women have risen to the top in many essential aspects of life. Women are supreme court justices, surgeons, philosophers, theologians, astronauts, prime ministers, athletes and pop stars. Gender has no bearing on ability.

In our religious congregation I live with many good men who don't come close in either intelligence or ability to the women I work with in journalism, broadcasting and in the spiritual life. Successful women have to work harder. They have encouraged me to be more open and to cultivate emotional intelligence as well as a spirit of adventure. For a peaceful life I leave most of those qualities outside the door of the monastery.

I cannot blame women (in fact I admire them) who complain about the utter irrelevance of the liturgies they attend. They genuinely fear that their children, particularly their daughters, will be contaminated by what they experience in church. So they make the logical decision to protect themselves and their children. They are inspired to make other choices about their lives and their futures.

The Second Vatican Council encouraged women to play a full role in Church life. It led to the opening up of seminaries and Catholic universities to the gifts and abilities of women. We are now into the third generation of women theologians, and they are engaged in educating the fourth generation.

Women teach in seminaries now. However, when they go back to their parishes they are forced to sit silently in the pews to experience uninspired liturgies and deficient communities. It is an unforgivable abuse of power and a waste of some of God's greatest gifts to the Church.

In my earlier memoir, 'a Different journey', I tell the story of how Bono famously asked me: 'Why the f*** are you still a priest?'

As I reflect during this memoir I have to ask myself why I remain a Catholic in such a dysfunctional organisation. So many others see clearly that there is something radically wrong; so what prevents me from seeing it?

I have no definitive answer. However, I know there is an enormous treasure of goodness and grace contained in the Church I love and belong to. I refuse to deprive myself of that gracious treasury.

I'm really saying that the clerical club is not the Church. We all have a God-given duty to rescue our beloved Church from their hands. None of us should allow them to think they are the Church. We should not walk away from the gift of Eucharist or the consolation of the sacraments. We cannot allow them to steal God's saving power from us. They have no right to do so and we have no right to allow them to do so.

That's why I stay a Catholic and a priest. I have faith in the power of Jesus Christ and I still want to be a faithful disciple in these difficult times. As I've shown here things do change, and things will change.

To leave the priesthood or the Church would be for me to disown a part of myself that was created and nourished by parents, family and countless thousands of good Catholics during the past fifty years of priesthood.

I will not allow the dysfunctional leadership of the institution to prevent me from journeying on the road to eternal happiness which has been mapped out for me in the Passion, Death and Resurrection of our Saviour Jesus Christ. I really have no choice but to continue in this faltering ministry.

Chapter 45

FERMANAGH AND ME

I am proud to be a Fermanagh man. They say pride is a sin and it could be if I thought I was better than somebody else. It could also be a sin not to be proud and grateful for the gifts given to me by God.

As a Fermanagh man I'm no better than anyone else – but I'm no worse either. I was blessed to be born in Fermanagh. I was privileged to live and work there for half of my life. I hope and pray I'll die there. I certainly want to be buried in Fermanagh because it's such a short journey from Lough Erne to heaven.

I try to promote Fermanagh in any way I can. It's a glorious place to live and the people are as good as you'll get. As a county we've had our share of little successes but not as much as we should have. In Gaelic football we've won two major All-Irelands. In 1959 we won a junior All-Ireland championship, beating Dublin and Kerry on the way. As a youngster I stood beside my father in Croke Park when we beat Kerry in the home final.

I waited sixty years to see Dominic Corrigan's St Michael's College, and my alma mater, win the college's All-Ireland Hogan Cup in Croke Park in 2019. It was the first time our college won the title. Two All-Ireland successes in Croke Park sixty years apart and I was there for both of them.

Guess who won't be there if we have to wait another sixty years for national success. We Fermanagh supporters follow the team and take the wins and losses as part of the journey.

I make a point of doing whatever little I can to encourage young men and women who wear the Fermanagh jersey. I follow them, go to training sessions, console them if we lose, and rejoice with them when we win. The loyalty and dedication shown by these young adults is mind-boggling. I wish supporters realised the sacrifices they make in pursuit of excellence. They do it knowing the odds of them ever winning a trophy are stacked against them. Their only goal is to be the best they can be and to represent their county with pride.

Over the years I gave my absolute support to Fermanagh senior football managers, among them Terry Ferguson, Pat King, John Maughan, Dominic Corrigan, Charlie Mulgrew, Malachy O'Rourke, John O'Neill, Peter Canavan, Peter McGrath and Rory Gallagher. Every single one of them gave their all to the cause in good times and bad times. I have the utmost respect for all those men.

I've been asked to give talks, to offer Mass and to help out if a player needs a comforting word. Not every player can be successful but it takes a strong person to put their name forward and accept the consequences. Anything is better than a hurler on the ditch.

I've given speeches to teams in dressing rooms and hotel rooms; I've spoken before dinners and after dinners; I've consoled losers, congratulated winners and sometimes at Masses for the teams I gave a team talk. It's not because I'm good; it's because I'm cheap.

These days I don't like making speeches. I turn down most offers because I know my best days are over. As Willie Nelson sang: 'I've a wonderful future behind me.'

John B. Keane, a delightful and wonderful man whom I was privileged to call a friend, came out with these delightful lines sitting in a snug in his pub in Listowel. 'The most dangerous animal known to mankind is a forty-year-old, white-legged, junior cornerback with varicose veins.'

He told me that was a good way to captivate an audience at the beginning of a speech because every club exists on the dedication of forty-year-old former cornerbacks who are always willing to put their bodies on the line for the club and the community. He was right too.

John B. also told me: 'You should make a speech which is succinct, uplifting, profound and humorous. Make them feel at the end of it that you have been worth your fee.' I can't guarantee anything uplifting, profound or humorous, but I can guarantee I'll be the cheapest guest anyone ever had, so being worth the fee doesn't bother me. There never is a fee and never will be.

Groucho Marx said a successful speaker should aim to have honesty, sincerity and integrity above all else. And, he concluded, if you can fake honesty, sincerity and integrity you have it made.

As in many rural areas now Fermanagh people are beginning to appreciate their potential. I believe we have abilities beyond our numbers. We have achievements in every walk of life that rank with any other county in Ireland even though we have a smaller population than most.

But I also believe we have a tendency to give up too easily, to be comfortable with the title of gallant losers. We're far too content to be satisfied with the odd win. We have too much respect for the ability of others and not enough respect for our own talents. We are friendly people and that seems to make us happy to play the martyr and be likeable losers. We accept defeat too often and too easily.

There are noticeable exceptions but it is a trait we'll have to change.

The mere mention of my Sunday World colleague Pat Spillane usually results in a severe form of apoplexy. Perhaps it's another example of our inability to learn from constructive criticism. Back at the beginning of the noughties Fermanagh played Kerry in the qualifiers in Portlaoise. They slaughtered us and showed no mercy. They piled on the scores just because they could. It was a dreadful day to be a Fermanagh man and it wasn't much better for Kerry people. Earlier in the day I was concelebrating at a funeral for another friend, the late Pat Quigley, who was the sports editor of The Sunday World. He was a close friend of Pat Spillane's too. After the funeral and before the match I walked into the hotel and met the only man in Ireland I did not want to meet that day, namely Pat Spillane. We chatted about the match.

He said he was genuinely worried that Fermanagh would get a good start in the game because, as he said himself, 'If you get a good start you might realise how good ye are. Our plan will be to kill you off in the first ten minutes and we will have no bother after that.' He went on to tell a story which he meant as a compliment but I didn't take it that way. When the draw was made in the RTÉ studios, Joe Brolly and Spillane were laughing at the ludicrously facile task Kerry got in drawing Fermanagh. Pat said Fermanagh had some good players. Joe Brolly said Fermanagh would never win anything. Pat didn't say it viciously and this is where we have got to learn. His theory was that Fermanagh will never win anything because they are too nice and give up without a fight.

Pat Spillane was not insulting me. It was a genuine observation that we had neither the character nor the attitude to be winners. I was annoyed at the time but have thought about it for years on end now. It's probably truer than I'd like to admit. Too nice is shorthand for too lazy, too uninterested and too ready to accept defeat.

I believe Fermanagh as a county, and particularly our GAA team, can change that attitude. I've often said I would die happy if Fermanagh could win the Ulster senior championship; it had better be soon because I'm suffering from a fatal illness – too many birthdays!

I believe we can win an Ulster title in the not too distant future if we get the structures we need. Success is not an accident. First and foremost we have to unite. We have got to learn from others and make the necessary sacrifices. We have to give our players, who are the lifeblood of the GAA, the treatment and respect that any young gifted athlete deserves.

The proper psychology is to encourage, be positive and challenge the individual and the team to realise and to achieve their potential. Rather than reminding players of their lack of success in the past it's more effective to challenge them to be convinced of their potential and to ensure that potential is realised.

I want Fermanagh players to have the same facilities and the same professional care as Dublin, Kerry or Tyrone. Our players are as dedicated as their players. But they must be given the opportunity of the best training facilities, proper food, dieticians, gear, blazers, travel expenses, time together, the accepted number of physios at training sessions, a doctor, sport psychologists, coaching and respect. These are not luxuries; these are the normal tools of success in the modern era.

We are a small county with fewer than twenty clubs and a playing population that other counties deride, but with a loyal support base. We make the best of what we've got. Essentially it's about fulfilling potential and building community.

The famous American author M. Scott Peck believed that good communications are the way to encourage community-building. He outlines four stages of community-making.

First there is what he terms pseudo community. People come together instantly. They begin by being pleasant to one another. They avoid friction, conflict and so the relationships are pretence and fake. When differences happen they have to move to the second stage which is a form of chaos.

Chaos is when differences come into the open. It's a time of struggle and fighting but instead of trying to hide or ignore them, they deal with them. The two ways out of chaos are organisation – which often appears to be community but isn't – and willingness to journey through the third stage, namely emptiness.

Emptiness is the bridge between chaos and community. It's a difficult and painful part of the solution. People empty themselves of the barriers to communication; they empty themselves of expectations and preconceptions; of prejudices; of the need to fix, convert or control. We accept one another as we are with all our light and darkness and still maintain respect.

The final stage is when the group moves from emptiness into community. That's when unity of purpose and respect for difference are harnessed into achievement. A team cannot come together overnight. It takes hard work and compromise. It demands that the individual's talents are placed at the service of the group.

The outcome of the hard work, the wins and losses, the comings and the goings within the panel is the achievement of results the team never even dreamt of. The achievement of the team is greater than the sum of the talent of its individual members.

Sports clubs in general and the GAA in particular, are fast replacing the Catholic Church as the glue which holds society together.

One of the most memorable quotes come from Marianne Williamson's famous lines. These words apply to all teams but particularly what are called 'weaker' teams. They have to create their own tradition of success. Losing becomes a habit but so does winning.

Our deepest fear is not that we are inadequate

Our deepest fear is that we are powerful beyond measure.

It is our light not our darkness that frightens us most ...

Your playing small doesn't serve the world.

There is nothing enlightened about shrinking

so that other people won't feel insecure around you.

We are born to make manifest a glory that is within us ...

Chapter 46

POP GOES THE CHAPLAIN

The Clipper Carlton Showband was the first showband ever. And it came about, as most good things do, by accident. The band members were from Strabane in County Tyrone. There was a man called Hughie Toorish who had a band in that area. It was a typical band of the time. The members dressed in dickie bows, black suits and white shirts, and they sat behind music stands playing everything in strict tempo. Toorish was the leader of the band and the piano player. In an interview, he described them well: 'We were like undertakers arriving for a dance.'

But, as usually happens in show business, a row broke out in the band about money and who was getting more of the limelight. The whole band walked out, leaving Hughie in a predicament because he had a big dance booked that Saturday night in the local hall in Strabane. He went around on his bicycle and gathered young musicians that he had heard of, and asked them to play. They told me they knew only about ten tunes to keep them going all night! In those days it was a five-hour gig. They got through the night mainly because Toorish himself kept it going. But it couldn't last. Because they were young and inexperienced they tried something different. A couple of them had been in amateur dramatics and knew funny sketches. In local halls the big play was preceded by a funny sketch. They began to do their routines in the middle of the dance and were surprised that people stopped dancing to look at them.

The band knew they'd hit on a good idea. Because they didn't have enough tunes, necessity became the mother of invention and so they built a show around their music. They were not yet called a showband. One night they were in Fintona in County Tyrone, in the early 1950s. The local priest, Father Carty, was raising money for the parish, and said, 'Why don't you get a proper name for yourselves?' They agreed to organise a competition in the hall that night to find a name for the band, with the winner getting half a crown. Various people wrote suggestions on the back of cigarette packets. One of them was, 'The Sweet Afton Band – because there's not a Player among you.' However, somebody else had written 'The Clipper Carlton Band'. Clipper was the name given to American planes during the war that landed on Lough Erne. It created an image of flying across the Atlantic: it was daring, different and glamorous. That man won the half-crown.

Hugo Quinn was a member of the band and a signwriter. On the way home he doodled with a sign. He thought the double C would work well so they called themselves the Clipper Carlton Band. They travelled one night to Dundalk and an enterprising proprietor recognised an opportunity. He advertised on a wall: 'Playing tonight: The Clipper Carlton Showband.' The name stuck. That's how an industry began.

The Clipper Carlton Showband brought joy and enthusiasm to everything it did. The five-hour show included not just music, but miming, Laurel and Hardy sketches, King Kong and Al Jolson, plus everything that was popular on the music scene.

It was the first band to bring glamour to the business. The band members deliberately chose brightly coloured suits. The only place they could get material for such suits was in drapery shops that sold curtain material. I'm letting their secrets out, but that's what their gaudy uniforms were made from.

As a band, the Clipper Carlton was out on its own. The band members had their instruments highly polished and well presented. They worked out a show that entertained people even when they weren't dancing. They were the first to throw away music stands and to stand up for the entire night. They brought excitement and a whole new world to the people of Ireland. Others followed and surpassed them but they were the pioneers.

Elvis was the up-and-coming star at the time. Music changed and bands were travelling juke boxes introducing the pop stars of the world to the most rural parts of Ireland. The clergy, however, were slow to change. The Clippers told me they once travelled from Strabane to Kerry for a dance. Of course people hadn't got used to that sort of band in the different regions of the country. In Kerry Mickey O'Hanlon was drumming. All he could see from his position on stage were bicycles going by him. He couldn't figure it out. There was a room at the back of the stage where the people could park their bicycles for safety. They came into the hall, paid their money, rode their bicycles up the hall and parked them at the back of the stage.

There was a priest in the area who had this idea that music raised the passions too easily at dances. He instructed bands that, after every three songs, they were to stop for precisely two minutes. He stood at the edge of the stage all night with his stopwatch in hand. At the end of the set, he'd say, 'Wait for two minutes,' and at the end of the two minutes he'd shout, 'Go now.' That was his way of keeping his parishioners' passions under control.

The showband era made a huge contribution to the opening out of Ireland. It brought fresh ideas; North and South became one. People followed the bands, so travelling was important. The Dixies from Cork played in Belfast. The Freshmen from Ballymena played in Cork. It was a cross-fertilisation that had never taken place on the same scale before. There were lots of people in bands whose religion I never knew or wanted to know.

The Freshmen were largely Protestant because the band members were from Ballymena, but there were Catholics in the band too – all were accepted as brilliant musicians all over Ireland. I did a series of sixteen programmes for the BBC and RTÉ on the history of the showbands and I interviewed all the major bands of the era. I did a forty-five-minute radio documentary on each one of the bands. I spoke with the late Billy Brown, who was a musical genius in the Freshmen. He was a Protestant from Ballymena and had a stutter. I said to him one time, 'It must be very difficult when you have a stutter, doing all these interviews. What's the most difficult part of it?' He replied, 'My name,

B-Billy B-Brown.' That was the kind of black humour the bands loved. He went on, 'In the Freshmen, we thought we knew everything. We were Prods and used to being in charge of everything. But we realised very quickly that the Republic was an entirely different sort of place. Protestants from the North of Ireland were innocents abroad when we went down there. So we got a Corkman, Oliver Barry, to manage us, and that was a shrewd move. He told us we needed a good lead singer that people in cities and rural areas could identify with. At first, we took great exception to this. But because we wanted to make money, and because we wanted to be part of the bigger scene, we decided to follow his advice. We tried to work out what sort of lead singer would be acceptable; what a lead singer of a showband ought to be and what he ought to look like. We came to the conclusion that the perfect lead singer for a showband would be a fellow who looked like a clerical student, but with sex appeal.'

Who needs market research with genius like that?

They picked a young man from Strabane who was a trainee teacher in a Catholic training college. He looked like a clerical student – tall, black-haired, good-looking. They had to pick a name that was neutral from a religious point of view. They called him Derek Dean. Dean of the Freshmen, as it were. People in showbands worked out what people needed. They paid attention to the 'punters', as they called them.

There was a time when the transition from local bands playing in local halls to showbands who travelled the length and breadth of the country overlapped. Members of the Mighty Avons showband remember country halls where people threw paraffin oil on the floor to make it slippy. Can you imagine what a fire hazard that was? In those days people smoked non-stop in the dancehalls. You could see a blue haze of smoke rising from the hall as the night went on.

The country was economically poor back then. The main form of transport was the bicycle. There were no radios or TVs and very few phones. In most parts of the country there was no electricity, either, which meant there could be no amplification. The early showbands all remember having to improvise. They ran their amplification off a bank of car batteries.

They brought glamour, excitement and travel. Any self-respecting showband had a luxury van in which they travelled six nights a week around the country. The late Gene Pitney once said that a definition of hell for him would be travelling for an eternity with the same musicians in the same van. I understand what he meant.

One of the most famous men involved in showbusiness was Albert Reynolds, who subsequently became Taoiseach. Albert left school at seventeen and earned £4 a week in his first job. In 1955 he worked for CIE in Roosky, where the priest formed a carnival committee. As well as entertaining the nation, showbands were a golden goose for churches and committees. The carnival committee in Roosky was highly successful and after a couple of years they paid off whatever debts had accrued. On one occasion, the parish priest, unusually, wanted no more money and so asked Albert to cancel the bands. It was too late to do so and Albert said he'd run the dances himself. The priest was delighted to get rid of the headache and handed everything over to Albert. Out of that, he and his brother Jim eventually built an empire of fourteen halls at the height of showband mania. Names like Cloudland, Jetland and Roseland still revive dancing memories for those who frequented them. Albert admitted that the skills he learned as a promoter for showbands stood him in good stead when he had to deal with the IRA, Sinn Féin and many Unionist politicians in later life.

Monsignor Horan, who built Knock airport, first made his money running the famous hall in Tooreen. It was alleged that the devil appeared in that ballroom. Nobody's too sure whether it actually happened or whether somebody put out a rumour to damage his business. Of course we can prove nothing and it was a good story anyway.

The Royal Showband was another band that pioneered new markets. The first showband record was released in 1963. Since there were no studios here, the Royal Showband had to go to England and record in the Abbey Road studios, where the Beatles recorded some of their greatest songs.

Mentioning the Beatles and showbands reminds me of a story Brendan Bowyer recalls clearly. The Royal Showband had just received the Carl Allen Award for being the best band in Britain and Ireland. As a result of that, they were touring England. When they came to play in Liverpool there was a young band keeping the audience entertained until the Royal came on stage. That young band was the early Beatles. Brendan Bowyer remembers how Lennon and McCartney came to look at their luxury wagon. They wondered aloud if they'd ever make enough money to buy a bus like that. Brendan advised them to keep writing their own songs and they might.

And so it was that the Royal Showband released their first record, a skiffle version of Eamonn O'Shea's 'Come Down the Mountain, Katie Daly'. The flip side was 'I Heard the Bluebird Sing', a duet featuring Tom Dunphy and Jim Conlon

When the showbands began to record, it highlighted the need for a recording studio here at home. Bill O'Donovan, who went on to become head of 2FM, cut his teeth in the Eamonn Andrews Studios. It was Bill who produced almost all the great records of the era.

Eurovision also gave an impetus to the band business. In 1965 Ireland entered for the first time, with Butch Moore singing 'Walking the Streets in the Rain'. Dickie Rock, with 'Come Back to Stay' and Seán Dunphy with 'If I Could Choose', all did well in successive years. Dana, of course, won the Eurovision in 1970 with 'All Kinds of Everything'. That was the first time Ireland won it, but we went on to win it more times than any other country in Europe. We used to have a proud record there.

The Mighty Avons were the first showband to have a record in the Top Ten in the British charts. Jim Reeves was a famous country singer who was adored in Ireland. When he died in a plane crash in 1964, the famous Eddie Masterson had a song written within five minutes on the inside of a Sweet Afton packet. He persuaded the Avons to record it and they eventually did. 'Tribute to Jim Reeves' went into the Top Ten in the British charts.

Eddie Masterson, the man who got me involved in journalism, was at the centre of the entertainment industry in Dublin, and was legendary among showband people and sporting people. He was in a position to help striving musicians. A young fellow would come up from the country looking for a job in a band and Eddie would say, 'Paddy Cole's looking for a drummer. Go and tell him I sent you.'

There was another occasion when a young journalist who was working for New Spotlight magazine was looking to get into mainstream journalism. Eddie wanted to help him. So he rang me and said, 'You know Michael Hand in The Independent. Both of us do. I'm trying to get this man a job. They've given him a week to write for The Evening Herald. We have to get him good stories. I'll meet you tonight and we'll come up with some stories and give them to him so that he'll get the job.' After a dance one night, we sat down, the two of us, and earmarked a few good stories. This young journalist wrote the stories and the stories made the front page of The Evening Herald on successive days. He was hired immediately. He went on to become an editor with The Independent. That's how Eddie helped people.

Eddie was also well known for playing tricks on people. There was a great drummer called Mickey O'Neill who used to play with the Capitol Showband. Mickey was up from Castleblayney. It was a wonderful, glamorous opportunity for him – being a drummer in the top showband in Ireland. The band had been off down in Killarney and had come back up to Dublin and were staying overnight in Barry's Hotel.

Eddie was sitting in the foyer of the hotel at about six o'clock in the morning. He called Mickey over and spoke to him sharply: 'Listen, don't you ever use me like this again. There's a photo call for you in the Garden of Remembrance tomorrow morning at nine o'clock. I'll do it for you this time but if they ever want to send you messages like this again, get them to do it some other way. Be in your band suit at nine tomorrow morning outside the Garden of Remembrance.'

Mickey was delighted. At that time, the Capitol Showband wore fluorescent green suits; they were always red or pale green – anything but what a normal man would be seen in. So Mickey got dressed in his pale lime green suit and walked to the Garden of Remembrance. The whole of Dublin was passing by looking at this eejit standing in a pale green suit during rush hour at the gates of the Garden of Remembrance and everybody laughing at him.

Mickey was getting more embarrassed by the minute. And then Eddie walked past and said, 'Did they not arrive yet?' And Mickey knew he'd been set up. That was Eddie, full of harmless fun.

There are many hilarious stories, too, about bands who bought their own records. They certainly weren't beyond doing it. The bottom of many a river was polluted by the vinyl records dumped in them by over-enthusiastic showband managers wanting to make the elusive number one spot. It paid them to do it because a number one filled halls and coffers – in that order.

I don't know when it was that I realised how important showbands were to the people of Ireland. Like most things in life, I didn't appreciate them when they were in their heyday, or at least I didn't appreciate the significant contribution they were making.

By 1972 the showband era had peaked. That year I was in Nashville, Tennessee, in the company of Brian Coll, Ray Lynam and Larry Cunningham, Mick Clerkin, Pat Campbell from the BBC, Jimmy Magee, Seán Reilly and a few others who were fascinated by the connection between showbands and international country music.

Back then we loved our local heroes, but the international heroes were something special. People like Buck Owens, Merle Haggard, Charley Pride and George Jones were the heroes every self-respecting showband paid tribute to night after night on the stages around Ireland. But in Nashville I discovered that the country stars admired Irish singers and saw Celtic music as the basis of their country music industry.

For example, George Jones thought Ray Lynam's voice was one of the best he'd ever heard. Charley Pride wanted Brian Coll to go to America. He saw him as a natural successor to Slim Whitman. Pride's manager tried his best to encourage Brian to leave Ireland and work in Nashville. Brian was doing so well at home that he couldn't take the risk. Nobody will ever know whether he would have made it in Nashville or not, but the country music industry headhunted him openly. It proved to me that our singers were as good as any in the world. That was one of the great contributions the showband made to the Irish music industry. It gave everybody confidence.

When the Royal Showband went to Las Vegas, it seemed it would be the end of them as an attraction at home. Yet, years later, Brendan Bowyer could still draw crowds when he returned from Las Vegas to tour Ireland.

Elvis Presley also admired the talents of the Royal Showband. Late at night he often went to see them perform after his own show. One of the highlights of the show was Brendan Bowyer doing an imitation of Elvis Presley. Elvis loved that part of the show.

There were, at one time, 600 full-time professional bands playing up and down the country. And a whole business built up around them, because it meant work for hairdressers, for people who provided soft drinks, and for the fast-food suppliers who catered for these big dances. There were more people employed in it than in the beef industry, which was supposed to be our number one industry at the time. And out of it came recording studios, radio stations and the infrastructure on which today's music industry is built.

Showbands gave a break and sometimes encouragement to musicians who later became famous in other forms of music. Van Morrison played in a showband and so did Rory Gallagher. Terry Wogan remembers that he was hooked on the glamour of showbusiness after he watched the Clipper Carlton play in Cobh. Phil Coulter got his early education working with the Capitol Showband. The Corrs' parents were part of a showband in Dundalk. Even Louis Walsh, the mogul of pop today, cut his teeth working with showbands. Daniel O'Donnell is one of the biggest attractions in America. His early days were spent with his sister Margo, pretending to play guitar in her band around the country. He himself went solo and is now one of the most respected artists in popular music anywhere. He'd be the first to admit that without showbands he would never have got a start. His manager, Seán Reilly, so important to his success, served his apprenticeship in the halcyon days of the showbands.

Showbands reflected the Ireland of the time. They were mainly Irish. They were mainly male, the exceptions being Margo, Eileen Reid, Eileen Kelly and Susan McCann, and Philomena Begley years afterwards. Their aim was to entertain. They're often denigrated now, because of their copycat style. Yet in the space of one decade they made over 2,000 records. Not all of them were original, but many of them stand up better than their pop counterparts in England do to this day.

The real gifts showbands left to the people who followed them were happy memories and self-confidence. Dickie Rock, Joe Dolan, Seán Dunphy, Doc

Carroll, Brendan O'Brien, Larry Cunningham and all the others were role models for young stars. They brought a sense of freedom and joy to the country. They showed the people of Ireland that another world of entertainment and glamour did exist. They helped drag Ireland out of the dark ages.

The Church had its say, though. Every Lent, dancing in Ireland stopped and showbands crossed to England and America to find work. Bands had to go away from home and leave their families for six weeks. It was unfair in many ways but that's how Irish society was in the 1950s, the 1960s and, indeed, the 1970s.

As I've said, their main vocation in life was to entertain people. They did so night after night in a professional and wonderful way. It took talent, initiative, enthusiasm and stamina. The old motto for showbands was that people should go home happy and looking for more. It was summed up brilliantly in a phrase that has gone down in showband lore: 'Whatever you do, send them home sweatin'.'

Many of a certain generation will identify with the last dance of the night. The band working up to a musical frenzy, the men and the women charging across from their respective sides of the hall and hoping for one last dance and perhaps one new date. There's many a family that owes its existence to the showbands sending them home sweating. There's not a night goes by that I don't say a prayer for all those good people who taught me so much. It struck me recently that maybe it was their constant journeying with which I identified.

For those who lived through it, it was the best of all possible times. I know that it was the people in the showband industry that made it so. I'm thinking in particular of friends like Seán McGrade, Séamus McCusker, Peter Smith, Gene Stuart, Seán Reilly, Big Tom, Tony Loughman, Henry McMahon, Christy Gunn, Jim Aiken, Chris Roche, Matt Carroll, Con O'Mahony, Dermot O'Brien, Paddy Kennedy, Mick Nolan, Noel Carty, Donie Cassidy and Frank McCloon in Dublin. Too many of them are dead and gone but all of them accepted me and welcomed me into their ballrooms seven nights a week. I learned everything that was useful from those friends who were supposed to be 'phoney' showbusiness people. Far from it, they were generous, open, charitable and very loyal.

Looking back, there is a solid connection to the showbands at every stage of my life. In return I hope I helped their careers. I had an expert ear for picking hit records throughout the 1970s and 1980s. I was also useful when called upon to write sleeve notes for their albums. I still help them and am occasionally asked to write sleeve notes for CDs. The new generation of Nathan Carter, Lisa McHugh, Cliona Hagan and Michael English are still friends of mine. The late Joe Dolan once said to me that if I knew as much about religion as I did about music, I'd have been pope years ago.

The golden age of showbands began with the Clipper Carlton and who knows where it ended. It gave employment to thousands of people. The industry they founded grew in an entirely different direction and led to Thin Lizzie, the Boomtown Rats, U2, Westlife, the Corrs, Boyzone, and all the other fantastically successful Irish artists around the world today. Many of the people who made the biggest contribution are forgotten. Rarely are they given the credit they deserve. It would be ungrateful of me not to remember the friends who made me what I am today.

Larry Cunningham once summed it up to me brilliantly: 'In the old days we used to play to 2,000 people with a wee, small amplifier of barely 200 watts. Everybody heard every word we said and sang and they remember the tunes to this day. Now we play to 200 people and use 2,000 watts. The sound is no better but the fun goes on.'

If I was asked to say when the Golden Age declined, I would have to say it was when the Miami Showband were murdered. That's when the fun ended. The Miami massacre was tragic for a number of reasons, the main one being the death of three lovely, talented musicians – Fran O'Toole, Tony Geraghty and Brian McCoy. In the beginning, it was Dickie Rock and the Miami. Things moved on and we were coming to the end of the halcyon days of the showband era. Pop groups, ballad groups and folk groups took over. Pubs were replacing the ballrooms and the country was experiencing some prosperity. The world was a smaller place.

People went abroad on holidays. English newspapers were on sale. The BBC was available on televisions all over the country. Communication broadened minds. In Church, state, sport and entertainment the old order was passing. The 1970s is thus important as a period of transition.

The Miami incident was a reminder to us that things were changing in politics too, and that nothing was sacred. Showbands in the North brought all communities together. They crossed the sectarian divide. Depending on the area, the bands played 'God Save the Queen' or 'The Soldier's Song'. They had both anthems in their repertoires. It was always a running joke in the bands. One of them on one occasion didn't know where they were. Half the band played 'God Save the Queen' and, simultaneously, the other half played 'The Soldier's Song' and both sides turned on them. That was the worst of all possible worlds.

The Miami was truly a mixed band. There were Catholics and Protestants in the band. There were Northerners and Southerners. There was one from Cork and one from Ballymena. It was just about the most perfect mix you could get. If you were going to attack a band for sectarian reasons, the Miami was the worst choice you could make. They were young and fresh with no history behind them. Fran O'Toole was an up-and-coming young star, one of the new breed. He was writing his own material, performing his own songs. They were a perfect example of where music and Ireland were going. Furthermore, up until then, showbands were untouchable. In the worst days in the early 1970s, when tit-for-tat murders paralysed the North, the bands never stopped going there because the Northerners always supported the bands. Bands loved going there. They always said the Northern audiences were special because they really appreciated the chance to enjoy themselves.

The Miami were travelling home from Banbridge the night they were killed, 31 July 1975. Briefly, they were stopped on the road outside Banbridge, by what seemed to be a legitimate UDR road check. They were taken out of the van because somebody with an evil mind decided to set up the Miami as bomb carriers. The plan was that this bogus road check would put a bomb in the Miami van which would explode somewhere down the road. It would then be said that showbands from the Republic were smuggling explosives across the border. That was the evil plan. In fact, the bomb went off while the bogus UDR group was planting it in the van. One of the band members who survived, Stephen Travers, to this day insists that the leader was not a bogus UDR man, but a soldier with an upper-class English accent. In other words, it wasn't just a group of terrorists who did it. Some of them were terrorists, but they were helped by members of the security forces.

The bomb went off and three of the band were blown to pieces. Others were badly injured but survived. Some of those planting the bomb were also blown up. There's an amazing sequel to the night of terror. One of the people tried for their murders was identified by his spectacles. The force of the blast blew his glasses off and a small fragment of the lens was found at the scene. Even in those days, forensics proved that it was a very rare prescription. There were only a few of them in Northern Ireland, all of them easily identifiable. They were thus able to convict him from that fragment of his spectacles.

For me, the Miami massacre was the day the music died. It was the day innocence died. The showband scene never recovered. Many of the big bands stopped going north. The entertainment scene changed completely. The innocence of the whole showband era, which had been thriving since 1955, was now sullied. Everything changed and moved on. It was a sad time which brought home to me that life changes us, whether we know it or not.

Part of my job then was to help with the funerals of both Tony Geraghty and Fran O'Toole. Fran O'Toole's wife and their two little children were devastated and emigrated shortly afterwards. I remember going to their house in Bray in the weeks that followed and finding a family utterly paralysed by grief. I wondered then, as I do now, whether those who commit murder ever think of the grief-stricken relatives. Fran's parents and brother also suffered greatly and all of them died too young.

It was devastating for the McCoy and Geraghty families too. Their lives changed for ever on that fateful July night. With the Miami massacre the last untouchable group fell victim to the terrorists' evil. There were no more boundaries after that and so many died needlessly. That's what war does. It destroys the most artistic, the most innocent. It destroys even those whose only ambition in life is to make other people happy.

The showband age is over and gone for ever. It's nothing but a memory. When I was a young priest I went to dances seven nights a week in Dublin. I thought it would never end. But it did end. Life moves on and there's nothing we can do about it.

The showband era brought Ireland from dancing at the crossroads to taking its place proudly on the stage of Carnegie Hall in New York. There's so much more to be said about the showband era but my purpose is to show that these were brilliant, intuitive businessmen and entertainers who did much to brighten dark days. These were the people with whom I was lucky enough to mix from an early age. They taught me so many skills that I can never thank them enough. It's impossible to name names, but my closest and best friends in life are still the people who travel the roads as many nights as they can, making a living simply by making people happy.

Chapter 47

THE PASSION OF FATHER CHARLES

The Passionists, an Italian order, came to Ireland 150 years ago. We came to Mount Argus on 15 August 1856. Our most famous member was a Dutchman called Father Charles Houben. He's a perfect example of God writing straight on crooked lines. Traditionally Passionists are supposed to conduct missions and retreats and, through preaching, spread devotion to the Passion of Christ. Too often our preaching has emphasised that it was our sins that caused Christ's suffering. That meant scrupulous people were left with a crippling sense of guilt. It is more encouraging and accurate to see Christ's Passion as the ultimate proof of God's love for us.

Father Charles was born in the quiet village of Munstergeleen and his life could be seen as a series of failures. He was a slow learner in his youth, one of eleven children in a poor family. It was only after his mother died that he could think about entering the priesthood.

First, though, he was conscripted into the army and he was a failure there too. But out of that failure he discovered a Passionist monastery and felt the call to become a Passionist. And he did. Before his ordination, however, his father died and the family were so poor they couldn't afford to go to his ordination, because of the expense of the funeral. After ordination he was sent to England to help establish the Passionists there.

The priest the Passionists sent to found Mount Argus was a member of the aristocracy, Lord Longford's great-uncle, Paul Mary Packenham. He was a young man in his early thirties, a former officer in the British army, highly intellectual and competent. A born leader, he was the ideal man to be the first rector of Mount Argus. However, six months after he came to Ireland, he died unexpectedly.

They had no one else to send in his place except this Dutchman who knew little English and was so pedantic they couldn't allow him to say a public Mass. He never conducted a mission and his only suitable tasks were blessing the sick and hearing confessions. Yet Mount Argus monastery was built on the reputation of this apparent failure, while the one the Passionists considered the ideal man was taken by God.

Despite his failures, Father Charles had something people identified with and they came in their thousands to him for healing.

Every day, hundreds of people came to him in Mount Argus. It didn't impress his community in Mount Argus, many of whom didn't understand him. He became so popular with the people that the diocesan authorities, not to mention the medical profession, grew suspicious of him. They got their opening when a couple of Dublin rogues came to Father Charles and asked him to bless a barrel of holy water for them. They then sold it at a shilling a bottle as being 'blessed by the holy man of Mount Argus'. It's hard to beat the Dubs.

Poor old Father Charles was banished to England. Before he left, there were elaborate plans to build a new church and retreat house at Mount Argus. The foundation stone was laid before Charles was sent away, but during his eight years away, Mount Argus went downhill and nearly closed.

Eventually it was decided to bring him back to Dublin. When he came back, Mount Argus took off. People returned and Charles took up his healing ministry again. Mount Argus once more became so popular that they decided to resume building the church. The problem was nobody could remember where the foundation stone was laid, it was so overgrown. Nevertheless, because of Father Charles's ministry, Mount Argus was saved and the buildings we know today were completed.

When I entered the Passionists I had never heard of Father Charles of Mount Argus. But as a student I soon understood his appeal. Compassion for the sick and dying were the hallmarks of his life.

In time I got to know the real Father Charles from Mrs Cranny. Her father brought him in a pony and trap to bless the sick around Dublin in the latter part of the nineteenth century. She herself was blessed and cured by him when she was a child. It was an effective blessing because she lived to be 107.

She remembered him clearly and insisted Father Charles wasn't a severe old man, with dead eyes looking down at the ground, as he is often portrayed. On the contrary he was a smiling, friendly man and good fun. When her father brought him around Dublin to heal the sick, Charles always encouraged people to trust God to walk with them in their suffering, whether they were cured or not.

For Charles, God isn't the cause of suffering but neither is suffering a curse. If we accept God's will strength will come. He preached the Passion by telling simple stories about Christ's suffering and by reassuring the sick that their pain was linked to Christ's, and therefore never wasted. Mrs Cranny's father memorised his stories and repeated them to the family when he came home.

Unusually for a healer, Charles sometimes told those who came for a blessing that they wouldn't get better. There is a documented case where he said to a sick man, 'It is not God's will that you should get better. This is God's gift to you so that you should go home and prepare for your death.' The man, to his credit, accepted his advice and died a month later.

I experienced Charles's unusual way of answering prayers in my own life when my mother got sick. As I have already explained, we prayed to Father Charles for guidance and healing, but Mammy died despite all our prayers.

I was devastated that my prayers weren't answered then; later in life I realised that all prayers are answered, but not necessarily in the way we want. As the song says, 'Some of God's greatest gifts are unanswered prayers'. I keep insisting, if my mother hadn't died, I might not have been a priest and I certainly would not be the kind of priest I am.

My father worked on the railway but in 1960 he was told the railway was closing and he'd have to train to be a bus conductor. A short time afterwards, conductors were done away with and he had to learn to drive a bus. My father was fifty years of age, without a job, and he asked me to send him a relic of Father Charles. He trained as a bus driver even though the only thing he had ever driven before that was a tractor. He passed the test and for the rest of his working life drove safely. But he'd never leave home without the plastic relic of Father Charles in his coat pocket, which was his way of showing his appreciation of Charles's intervention.

When I was rector and parish priest of Mount Argus from 1983 to 1989, my biggest problem was the restoration of the monastery and church. In 1983 we discovered that the timbers and walls of the monastery and church were in an advanced state of dry rot. We had to take every slate off the roof, every rafter, every inch of plaster off the walls of both buildings. We had to lift all the floors in the monastery and restore the complete fabric from foundation to roof.

When Mount Argus Monastery was first built in 1863, the leading newspaper of the day said, 'Mount Argus Monastery is the noblest religious house built in these countries since the Reformation.' Later, when the church was completed, it became a famous and majestic landmark. In 1983 the entire complex was in danger of collapsing.

At first we thought about demolishing it, but because it was such a historic building, that was not possible and, anyway, the most economical solution by far was to restore it. There is a fascinating and varied meeting of cultures in the history of Mount Argus. James Joyce mentioned it as a centre of spiritual comfort in Ulysses. Both Brendan Behan and Christy Browne came regularly to Mount Argus, and mentioned it with affection. The leader of the 1916 Rising, Pádraig Pearse, came to Mount Argus to make his peace with God and brought many of his comrades with him on Good Friday 1916. James Pearse, Pádraig's father, was received into the Church in Mount Argus in 1877, and his firm made and installed the pulpit that's in use in the church to this day. On the other hand, the first rector was Father Paul Packenham, who hailed from the British aristocracy. Before the founding of An Garda Síochána, the Dublin Metropolitan Police took Mount Argus as their church. After 1922, An Garda Síochána continued the association with Mount Argus.

Of course the reason it survived at all was the saintly Charles. In his lifetime 300 people every day came to be blessed by him and 20,000 attended his funeral. Mount Argus had such an important heritage that it had to be saved.

It's difficult for somebody who wasn't there to understand what an impossible task it was at the time. There were over eighty priests, brothers and students in the community.

In the 1980s Ireland was an economic mess. Unemployment was high; the best of our young, educated people emigrated to find work and a future. A government minister actually said that the island was too small for the number of people living on it and that it was a good experience for our talented graduates to emigrate. It was the worst possible time to ask people for money to restore a church and monastery.

Father Charles was the man I put my trust in. I lived in a wee room next to the room where he died. I discovered then what a friend I had in Father Charles. I had to raise £2.5 million to save the buildings. It was as part of that fundraising process that I appeared on The Late Late Show.

Pictures of the decaying monastery appeared in The Sunday World and Gay Byrne couldn't believe the conditions we lived in. He sent his researcher Brigid Ruane over to Mount Argus to check it out and she reported that it was even worse than the pictures. As a result of my Late Late Show appearance, hundreds of thousands of pounds were donated from all over the country. The showbands came on board and raised thousands more. So did the Garda. Every county in Ireland contributed to the fund. To me it was a miracle it was ever completed and Charles was the miracle man.

Towards the mid-1980s, we had to begin a major project in the church. We decided to split the church in half and keep services going in one half whilst the other half was being restored. It was nerve-wracking for me because there was no money to finish it and I wasn't even sure if we'd ever re-open the church.

The work began at the end of September, the Monday after an All-Ireland final. When I finished eight o'clock Mass I went to introduce myself to the workers arriving on site. Kerry had beaten Dublin in the All-Ireland football final the day before.

We decided there had to be Dubliners employed on the building, otherwise security would have been impossible.

Three or four 'real' Dubs appeared on the first morning. One of them was a tough little bearded man. He had bloodshot eyes and black hair and he'd obviously been on the tear the night before, drowning his sorrows after Dublin's defeat. He wasn't interested in a sermon from anybody.

I was on the steps of the church and I spoke a little nervously about the ground rules. 'Listen, lads, I know it's a building site, and I know that I can't expect you to behave as if you were in a church all the time. I know that. Can you do a few things for me? While you're working here, Masses will be going on in the church. At least during the Masses, mind the language, keep the noise down. Weddings will be going on. Remember that it's their biggest day, so don't spoil it for them. Funerals will be going on (this was my big line). Funerals will be going on and it's a sensitive time. If your own mother was being buried, you wouldn't want to hear effing and blinding and shouting and roaring during the Mass, would you?'

The wee Dublin man with the squinty eyes looked up at me and says: 'Ah, you needn't worry about us, Father. You'll hear no f*****' cursin' from us.' The rest just laughed.

There were moving statues all over the country at the time and, as a joke, I said, 'By the way, if you see any of the statues moving, for God's sake don't mention it to anyone.'

And the ever-ready Dubs were up to it: 'Jaysus, Father, if we see any of the statues movin', we'll hand him a bleedin' shovel.'

We got on the best after that.

By 1987, good will towards Mount Argus was exhausted. We had been going for over four years and we simply succumbed to charity fatigue. We ran one last draw, the fifth in all. Some 3,000 participants paid £100 each into what was supposed to be a massive draw. It turned out to be a disaster. The committee was afraid to tell me how bad it was. The leader, Joe Morris, called me into the office one morning and told me we were going to lose thousands. I had always said that if Father Charles wanted Mount Argus to be restored, it would happen. All we had to do was the same as he had done: trust in God. But I was in no humour for pious thoughts that morning and in an offhanded way I said to Joe, 'Wouldn't you think, if Charlie wanted Mount Argus restored, he would get off his backside and help us.'

Poor Joe was shocked at my disrespectful attitude to such a saintly figure.

I went on to RTÉ to do an interview with Mike Murphy, but when I came back two hours later I was told that Rome had phoned in my absence to inform us that Father Charles would be beatified in a few months' time. That was his way of telling me that he was still in charge.

Needless to say the draw was filled, the church was completed and we were even able to build a shrine to Blessed Charles as well.

Father Charles had three simple rules about suffering: he told the sick to thank God in the midst of their suffering, to offer up their suffering to God, and to expect God's help and sometimes healing. He believed that Jesus walks with us during our suffering. It is a Way of the Cross. On the Way of the Cross Jesus fell three times but got up each time. He needed help. He needed Simon. He needed people. He needed a mother to touch him. He needed a towel from Veronica. He needed compassion from the women of Jerusalem. After his resurrection he proudly displayed his wounds to Thomas.

Thomas is often referred to as 'Doubting Thomas' as if doubting were a sin. Doubt is not the opposite of faith; certainty is. Thomas wanted to see the wounds of Jesus. And when he did, he believed totally: 'My Lord and my God,' he said, before going on to give his life to spreading the Gospel. Because of Thomas's doubts, we know for certain that Jesus carried the wounds of his Passion after his resurrection, showing that the new life of the risen Jesus was won by the wounds he still bore. St Peter later summed it up: 'By his wounds we are healed.' That's what Charles believed and, furthermore, he was convinced that our own woundedness as well as Jesus' wounds save us. He knew that we don't need to be able to make sense of suffering, as long as we remember that 'Nothing is impossible with God'.

The Dutch artist Vincent Van Gogh also said that God always sends works of art so that we might recognise ourselves in them. 'Christ is the greatest artist of all. He works not in canvas but with human flesh,' he concluded. Charles, for me, is a wonderful example of a human canvas that God made into a work of art. He was a poor preacher, ridiculed by those who lived with him. At the end of his life he suffered pain but remained human enough to have a sing-song and a glass of whiskey when he needed it. He's my kind of saint.

He called himself 'poor old Charlie' as he walked along the corridors. One lasting memory that Father Eugene Nevin (a contemporary in Mount Argus) had of Charles, was his fear of death as he hobbled down the fifty-nine steps from his cell on the top floor to bless the sick in the parlours. All the while he would be repeating the second half of the Hail Mary: 'Holy Mary, Mother of God, pray for us sinners, now and at the hour of our death, Amen.'

In theory, Charles was not the ideal model of the perfect Passionist. Yet of all the Passionists who've lived and worked here for over 160 years, he's the only one to be canonised.

Through the bad times, Charles still keeps me going. There have been many times, and I'm sure there will be many more, when I wondered why I remained a priest or a Passionist. And I still do to this day. These days as I look back and reflect on my life honestly, there isn't much to enthuse over. But then I think of Charlie. An old man full of pain praying for a happy death, recognised by the people as a holy man but not really by those in his own house. And now he's a canonised saint in heaven. That's what keeps me going. Even broken failures like me can be a work of art when I allow God to work through me.

Even though Charles was canonised in June 2007 and is forever Saint Charles of Mount Argus, he's still a friend to me.

CHAPTER 48

TO WED OR NOT TO WED

In 1994, on live radio, Joe Duffy asked me if I had ever fallen in love with a woman. Many people were shocked by the question. To me it was no big deal. I was getting used to being fifty then and answered, 'How could any normal man arrive in middle age without falling in love?' Of course I fell in love.

In recent years I haven't talked much about personal relationships of friendship and love in public because it's not fair either to myself or to my friends. I simply state the facts: I know what it is to love another human being who also loved me, but I have never known sexual love.

Love was an experience that was beautiful and holy and was never given sexual expression through making love. It annoys me that sex and love are so confused in the modern mind and so I make no apologies for saying that chaste love is possible and desirable.

For a couple committed to each other for life, sexual love is their greatest prayer. But there is another experience of intimacy that is not sexual intimacy. There are experiences of deep, loving friendships which are precious gifts from God and don't lead to sexual intercourse.

As a religious and priest, I'm not free to commit myself to anyone but God and therefore I cannot and should not mislead others or myself about that. I have found it hard and I know that those who loved me found it impossibly difficult too.

When I entered the monastery all those years ago, I knew in theory that I would have to give up sex and marriage. That was easy enough to do at eighteen. It was the sacrifice of intimacy and companionship that proved to be the real challenge. It took me a lifetime to recognise that God takes no pleasure in unnecessary loneliness.

As novices and students the constant mantra by which we had to live was 'to mortify your eyes'. We were trained to walk with our heads bent down and our eyes cast to the ground. If for some reason we looked out a window during our novitiate, we had to confess in public before all the community that we had failed 'to mortify our eyes'.

It was also part of the unspoken assumption that women were bad and would always be a danger to our purity. Think of the implications of that attitude being implanted in a teenager's young psyche. The practise was to suppress normal human emotions rather than to cope with them healthily.

Even now I struggle daily with the need for emotional maturity, friendship and integrity in my life. I don't always live up to my principles. But the struggle must go on. My first duty as a priest is to live in truth, to hold on to decency and honesty, to try to live the Gospel before preaching it.

Throughout my life I have had to come to terms with the fact that I need close friendships with women as well as men. When it comes to close friendships, it's important that boundaries are absolutely clear. It's unjust to mislead anyone into believing that there is the possibility of a long-term, married relationship on offer. If I do that I should leave the priesthood or leave the relationship. It is unnecessary and harsh that I should have to make that choice, but with Church laws as they are, there is no other option. I used to think it was a pity. Now I consider it a scandal.

The most advantageous and challenging parts of my priesthood have been the genuinely good, loving friendships I have with women. There are women in my life who know me better than I know myself. They are the people who encourage me and drive me to be a better man. If I can be a better man there is every hope I will be a better priest. I can never thank them enough for their love and their patience. They are the greatest gifts God has given me, a holy communion.

A greater danger perhaps is that we priests use women. It is a terrible crime to destroy a woman's future or a woman's life for selfish reasons. Worse still is to keep a woman hanging on because we can't or won't make up our minds, or with the impossible hope that priests will be allowed to marry some day.

My greatest fear, apart from the horror of wasting a good person's life, is that I would end up a solitary, disillusioned,old bachelor. I never want to spend my energies being celibate instead of striving to be a good priest. I believe it's achievable to have close personal friendships with special people in our lives without crossing the boundaries, without abusing or misusing friends and without displeasing the loving God we'll all have to meet. As with any of God's special gifts, we should be grateful for them but we must be scrupulous not to misuse them.

I know now that I would have been a far better priest and a far better human being had I been allowed to marry. That's a fact, not a moan. Nothing in life is perfect and I hope I have tried my best to be as normal, as healthy a human as is possible in a situation that does not lend itself either to honesty or maturity.

I would have preferred to be able to choose both priesthood and marriage in the circumstances, but couldn't, and ended up making the choice for priesthood. I still don't know whether that was the right decision, but it was the best choice I could make at that time. Most days I don't regret the choice I made, but I do regret having to make it. I've been able to live with reasonable peace of mind. But the choice had to be made. If I had drifted in life it would have been unhealthy and upsetting, not only to myself, but also to the person who was good enough to love me.

It was only when I really thought about it for this book that I realised the time I was close to leaving was when my best friend in the Passionists, a one-time classmate for whom I have enormous respect, decided to leave and marry. We are still close friends. He and his wife are so good to be with and are obviously people who have grown together in love. When I meet them I enjoy their company but there is a great sadness in my life as I drive home to my single bed in the monastery. Perhaps I could have been as happy as they are and have done as much good work as they do had I decided to marry twenty-five years ago.

At times like this I console myself that in life we make the best decisions we can at the time. After a period of wrestling with their pain, my friends made an honest decision that took them to a wholesome place. I also made the best decision I could to remain a priest. I can only leave it with God, stop beating myself up, and hope I have done the right thing in God's eyes.

Now, to get back to that famous disclosure on radio and its aftermath. It was a run-of-the-mill radio interview with Joe Duffy. At that time Joe was sharing the morning slot with Gay Byrne. He had moved on from being a reporter on the Gay Byrne Show to hosting the programme a few mornings a week.

I can't remember the reason Ann Farrell, the producer, asked me on the show. Maybe it was because I'd just come back from South Africa. I'd gone there deliberately to rest, pray, reflect and, most of all, to avoid my silver jubilee as a priest at home.

The interview was typical Joe Duffy. He was informed, knew where he wanted to go, his questioning was gentle and conversational but penetrating. As always with Joe, he knew the answer I was going to give before he asked the question. Skilfully, and when it suited him, he slipped the question in. 'Brian, you strike me as a very normal man. Have you ever fallen in love with a woman?'

I answered it as honestly as I could. Yes, I had fallen in love. I added, as I always do, that thanks to the grace of God and my mother in Heaven, I had not broken my vows. I went on to explain to him that for a man just turned fifty, it would be more than unusual not to have fallen in love, given that I considered myself still a reasonably normal human being. I thought nothing more of it. At the end of the interview Joe thanked me graciously for being so honest.

The way things work in communications these days is that when people in radio or television know they have a story, they inform the papers. It's good publicity for them and helps in the ratings battles. And so the headline a couple of hours later was, 'Father Brian admits to falling in love.'

I don't have a problem with journalists doing their job. But why do they make being in love sound so dirty? Journalists, like bishops and priests, seem to think all sexuality is bad. The next day it was all over the papers, and once again I felt guilty, ashamed and a failure. By now it was 'admits to affair'. It was not an affair and I really resented them cheapening a good, painful and worthy decision.

When I saw the word 'affair' in black and white it really did upset me. It sounded nefarious; it sounded dirty and it sounded to me definitely sexual. It also had implications of being illicit. None of those things was part of any relationship I've ever had. I was so annoyed about it that I sought legal advice. The senior lawyers I spoke to confirmed that the legal definition of 'affair' had all these connotations. I was told that in law I had a case but was it worth the hassle? Probably not.

I need to be careful not to be too negative, because overall this was a positive, developmental time of my life that helped me to be in touch with myself and to experience a kind of emotional intimacy without a sexual intimacy. I was able to be with another without the usual masks and defences. I was free and safe to share fears, anxieties and failures as well as dreams and visions. I was able to grow emotionally.

To be fair to myself and to others, too, I need to say something more about 'falling in love'. In the modern world the words sex and love are taken to mean the same thing. I don't like it and I consider it demeaning to genuine love. Yet I have to live in the real world and I fully realise that when I 'admit' to falling in love, the normal person's mind races to one conclusion: 'He's had sex.'

When people close to me presumed the same thing, I was horrified. Ever since, I've had to add that I never broke my vows.

I feel demeaned having to use such language and to write so publicly about something that should be nobody's business but mine. Yet I realise that, unless

I tell it like it is, there will be those who will add two and two and get twenty-two. I also realise that it is part of being in the public eye these days, as well as part of talking publicly about personal issues, as I have tried to do all my life. Regrettably, it comes with the territory.

Many of my priest colleagues thought Joe Duffy's question was a very unfair one and were angry with me for answering it honestly. I should have protected myself from such intrusions, they argued. It meant that whoever was asked the question in future would be obliged to answer it in a straightforward way or be looked upon with suspicion.

Once again my family thought I was on the verge of leaving the priesthood. And those who worked with me closely, especially the laity who keep me going, were frightened that I had spoken too openly for my own good. Over the years they have learned, as I have, that most of these things are a one-day wonder. It took me months to come to terms with the public knowing so many details of my life. But people gradually realised what I was doing and have supported me ever since. It took them some time to realise that priests are human and that falling in love is normal, even for priests and religious.

To be honest, I didn't find the question offensive at all. It really was a first, though. Until then there were some areas private enough not to be asked about in public. A priest's love life was definitely a no-go area. But after Eamon Casey and Michael Cleary the boundaries changed. If we priests had spoken dogmatically about how others should behave in bed and out of it, then people felt – rightly in my opinion – that they should know how chaste and how normal we ourselves were.

Joe had the right to ask me that straight question because of the scandals that had happened. Gay Byrne, twenty years earlier, asked a priest on the Late Late if he had ever fallen in love, and the country was up in arms that he would ask such a question. But in the mid-1990s, Joe Duffy slipped the same question in and it was easy for him to do it because of the breakdown of that image of the priest as one who didn't have problems, couldn't have problems and never wrestled with personal sin.

Eamon Casey, Michael Cleary and, in a totally different way, Brendan Smyth, with a plethora of others, were priests with human foibles and failings. Even though I didn't want it put in that context, in people's minds that was the context in which Joe Duffy was able to quiz me. Priests were no longer seen as perfect. Twenty-five years on, nobody cares much about what priests do; we're not that important any more.

What I'm trying to say now is this. There is a context in which there are genuinely loving relationships for people who are celibate, which can be life-giving, spiritually uplifting and fulfilling, and are in no way scandalous. Thomas Merton put it perfectly when writing of his loving relationship with a young nurse: 'I do not regret at all my love for her and am convinced it was a true gift from God and an inestimable help to me.' (5)

In those few years people's attitudes have changed. They now accepted that just because we take a vow of celibacy, it doesn't mean we become angels overnight without feelings or failings. Nowadays the vast majority of people are angry that priests can't marry. The harsh law of mandatory celibacy is fast becoming a scandal in itself.

Only recently I realised that St Clare and St Francis loved each other deeply. If they were living in the present time, they could have been on the front page of the tabloids. Yet they were two of the great founders of religious orders, the Poor Clares and the Franciscans. They were able to do it with such incredible beauty and yet, at the same time, they had to ensure they didn't let their love for each other degenerate into something that would spoil their great work. That's 800 years ago and things have hardly changed.

Wrestling with loving relationships should be part and parcel of a healthy celibate's life. I believe that even those who choose celibacy need close friendships as human beings. That doesn't mean a sexual intimacy.

Freely chosen celibacy is difficult but can lead to a singularly dedicated life. It is even more difficult if lived outside community. My experience is that even within community I have met very few healthy, mature men who are better people because they are celibate. In over fifty-seven years of religious life, I could count on one hand the number of healthy, mature, well-developed men for whom celibacy is as an enhancing gift.

There is an ongoing debate throughout the world about the value of mandatory celibacy for Catholic priests, even though officially the Church has said there should be no debate about this issue. Obviously the Church is bringing itself into disrepute. You can't prevent a debate on an issue as vital as this. And why would anyone not discuss it if there are rational arguments to be heard?

There is a tradition of celibacy for Roman Catholic priests going back hundreds of years and it must be respected. There is also a long history of married Catholic priests and that's a position that deserves respect as well.

In my view the debate is already over. The Church has accepted the principle that there can be married priests in the Roman Catholic Church. There are considerable numbers of married Anglican ministers, most of whom disagreed with their own Church's policy of ordaining women, who became Catholics and were ordained as Roman Catholic priests whilst remaining married. They are active in parishes throughout the world and they maintain wives and families whilst continuing parish work. So there is nothing in principle against having married priests in the Catholic Church today. They already exist.

Voluntary celibacy is a treasure in the Church. Irrespective of any changes there will be many priests that will remain celibate. Even if mandatory celibacy is removed, some diocesan priests will still choose to be celibate. In my opinion, that would actually add to the standing of celibacy in the Church. If people are free to marry and on principle choose to remain celibate, then that in itself is a wonderful witness. On the other hand, mandatory celibacy has no worthwhile witness value at all. On the contrary it has turned the priesthood, in many people's minds, into a weird group of bachelors, to be viewed with suspicion.

There are married priests today, and for most of the Church's history, married clergy were part of the priesthood. Indeed, Clement of Alexandria, who lived in the third century, refused to have unmarried clergy in his Church because it implied a rejection of the value of marriage.

It is worth outlining briefly the history of celibacy in the Church. According to the New Testament at least some of the apostles were married. Peter had a mother-in-law, for example. According to early writers in the Church (e.g. Eusebius), Peter's wife was a first-century martyr. Philip had four daughters. Read the Gospel of Matthew or the First Letter to the Corinthians or even Timothy and Titus to discover repeated references to married priests and bishops. In fact, it is St Paul's opinion that bishops and priests should be good at running their own families before being accepted into priesthood.

Things began to change in the fourth century for many reasons. The arrival of early forms of monastic life was one of them. But there was also a view that sex was incompatible with holiness. This is clear in some early rules and regulations that laid down that a priest should abstain from sex with his wife on the night before he celebrated the Eucharist. They obviously had a bad theology of sex and an even worse theology of the Eucharist.

Later other reasons emerged. It was easier to have control over single men. A priest who was married would have to listen to his wife and family. A bishop could manipulate a single man more easily.

Property was also an issue. Early on in the Church's history, Church property got confused with personal property. Customs were different then, and there are even instances of priesthood itself being handed down from father to son. Many claim that this was how St Patrick became a priest.

Underlying all of these arguments, though, is an emerging view that sex is tainted and that those who gave their lives to God as celibates were holier than people who married. This has been one of the great tragedies in the history of Catholicism.

It was after the Reformation, however, that the rule of celibacy was strictly enforced. This had much to do with counteracting Martin Luther's views and less to do with spirituality. It was at this time that mandatory celibacy became the badge of priesthood.

Theologian Dr Thomas O'Loughlin sums up the history of compulsory celibacy: 'Celibacy is a classic example of how an idea from one period, if it gets lodged in law, can become self-perpetuating and eventually be seen as an ideal.' (6) That's why it's time to debate the value of, or necessity for, mandatory celibacy.

On a practical level, some of my best friends have left the priesthood to get married. It has been sad to see their talents and their vocations lost to the Church. Over 100,000 (at the very least) former priests were forced to make an unnecessary choice between the love of the priesthood and the love of a woman. There have been occasions when that same choice has stared me in the face. I'll never know if I made the right decision when I chose to stay a priest or if I would have been better to marry.

What I do know is that many of those who left would have become exceptional leaders in our Church today and we would not be in the mess we're in. They were leaders, they were compassionate, they were open and vulnerable and by that very fact were deeply spiritual men. Most of them were the cream of the priesthood. We rejected those gifted priests needlessly. We chose a man-made discipline instead of a God-given gift.

CHAPTER 49

MUSIC LIFTS MY SPIRITS

Every generation needs creative people to challenge our principles and our prejudices. The arts should encourage us to reflect on undreamed-of possibilities. They do so through song – Kris Kristofferson has been creating a vision for me for thirty years or more. Kimmie Rhodes, Kieran Goss, Brendan Graham, Guy Clarke, Leonard Cohen, Tom Russell, Gretchen Peters, Tom T. Hall, Johnny Cash, Kate Campbell and Beth Nielsen Chapman are just a few of the writers who inspire me today. They write the real hymns.

Poets do it: from Kavanagh to Yeats to Brendan Kennelly to Heaney to Denis O'Driscoll. Painters like Van Gogh and Craigie Aitchison give life to my spirit. An occasional article or book, such as The God of Surprises by Gerard Hughes, has kept me sane in a mad world. I hope the odd article in The Sunday World over the past forty-four years has helped a lost soul along the way. God works mysteriously and wonderfully through anyone who endures the pain of being lost. And I pray this book will help someone to realise, 'You're loved. Just because you're lost doesn't mean you're bad. You have to be lost to search meaningfully.'

Patrick Kavanagh's insights inspire me when I realise that the ordinary is spirit-filled. Like myself, he was a bogman who walked to Mass on crispy ice of a Christmas morning. He was a bogman who recognised the God of the gaps, who found poetry in setting spuds, cutting turf and ricking hay. Those were not the topics of the poets I grew up with, but he made the ordinary sublime. He also preached a unique theology. How or where he got his insights I don't know. It must have been the Holy Spirit. Imagine how frustrated he must have been, locked into the small-mindedness of a country parish. It's no wonder he became a cranky old man, but poetry gave him his freedom, and is the real Kavanagh. Poets see things we don't see, express things we cannot express, understand feelings we don't understand and allow us to reach and express emotions we didn't know we had. They give us language and insight.

Kimmie Rhodes is a talented, thoughtful singer who writes challenging yet peaceful songs. Her concerts are a spiritual experience. I went to see her once in Lurgan. As well as being a lovely night, it gave me a good example of this changing Ireland. The concert was held in a former convent that is now a residence for young people from broken families, who find life difficult. Because there are no vocations the nuns moved out and the former convent became a place where dysfunctional adults could learn to be independent again.

There's an intimate little theatre that once was the nuns' chapel. It was a sobering experience when I thought of the irony. The nuns were gone, leaving not a single trace of their lives of virginal dedication. Yet an American lady with a couple of failed marriages, and one very fulfilling one, with her fruitful struggles and a freeing spirituality, used their chapel to evangelise a broken world. This is the word of the Lord. The word truly made flesh.

Kimmie gave me pause for thought on many occasions.

One night she and I were guests in the home of Kieran Goss and Annie in Sligo. We had a pleasant, though deep, conversation in front of a roaring log fire. Songs and life were the topics. There were bypasses into religion, love, failure and humour. I must have been revealing more of myself than I knew because Kimmie gently borrowed Kieran's guitar and sang the song she thought put words on my searching.

Life has led me by the hand
Time has helped me understand
I'm headed to the promised land
With the heart of a believer.

I believe my dreams are safe
Faith that's blind will find its way
Doubts will leave me when hope remains
In the heart of a believer.

A star is just a ray of life
Finding its way through the night
It's travelled light years just to shine
For the heart of a believer

A pearl is just a grain of sand
A tree is just a seed that lands
Every miracle began
In the heart of a believer.

'The Heart of a Believer' was just enough to get me thinking on my journey home through the wet and windy winter night. By the time I arrived at The Graan, 'A tree is just a seed that lands' blotted everything else out of my consciousness. Hope for the journey indeed. Sometimes the simplest inspiration gives me life.

Singer John Randall wrote in his 2005 Song of the Year,

I'm finding new faith in the arms of old friends
I'm walking among the living again.

After Kimmie's show in Lurgan that night, we took up the conversation again:

'You don't know how much your presence means to us entertainers when we come over here,' she said reassuringly. 'We were hoping you'd be here simply because you understand our life and our vocation. We feel at home when you're here. It doesn't matter where we are, we need people to make us feel at home and you do that.'

It was a complete shock to me. I thought I was there to enjoy the music. She said I did more – I understood the music and thereby gave meaning to her search.

She continued: 'Kris Kristofferson comes and you talk to him about his songs. For him to hear from a man of the cloth that you have given sermons about his songs makes his life worthwhile. A record company is interested only in a commercial success. Commercial success is necessary but the fact that you understand his thoughts makes his suffering, his pain, his struggle and his life worthwhile.'

Johnny Cash was the same. He always asked to see me when he came here, and in later years he asked me to introduce him on stage because he felt safe and fulfilled when I did it. He saw it as significant when 'The Man in Black' introduced the world's most famous 'Man in Black'.

The last meeting I had with Johnny Cash was after I introduced him on stage in Ireland. As always when he came here, I got to as many of his gigs as I could. I always knew I was in the presence of a legend, but a vulnerable man too, whom I could not be sure of seeing again. It was his vulnerability that made him beautiful.

Walk the Line, the film of Cash's life, doesn't deal with the man I knew – the mature, focused and loving husband in the golden days of his life.

Each time we met – over a thirty-year period – we talked more and more about life and less and less about music. My first conversation with the great man took place in Nashville in 1972 when he invited me to the premiere of his film Gospel Road. Religion was always central to his mission.

It is difficult to put Johnny Cash's talents into a single category. He wrote and performed far too many average country songs. But he also wrote and performed some great classics that will live for ever. The more mature he became, the freer he became and the more powerful his music was. He told his stories in exactly the same down-home way, whether he was performing to a country audience or a rock audience. The fact that he was accepted into the Hall of Fame in both country music and rock music is a testament to his extraordinary appeal. Bob Dylan, Bruce Springsteen and Bono adored him. Johnny always called Bono 'a true visionary'. He appreciated his genius for prophecy before most. Johnny came to believe that his job as a writer and singer was messianic. That was why he dressed in black.

Kris Kristofferson told me that Johnny Cash was the spiritual father to a whole generation of musicians, himself included. He was the man who helped launch the career of Bob Dylan and persuaded Columbia Records to sign him. That's some legacy to music and to life.

In latter years Cash unquestionably recorded the best tracks of his career under the guidance of Rick Rubin. The voice wasn't what it used to be, the man's outward strength had disappeared, but his vulnerability gave a depth to his music that was at once frightening and inspirational. His rendering of 'Hurt' – which Cash himself reckoned to be the best anti-drug song ever written – is truly a masterpiece, full of excruciating tension as it highlights the fight between good and evil. What makes it outstanding is the certainty of redemption through weakness. Cash didn't want to record it at all because it was a pop song, but after listening to it more than 100 times, he knew the message he was determined to get across.

Cash lived the hurt in his own life. He and his great friend Waylon Jennings were rebel companions in the 1960s when they roomed together. Tragically, both of them wrecked their bodies by substance abuse.

Fifteen years before his death, when Cash entered hospital for a bypass operation, Jennings came to visit him. Cash advised Jennings to have a medical examination, since, 'You have lived every excess I have.' Jennings did, and had to have emergency bypass surgery there and then. Both of them recuperated side by side and Cash admitted they both dreaded the arrival of their mutual friend Tom T. Hall. If he saw them in this condition he would immortalise the pair in one of his brilliant story songs.

No mention of Cash would be complete without a tribute to his wife, June Carter, who died a few months before him. June Carter, according to Johnny's daughter, Rosanne, went to the man she loved each day and asked one simple question: 'What can I do for you today, John?'

What she did for John was keep him alive. Over and over he paid tribute to her. He recognised that each new day was a gift not only from God but also from June.

She was a vulnerable lady herself, who seemed to attract flawed genius. She was a confidante and friend of Hank Williams. Williams had a back problem, for which doctors prescribed addictive painkilling drugs. He died at the age of twenty-nine, having written some of the most poignant songs of the last century.

June also befriended Patsy Cline, another outstanding singer, who was addicted to alcohol before she was killed in a plane crash.

Elvis Presley was a friend, at both the most successful and most pathetic times of his life.

When June married Johnny Cash in 1968, most people thought he'd be dead before he was forty. She kept him alive past the three score and ten.

It was entirely predictable that, when June died, Johnny wouldn't want to live without her. Four months after her death, he joined her in the heaven he was certain of going to. He told me once that he gave his life to God at the age of twelve. He said, 'Whenever I hand it over to him, I have an inner peace that only he can give. When I try to run it myself I end up in a complete mess.'

The last time we met he brought June and her sisters into a small room to ask God's blessing for the show they were about to perform. I always remember his final prayer: 'God give me the strength to remember my weakness.' That's how I like to remember him.

On one of his early visits to Ireland, we spoke at length about the value of music in communicating with young people. He believed, as I do, that the best songs express the values and doubts of their generation.

Johnny was so convinced of that fact that he volunteered to talk to me about his life and songs, if I would make a tape of it and distribute it to young people in schools. We subsequently did three educational and highly entertaining tapes about his own music and that of other contemporary writers.

He was not proud of his early life and regretted the hurt he caused so many, especially his first wife, who as it happens, died just before the film Walk the Line was released.

Cash had many crises in his life but he maintained his honesty and his integrity. He struggled with life yet always believed. He was, as Kristofferson famously wrote in 'The Pilgrim Chapter 33':

a prophet and a preacher ...

and a problem when he's stoned.

He's a walking contradiction,

partly truth and partly fiction ...

taking every wrong direction

on his lonely way back home.'

In other words, human, just like us.

When it comes to people who have influenced me, Kris Kristofferson is near the top of the list. I am not just a fan; I'm mesmerised by his way with words and his ability to express emotional searching and sometimes emotional devastation. As far back as 1970 I reviewed an album whose original name I can't recall now, but within months it was reissued under the title Me and Bobby McGee. His songs did something to me. They touched me in a way no other works had.

For fifty years his songs have become old friends which get me through bad times. His imagery, his ability to capture feelings, and his descriptions captivate me. I've been lucky enough to talk with the great man often enough to glean new insights into the suffering that produced them. Years ago he told me that the low times in his life produced the most powerful songs. When life is good, his songs are different. He needs to write from anger and despair. It's a cross to bear.

He has an unusual background for a songwriter in the country music tradition. His father was in the United States Air Force during the Second World War and was later in charge of airlift operations during the Korean War. Kris was brought up on a base in Brownsville, Texas. A huge influence in his life was the Mexican nanny who looked after him like a mother. He spoke Spanish before he spoke English and she gave him insights into how the poor live and think. He was bright. Not many win a Rhodes scholarship. He did, and attended Merton College, Oxford. There he immersed himself in literature, finishing with a PhD.

'For the first time in Oxford I got in touch with some wonderful, mind-blowing people like Shakespeare and William Blake,' he told me, at a time when I wasn't too sure who Blake was.

'It was a great experience for me, but I went from there into the army carrying all of this inside me and I'm lucky I'm alive today. I did everything I could to be self-destructive. I spent three years in Germany and volunteered for Vietnam – I was absolutely suicidal.'

I really liked his version of 'Sunday Mornin' Coming Down'. What descriptions, what insights! The Johnny Cash version gave Kris his first taste of chart success.

He once told me that he considers 'Jodie and the Kid' the first good, commercial song he ever wrote. At the time Kris brought his little daughter Tracey with him as he toured the bars trading songs. His then wife didn't see much future in their relationship, and before the final split, Kris took Tracey around with him to say goodbye to all the old guys they'd become familiar with.

'One old man saw us come in and said into his beer, "Look, yonder comes Krissie and the kid." I couldn't write it like that so I changed the name to Jodie,' he recalls. I liked the song because there is a heartbreaking sense of loneliness about it.

The first time I saw Kris live was in the National Stadium in Dublin in the 1970s when the amazing Rita Coolidge was his wife. They sang 'Help Me Make it through the Night' with passion.

The next time I met him was when Jim Aiken brought him to the RDS. It was a packed audience and I was backstage talking to Kris when Jim called me aside. He asked me to stay around, as there was bad news for Kris. His daughter – the very same Tracey of 'Jodie and the Kid' – had been in a car smash somewhere in California. She was on life support, not expected to make it.

Kris was distraught. I'd never seen a hero so broken. We chatted for a while, and even got through a mouthful of prayers. The show was cancelled as he headed for America. It was a decade before I met him again. This time it was when he toured with lifelong buddy Johnny Cash. I was sitting round with the Cash crew when Kristofferson came in.

I asked him for an interview and he was delighted. Johnny left us and twenty minutes later we were locked in discussions about lyrics, melodies and meanings. Before turning on the tape I reminded him of the last time we met – obviously he had no idea who I was. I asked if Tracey had survived. His eyes opened and his face stiffened as the blood drained from him. I wanted the ground to open and swallow me.

After a few moments, he composed himself. He was thrilled that I remembered and he called his travelling companion into the conversation. 'This is my manager now,' he said, 'the very same Tracey who survived the wreck.'

It's amazing what's in the life of a song.

I have always found Kristofferson a courteous, shy, thoughtful man, especially if you can talk about his songs.

Another night I was chatting to him in the Ulster Hall in Belfast after a show. We must have been talking for an hour – and that was probably about only one song. The band were having a few beers and grew ever more noisy. It annoyed the hell out of Kris. You could see him thinking. Suddenly he shouted, 'Can't you see I'm talking seriously to the man. If you want to party, go somewhere else.'

Another side of a real human hero – the way I like them.

He insists he's not a religious man in any conventional sense but then so do most modern saints I meet. They have a real relationship with their personal God but don't want the encumbrances of organised religion. He's a Christian with a personal faith in Jesus and, after all, he did write 'Why Me, Lord?', not to mention 'One Day at a Time' – both of them in their own way expressions of faith.

The song that introduced Kristofferson to the widest audience of all was 'Me and Bobby McGee'. The first hit version was by the late Roger Miller. At the time Miller was the biggest country star in the world. He came to Nashville to record, and Kristofferson, who had given up the academic life to follow his musical dream, volunteered to work the weekend as a cleaner just to get close to the legend.

'I was working in Columbia Studios and Miller rolled in,' Kristofferson remembers. 'He was all over the place. Those were the days when Miller was a living testament to better life by chemicals. He rattled. He was climbing the walls. He pulled out a suitcase and pretended to talk into a phone. He didn't record a thing. He was high. A short time later he remembered me and invited me to Los Angeles to write new songs for him. In fact we spent all day, every day, by the pool and not one song was written.

'We were on the plane back home and Roger said to me, "I hear you have a good song; let's hear it." I taught him 'Me and Bobby McGee' on the flight to Nashville. We went into the studio and recorded it and that was the start of big stars recording my material. I owe a lot to Roger Miller.'

Janis Joplin also had a million-seller with the very same song, and that's the version Kris prefers, but then he adored Janis, and was rocked to his foundations when she fell victim to her crazy lifestyle and died.

He was always close to Johnny Cash. There's a wonderful story about their first meeting. Cash lived a quiet, guarded life in Hendersonville, near Nashville, especially after he and June were married. Kristofferson sent him songs but didn't even get a reply. Cash 'wasn't listening', as they say. So Kristofferson hired a helicopter and piloted it himself. He landed on Cash's lawn. June thought they were being robbed and phoned the police. Cash, though, was more impressed. He thought that if a songwriter was that proud of his material, he deserved to be listened to. It was the beginning of a long, close friendship between the giants of songwriting in the twentieth century. Cash protected Kristofferson.

When Cash died Kristofferson penned a tribute, which highlighted the point I am making about songwriters being modern-day prophets: 'Johnny Cash has always seemed larger than life to me. He's a true American hero, beloved the world over, as much for his kindness and compassion and championing of the underdog as for the power of his art. He's been my inspiration, my faithful friend, my oasis of unconditional love and support. His fierce independence and free spirit, balanced with his love of family, children, and his fellow man would stand as a shining example of the best of what it means to be human. And he was damned funny, even in the darkest times.'

If I were ever asked to write a tribute to a hero like Kristofferson, it would be pretty damned close to that.

There were only a few artists in the world I would like to have met and didn't. I hadn't met Frank Sinatra but towards the end of his life I did and heard him perform. He was still magical, and even though the voice wasn't what it used to be, his insight into the power of lyrics was amazing.

The only artist that I really wanted to meet and didn't was Elvis Presley. He had been so much a part of my youth and I adored his music, his charisma. Then, in the early 1990s, I went on a trip to Nashville.

One morning I booked a one-day, cheap flight to Memphis. When I arrived I went directly to Graceland, the home where Elvis lived in supposed luxury for the greater part of his life.

The omens weren't good when I got there. It had all the hallmarks of a professionally run tourist attraction. It was a smaller house than I imagined. But then in our mind's eye the word mansion has its own connotation. Obviously in Tennessee mansions didn't mean the Big House.

Instead of having a human guide taking tourists from room to room in groups, we were each handed a Walkman containing all the information about the house, which I was able to control myself. And so I spent the next three hours going pensively from room to room listening to the commentary and taking it all in. As the tour progressed, I got sadder and sadder. I saw the room downstairs which had carpet on the floor, up the walls and across the ceiling. This was the place Elvis met and sang with many of his buddies.

The bedrooms, the studio and the TV room all looked so ordinary by our standards today. I had to keep reminding myself that Elvis was almost twenty years dead by this time and Graceland had been a luxurious place by the standards of the 1960s. I was impressed, though, by those who were in charge of Graceland at that time. It wasn't cheap or tatty. It wasn't a rushed tour and you had time to look at the significant memorabilia in the house, all of which brought the hero of my youth back to life. The songs he sang, the memories they evoked, the poignancy that a huge superstar actually led such an ordinary, sad life. By some standards it may have been a wasted life too.

Outside were Elvis's jet planes, and the room where he died had over 260 gold discs decorating the walls, yet despite such success he died lonely and tragically in August 1977.

It was the little graveyard out in the garden, however, which really got to me. There his mother's memorial lay alongside Elvis's own. There was even a memorial to his twin brother, who died at birth.

I have often been ashamed to admit this, but I sat in a corner and cried my eyes out. I wasn't the only one crying and that was a comfort. To this day I don't know what the tears were about. They probably were about Elvis but they were more likely to have been about my own lost youth.

I love Brendan Kennelly's writings. Brendan, in one of his works as I mentioned earlier, has a theory that memory is all-important. As long as we are remembered, we never die. He links it in with Christ's death and his plea on the night before he died: 'Do this in memory of me.'

As an example of memory keeping someone alive, Brendan wrote a beautiful poem about his father. He remembers him dancing in the kitchen and whistling his own dance music. It's a magnificent memory – evocative, real and not at all deathly. It makes his point brilliantly that when we remember, we keep the person alive and furthermore the memories we ourselves leave behind will keep us alive.

In that sense Elvis really is alive. Graceland evoked for me very precious and wonderful memories of a rebel singing music, the kind I'd never heard before, which stirred something inside me that is still alive to this day.

Richard Thompson wrote 'From Galway to Graceland', which Eleanor Shanley performs to perfection. Every time I hear that song with its mysterious and almost ridiculous storyline, I find myself back in Graceland on a sunny afternoon, on my own in a corner, crying for a man I never met.

Later that evening in Memphis, Al Gore, who was then vice-president, was on a walkabout visit. I shook hands with him, and if you were to put a gun to my head at this moment and asked me to describe what he looks like, I could not tell you.

Later still I visited BB King's great Blues House in Downtown Memphis. It was a wonderful night and the music, as always, was superb, but the loneliness of a fallen hero, lying in a graveyard, with tourists sifting through his memorabilia, said everything there is to say about the passing of fame. As the old Latin phrase has it, sic transit gloria mundi. That, roughly translated, means everything in this world is transient.

CHAPTER 50

MASTERS OF THE AIRWAVES

In fifty years of broadcasting, I've met and worked with most of the legendary names here and in Britain. Most of the greats were Irish.

The late Eamonn Andrews paved the way for Irish broadcasters in Britain. In my youth I got up in the middle of the night to listen to him commentate on world heavyweight title fights. It seemed a glamorous and important job, and it gave me a sense of pride to know an Irishman was that important.

He moved through journalism with the BBC and ITV to become the host of the hugely popular This is Your Life. When I got to meet Eamonn later he was, like many of the great broadcasters, a shy man away from the camera and the microphone, but became a different personality as soon as he got on air. He didn't like talking about his glamorous life and would much rather talk about normal life in a quiet corner away from the limelight. The hallmark of really successful broadcasters, communicators and people in the public eye is that they know when to come alive and when to switch off. Artists who are never off the stage are a bore to be with. Eamonn Andrews was never a bore.

Another advantage I have is that I grew up, professionally, with many of the top broadcasters on these islands. I have freelanced in RTÉ and the BBC for close to fifty years.

I broadcast with 2FM on the day it first aired, 31 May 1979, and continued with that station for more than fifteen years.

I've worked regularly alongside such luminaries as Gay Byrne, Mike Murphy, Treasa Davison, Ruth Buchanan, Pat Kenny, Ronan Collins, Marty Whelan, Larry Gogan, Alan Corcoran, Paschal Mooney, Gerry Wilson, Aonghus McAnally, Maxi, Marian Finucane, Joe Duffy, Henry Kelly, Derek Davis, Sean O'Rourke, Miriam O'Callaghan, Mary Kennedy, Brendan Balfe and Val Joyce. All of them were contemporaries and I have been part of their programmes and they have been part of my life since the 1970s.

I learned from each of them and some might admit to learning a little from me. The nature of broadcasting is that every time you go into a studio you learn something new; you never take success for granted. Live shows are the best. The adrenalin does wonders for the pace of broadcasting. On Millennium night, I hosted a five-hour live show for BBC Radio Ulster. I was in my element. Later, when I chaired a live current affairs programme for BBC Choice I revelled in the discussions. Straight Talking with Brian D'Arcy was my favourite programme for two years.

You cannot prepare enough for broadcasting. I was part of RTÉ's radio team at the state funeral for Charles Haughey. I sat up most of the night reading background material even though I knew I would use less than six or seven minutes of it during the entire service. I could have talked for seventy minutes if necessary. That's the only way I can relax and feel confident – be on top of my subject.

Many broadcasters don't write scripts for music programmes. I need to have the programme fully mapped out so that I have pace and balance. Random selections rarely work. It's the same whether I'm doing a ninety-second broadcast on Pause for Thought on BBC Radio 2, or an hour-long broadcast for BBC Radio Ulster.

Pause for Thought (PFT) is by far the best thing I've done on radio. I did over thirty spots a year on what was the biggest radio show in Europe with over eight million listeners daily. The feedback was incredible, mostly from people who never enter church, mosque or synagogue. Terry's listeners were unique. They were all fans of Terry (and his producer Paul Walters) and we on PFT borrowed them for a few minutes every morning. What makes it really worthwhile is that Terry and Paul (as well as Alan Boyd) made me so welcome and made me feel part of the show. To do PFT well I have to listen to the whole show, so that I am across the running banter.

I get hundreds of requests for scripts and every summer dozens of English visitors called at The Graan, just because it was mentioned so often on Wake Up with Wogan.

I began to do the show from my bedroom, on ISDN phone line or, as Terry put it, 'Here's the man who won't even get out of bed to talk to us.'

Terry always made a helpful little joke which set me up positively. When he wasn't on I had to work harder to win over the listener. If I never preached a sermon in church I still would have spoken to more people than a 1,000-year-old missioner on Wake Up with Wogan. What a privilege!

I'm often asked who is the broadcaster I admire the most.

The broadcaster I listened to most was the late Alistair Cooke. His Letter from America ran for close on sixty years. He was over ninety when he stopped broadcasting, weeks before he died. I still have tapes of his programme, which I listen to frequently. His style, his delivery, the pictures he paints, the gentleness with which he makes serious points and, most of all, the flow of language are inspiring no matter how often I hear them. For honest, basic professionalism, talking to microphone, no one comes close to Alistair Cooke.

It's a cliché to say that the pictures are better on radio, but it is true. I spend hours most days in my car. I listen to sports events, particularly soccer matches, night after night, as I travel around the country. Now I would much prefer to listen to a soccer match on radio than to watch it on television. It's just that the pictures I have in my head are more interesting than the actual pictures on television.

Gay Byrne is another professional whom I admire. He's a consummate broadcaster, well prepared, professional, but most of all highly aware of what listeners want. For all the years I've known Gay, he is always a pleasure to meet

– a man of knowledge, of wisdom and as far as I'm concerned, unfailingly helpful.

I can never forget what he did to help me when I was restoring Mount Argus. Without my appearance on the Late Late at the start of the campaign and his continued support throughout, it would have been next to impossible to achieve.

On the weekend after that appearance in October 1983, thousands came to look at Mount Argus, from every county in Ireland. The first day brought IR£60,000 in the post and by the end of the week, IR£250,000; all as a result of one, short Late Late Show appearance. That's just a hint of the power Gay Byrne's Late Late Show had.

One of the absolute gentlemen in broadcasting whom I've had the privilege of knowing all my life is Larry Gogan. Larry is the best pop DJ I've ever heard. Apart from that he's a shy, kind and good man who has been a friend, a colleague, a helper and an inspiration since I first met him in 1968.

The broadcaster most people ask me about today is Terry Wogan. Even other broadcasters are fascinated by his genius and want to know what he was like to work with. (I shared some of my thoughts in Chapter 23 yet I need to give the great man his proper place here too.)

Terry Wogan was not only the best broadcaster I've ever met, he was also one of the kindest people I've ever met.

Not many know this, but Terry was, first of all, a frighteningly well-read man. I never talked to Terry Wogan without being astonished and a little bit bemused at the breadth of his knowledge and ashamed at how little I know. He could speak French, German and Spanish excellently. And of course he used the English language as nobody else could. That's because he read insatiably. Not only was he well read but he had a memory like an elephant. He could remember large chunks of Latin as well as long passages of poetry from his school days in Crescent College in Limerick and later in Belvedere College in Dublin.

When I was editor of The Cross, in 1972, I did an interview with Terry in which he outlined his philosophy of broadcasting. It's still valid forty-seven years later, even though the medium has revolutionised itself in the meantime. Terry Wogan became the reliable companion to those who were hassled by life; to people who wanted to get away from the bickering of the Today programme on BBC Radio 4, or whatever local row there was on morning radio across Britain. More and more people listened to Terry Wogan simply because he was an escape from the boredom of the scraps we have to endure daily.

Terry never scripted his morning shows, but he was quick to admit that he had the best scriptwriters in the world – his listeners. I often sat in the studio waiting to go on air for PFT and heard the continual hum of the printer, running off hundreds of emails from all over the world. The producers, Paul Walters and Alan Boyd, spent their time going through emails and selecting the most suitable for broadcast. I was often envious, as dozens of wonderful scripts were dumped in the wastepaper basket because there was no time to use them.

As a friend he was helpful, encouraging, insightful, and always interested in the affairs of Ireland. What's more, he never forgot his friends. Most days when I spoke to him he continued to ask for his old friends, many of whom were on air before he went to England at all.

Terry Wogan was the first person to explain to me the essence of good radio broadcasting. He pointed out that everyone should be able to broadcast on radio, because everyone is able to talk on the phone. Think about that. Each of us has a conversational style that is exactly right for radio, which we use day in and day out on the phone. Yet if somebody thrusts a microphone in front of us, we 'put on' a voice. Terry suggested that I talk to the listeners as if making a personal telephone call. That's sound advice. You are speaking to a mass audience made up of groups of two or three.

'Think of those small groups, not the millions. That's why I never work from a script. If I wrote it down my sincerity would be gone. If I'm wishing somebody a happy birthday, then I wish it with all the joy and enthusiasm I can muster at that moment. To do anything else would make it all sound flat.' Obviously Terry Wogan was the broadcaster I've worked most closely with and from whom I learned most. As I look back now on a lifetime of broadcasting and television work, however, I can't think of a single person that I would not broadcast with again.

Broadcasters and journalists who last the pace are always well prepared, thorough, fair and professional in their approach. Those who aren't are soon found out.

It is often said about me that I'm always looking for notice or that I look for the attention of the media. After fifty years I don't need to defend my role. Others say I am not a real priest because I write and broadcast. I see communication as part of my priestly work and an essential part of it at that.

At those times in my life when it seemed much easier to leave the active ministry I was offered, on many occasions, full-time posts in broadcasting and on national papers, in Ireland and Britain. Some senior BBC producers would have been well pleased if I'd broadcast with them full-time. I always resisted. Broadcasting, journalism, chaplaincy to the entertainment industry, and interest in sport and music are all part of my priestly life.

There are many ways to be a priest. One of them is to run a parish, which I've done. Another is to present a programme or write a column for The Sunday World. These days my biggest congregations are on radio, the internet and The Sunday World. It's about finding the most effective way to be in the marketplace.

The central question for me is not, 'What do I want to do with my life?' It is one of the many questions but not the central one. The central one is, 'Where does God want me to be?'

Looking back on my life there have been so many providential twists and turns that I am convinced God brought me to this place.

I wish I could say I trust God blindly, or that believing comes easily. It does not. I wrestle, fight, twist, turn and look for different ways to satisfy my conscience. But eventually I come back to the fact that priesthood is in the marrow of my bones. I am convinced if I left the structure of priesthood tomorrow, I would continue almost every single one of my priestly activities no matter where I was, including broadcasting and journalism.

CHAPTER 51

MAN OF THE WORLD

In 1974 The Sunday World came on the scene as a loud, brash Irish tabloid. By today's standards those back issues are as dull as ditchwater, but they were gaudy and controversial back then. Hugh McLoughlin and Gerry McGuinness, both now deceased, did everything they could to grab headlines. One of their most famous ploys was to publish deliberately provocative articles that would be sent around the country in time to be condemned by priests on Sunday. Saturday evening Masses are not favoured by Sunday newspaper editors. Occasionally they hit the jackpot when someone of the stature of Bishop Lucey of Cork ranted about 'the filth' in The Sunday World. It was the best publicity possible and went a long way to saving the World in its early, shaky days.

A few weeks after it started I was visited in Mount Argus by Joe Kennedy, the first editor of The Sunday World, and Kevin Marron, who was one of the shrewdest and best journalists I ever knew. He had a genius for recognising an angle to hang a story on.

They asked me to write for the paper every week. I declined, mainly because I was too busy making The Cross a success, but also because I was afraid to risk writing for a hard-nosed red-top. The only way I could get out of it was to promise I would consider the offer if I ever left The Cross.

Two years later, I had moved on from The Cross, had left Mount Argus to live in Wicklow, and was lecturing, editing and producing in The Catholic Communications Institute, Booterstown. I was still going to dances every night and was writing a regular pop music feature for The Sunday Independent as well as working on radio and television.

The phone call came. 'Kevin Marron here. Now that you're not doing The Cross, you have no excuse. When can you start writing for us?'

I thought of every excuse in the book but two stood out. I really didn't feel comfortable writing as a priest for The Sunday World, given the kind of stories they did and the pictures they highlighted. The joke at the time was that in most papers you had to read between the lines to find the truth, but in The Sunday World you had to read between the legs!

Secondly, I didn't think I would be able to turn out an article every week.

Kevin's reply was devastatingly simple. 'I am offering you a pulpit every week to nearly one million readers, most of whom don't go to church, and you say you won't talk to them. What sort of priest do you call yourself? Anyway, try it for a month and if it doesn't work we can both walk away from it.'

I had no answer. I knew he was right.

The Sunday World has been part of my life now for forty-four years. Every Sunday since July 1976, there I am with a frozen, paper smile: 'Father Brian's Little Bit of Religion'. That's well over 2,500 articles (I've often had more than one piece per issue) and nearly three million words. It has spawned fifteen books, endless interviews, triggered heart attacks in over-anxious bishops and, I hope, has been a lifeline for those on the margins.

It was Kevin Marron who thought of the title for my column. He didn't waste time on long briefings. He kept it all in his brain.

Once, when he was a feature writer on The Sunday Press, he did an in-depth article about my work around the dance halls of Dublin. He came to Mount Argus to interview me. He drank cup after cup of home-brewed coffee, talked to me, listened to me, argued with me, but never once took a note. He sent a photographer to take pictures of me working the halls, but I dreaded what he would write. It was serious stuff and a body could end up with a single ticket to Africa for stepping too far out of line.

I needn't have worried; he wrote one of the fairest and most accurate articles any one ever did. And it was littered with quotes – every single one of them accurate.

So I knew how he operated. When I went to him to discuss what sort of column he wanted, his instructions were so precise that I think of them every time I sit down to write for the World.

'You can write about anything except religion. Write about human beings and the struggles they have, and that's all there is to religion. A little bit of religion is all we need,' he said. He stopped for breath. His eyes lit up and his dishevelled hair seemed to stand on end. 'That's what we'll call it: "A Little Bit of Religion".' That was the end of the discussion.

Gerry McGuinness wondered what I should be paid. I didn't want money. I have a vow of poverty as a member of a religious order and personal money doesn't worry me. Like all religious, if I left in the morning, I wouldn't have a penny to my name. I'm not putting on the poor mouth. I am well cared for now – though for years we lived in dirty, demeaning surroundings. As Father Edmund Burke – what an appropriate name for a man who was an expert journalist as well – an elderly Passionist renowned for being tight, once explained to me: 'In our day, they taught us to be mean and called it poverty.'

The Sunday World gave me the use of a car, which was the best payment possible – I could now get rid of my little Honda 50 motorcycle.

In all my time there I've had only one serious disagreement with The Sunday World and it certainly wasn't about money. They treat me well in other ways and when I was raising funds for Mount Argus Restoration Fund throughout the 1980s, I couldn't have done it without them. I have no complaints at all.

Yet when I began writing for The Sunday World, not many of my Passionist family were in agreement. That was understandable since I had reservations myself. The provincial gave his permission, reluctantly, but it is to his credit that he allowed me to write at all.

What I say in The Sunday World is what Brian D'Arcy thinks. I don't speak on behalf of the Church, or on behalf of the Passionists, or on behalf of The Sunday World. I write for those who read the paper, in a way they'll identify with, and about topics they are interested in.

Catholic Church authorities did, at one stage, go to my provincial arguing that since I am not a recognised theologian, all my articles for The Sunday World should be vetted by selected theologians before publication.

The provincial asked me what we should do. I told him I wasn't writing for a Catholic paper or indeed a Catholic audience. I write for all readers of The Sunday World. Some of them are Catholics, some are not, some of them have no religion at all. If the archbishop wants a Catholic article, for Catholic readers only, he should have his own publication. I'm a priest but I'm also a journalist hired specifically to share my thoughts.

I suggested that my provincial ask him to write to me personally if he had any further difficulties about it. I never heard any more about it.

It is up to others to assess the impact of my presence in The Sunday World. For the first ten years, every time I was interviewed, the same old question was put to me: 'Why do you write for that rag?'

I write for The Sunday World simply because it is the place a priest should be. Writing for a tabloid paper is a special skill. The language has to be simple and direct. Sentences must be short. The story has to flow. The theory was brilliantly summed up by our rival News of the World in its slogan: 'All human life is there'.

Any priest should be able to write an occasional article for a broadsheet, where there is time and space to develop a line of thought. That's not a luxury we have in tabloids.

A priest should write for The Sunday World for another reason. There are people who read that paper who never darken the door of a church.

Furthermore, many younger people get it and selectively read it for sport, fashion or pop. I don't claim they all read my column. But it's there and they have a chance to read it. As a priest I have to be comfortable in the marketplace.

Every week I get letters from people who are reading my article for the first time. They say it was a godsend to them. God can use people like me to be a voice of compassion and encouragement.

More and more I find complete strangers approaching me to thank me for being there and for what I say. They invariably tell me they read it now because their parents used to read it when they were young. More and more say it's the only contact they have with a God they can identify with. They feel I am someone like themselves struggling to find a place in an often unfriendly Church.

The late Cardinal Ó Fiaich was the only member of the hierarchy who understood why I wrote the way I did. I never once met him without taking away some sense that I was doing a good thing for the Church.

Whenever I met the cardinal at football matches, which was where I met him most often, he'd discuss the article in that day's paper. He used to confide that he couldn't be seen buying The Sunday World, but his housekeeper or driver always bought one for him. He often told me I was saying the very things he'd like to say but couldn't. His favourite encouragement was, 'For God's sake, keep writing for your people. You have a whole diocese of your own out there. Keep telling them they don't have to be perfect to be loved by God.'

When I was well established in the World, he invited me for lunch one day. Cardinal Ó Fiaich was sounding me out, or maybe filling me in. I can't reveal details but the gist was that I should think about grooming myself for consideration as a bishop. He said, 'The Sunday World isn't the best place to be noticed by the nuncio. Do you not think it might be better to stop writing for them?' He saw the look of horror on my face. When I left, I added as a parting shot, 'Anyway, to be a bishop now you have to agree that artificial contraception is intrinsically evil, be against married priests and not even speak about women priests. And you have to be passed by Opus Dei. On that score I'll be lucky to get a Christian burial, never mind be a bishop.'

The two of us laughed our heads off and went back to the serious stuff – who'd win the Ulster Championship. We agreed it wouldn't be Fermanagh anyway.

Shortly afterwards I was invited for tea with the papal nuncio at his Cabra residence in Dublin. It was interesting, but as I left, the nuncio firmly told me that what we had discussed was to remain confidential for ever or, as he put it, 'in perpetuum'. Obviously I have to respect that confidence but what I can say is that he and the cardinal had been talking and I can safely say that I will never be a bishop – thank God.

During the 1980s, in particular, I seem to have been public enemy number one in the mind of many clerics, because I was writing for The Sunday World. One priest in the North of Ireland was prepared to take out his anger at me on my family, which is always difficult. I was to do a relative's wedding. Everything had been arranged but when I drove up from Dublin it must have dawned on him who I was. He asked to make sure.

'Are you the renegade who writes for The Sunday World?' That's a difficult one to answer. Say yes and you allow yourself to be called a renegade. Say no and it's a lie. So I agreed that I was the journalist who wrote for the paper as well as being the parish priest and rector of Mount Argus.

'Well, you'll never stand on my altar,' he huffed. Remember, this was the day of the wedding and the groom was out in the church waiting on me to officiate. At the time I was timid enough to back down. And as a matter of canonical fact, a parish priest has to give his express permission to the priest who does the wedding for it to be valid in the eyes of the Church.

I asked if I could concelebrate the Mass. 'Did you not hear me?' he barked. 'You'll never stand on my altar. If I had my way you wouldn't even sit in my church.' That's the kind of thuggish behaviour that has destroyed the Catholic Church in Ireland. The heresy of my altar, my church, wasn't lost on the guests.

I sat in the church. My family were at first worried that I must be leaving the priesthood or be in some kind of trouble, and then furious that he got away with it. They were even more disgusted when he came to do the wedding. He kept asking the groom his name. That's the extent of the interest he had. Three times he shouted at the groom to speak up. He was more concerned about getting at me than he was with the couple's welfare. It is a classic example of how we priests abuse power and use sacraments as weapons. People today would recognise the ignorant bully for what he was and wouldn't put up with it.

I was regularly refused permission to do funerals of friends or even to concelebrate, but I survived and, to be fair, those priests were in the minority. Most priests tolerated me with courtesy and a few were kind and encouraging.

The point I'm making is that writing for The Sunday World has defined the kind of priest I have become. The fact that I resolutely wrote for the marginalised meant that I myself became marginalised. It caused me more suffering than anything else in life because I'm not a natural rebel. But I know the kind of priest I have to be and the kind of apostolate I have to work at.

When I was working in the Dublin archdiocese in the 1970s and 1980s, I was a representative on both the National and the Diocesan Council of Priests. That's where I encountered the career clerics. They had a prudent solution to everything but rarely thought of the pastoral needs of their people.

There were outstanding exceptions, many of whom are now married and referred to as 'ex-priests'. There is no such thing as an ex-priest: once a priest always a priest. They are good men who were forced to resign from the active ministry, usually because they fell in love with a woman.

I usually found myself on the pastoral side of the argument and because I wrote for the paper was never really trusted by my fellow priests, even though I never, ever broke a confidence.

Ironically, when I started going to meetings of the National Union of Journalists I was treated with great suspicion by fellow journalists who regarded me as a spy for the bishops. They wrote about me as the acceptable face of the Catholic Church. Little did they realise that I wasn't accepted by most of them, either.

Chapter 52

WORKING AT THE BBC

Back in 2012 the BBC celebrated eighty years of religious broadcasting. Director General Greg Dyke and Head of Religion and Ethics Alan Bookbinder hosted a lunch, which included a presentation of highlights from broadcasts since 1922.

There were some poignant moments from radio, particularly from the war years. The first national event to be broadcast on TV was in fact a religious event, namely the coronation of Queen Elizabeth II.

We looked at BBC interviews with John F. Kennedy and a prophetic one with Doctor Martin Luther King Jnr on the eve of his assassination. All of this showed how religious broadcasting was genuinely cutting edge back then.

Famine figured prominently, too, particularly the famous 1984 Michael Buerk report, which led to Bob Geldof's miraculous efforts through Live Aid the following year.

I was surprised to learn, for example, that when the funeral of Princess Diana was televised, a hard-to-imagine 2.5 billion people worldwide were glued to their televisions.

And, of course, there were many moving memories from the 9/11 tragedy.

It was while watching the package that I became aware, for the first time, how fortunate I was to be part of a team continuing such a unique tradition of broadcast religion. Despite the usual gripes from us broadcasters, the BBC still takes religious programming more seriously than anyone else.

In a fifty-year career in communications, I have to admit that the BBC is by far the best in its approach to religion and ethics programming. If you do your work professionally, they'll treat you with respect as a broadcaster and not as someone to be grudgingly tolerated. I have never been treated as a token contributor used to create an impression of balance. They don't seem to have the chip on their shoulders about religion that so many Irish broadcasters have.

I was particularly struck by two quotes from the archives on that day of celebration seven years ago. In 1936 the then Archbishop of Canterbury said, 'Religion is fading in today's world because God is not so much denied, as crowded out of life.' It struck me that every generation becomes pessimistic about the future of religion. Still, the need for God survives.

When the BBC initially planned to go ahead with their first religious broadcast, there was a debate in parliament whether it would be blasphemous to do it. One MP said, 'Religion can never be broadcast on radio, because it could happen that men would listen in pubs with their hats on.'

I have been working with the BBC's Religion and Ethics Department for thirty years now. I've done all kinds of broadcasts on both radio and television, though I prefer radio – probably because I have a better face for radio!

I've been one of the Pause for Thought (PFT) team, which is part of the breakfast show on BBC Radio 2 each weekday, since January 1990. Presently PFT goes out live at 9:15 a.m. each morning.

I started with the BBC when I was transferred from Mount Argus in Dublin to The Graan in Enniskillen. I did some selected broadcasts for them before that, but when I moved to Northern Ireland it was easier for them to hire me. I was living within their jurisdiction, as it were.

The first presenter I teamed up with on Radio 2 was Derek Jameson. Derek was essentially a tabloid journalist who began writing at Reuters and worked his way up to become editor of several tabloid newspapers. He hosted the morning show on Radio 2 and had a talk show on television as well.

He was always kind to me but his style was pompous and sometimes dismissive. I often joke that the only problem appearing with Derek was that any time I mentioned God, Derek presumed I was talking about him! Derek died in 2012.

When he moved on Brian Hayes took over. Brian is known as a phone-in presenter and, it seemed obvious to me, was never comfortable as a morning host. He never spoke to, or made contact with me in the studio. It was simply a 'Here is … That was … ' introduction. He didn't last long in the slot. He, too, moved on and had a long and successful career on air elsewhere.

After him I had occasional broadcasts with Sarah Kennedy, whom I found a delightful host and who took a great interest in what I said in my PFTs. In the days after the Omagh Bomb, I was called on to present a few PFTs as we all attempted to find comfort in what was a cruel and tragic act of savagery. Sarah stood in for Terry that week. It was difficult because both of us were on the verge of tears even thinking about what happened. I respected Sarah. She was a lady to me.

Things changed amazingly when the masterful Terry Wogan came back to radio after he finished with his evening television show. I was lucky enough to team up with Terry at the beginning of his second coming.

For sixteen years Terry entertained the nation, gently gathering ever more listeners for his show until it became the biggest radio show in Britain with eight million listeners.

It was always a privilege to be on air with Terry. He was the most welcoming host imaginable. He expected you to react to his banter and he respected you more if you spoke to him and lifted your eyes from the page occasionally, rather than having your head stuck in a script. His view was that if you believed what you were saying you should be able to speak sincerely without notes and without having to read every word from a page.

That was how he did it. He risked having silence on air; his listeners knew he was a real person talking personally to each fan who tuned in. He became everyone's favourite uncle. Gay Byrne used to say he was like a personal confessor to whom you could admit anything without fear.

Terry kept me on edge all the time because he was capable of making a comment that had absolutely nothing to do with what I'd just said. It was his way of ensuring the PFT segment was part of his show rather than an insert into his show. Terry gave a high profile to PFT, which made it the most listened-to religious broadcast on radio.

When Terry retired I just presumed PFT would die with him. At that stage I had done it for over twenty years so it was time to retire gracefully with Terry, I thought.

When Chris Evans followed Terry, I was convinced he would not want PFT. What I didn't know was that Chris had listened to us when we were on with Terry and knew who he wanted with him on his show. He had a totally different approach from anyone I've ever worked with. His mind worked in overdrive, darting off in unconnected directions. Words, images, ideas flowed endlessly from his fertile mind.

At the time he was settled into a new marriage with Natasha. His rebel years were behind him but his energy was focused on making The Breakfast Show a huge success. He admired Sir Terry immensely and desperately wanted to justify his faith in him. Many thought he'd lose Terry's older audience and he did lose some of them. But a huge number stayed on, gave him a chance and slowly grew accustomed to his madcap style.

He wanted everything to be sharp, clear and relevant. I took to it like a duck to water because essentially it was the tabloid style I was at home with.

It's hard to put words on how much I enjoyed working with Chris Evans. He was courteous, welcoming, encouraging and enthusiastic. He was interested in what I had to say; he questioned me on air and helped clarify the best bits for his audience. He had a natural connection with struggling people and knew instinctively what was helpful and what was propaganda. I had to change my style to fit the new model but it was effortless.

Chris himself devoured every morsel of self-help philosophy available.

He too made sure PFT was part of his show. I got more reaction from listeners during Chris's eight years than at any other period on PFT.

I was sorry he moved on from Radio 2. In fact we went for a very long breakfast one morning after his show to chat it through. By the end I realised he feared he might undo all of his good work if he stayed on. He knew what he had achieved and it was now time to move to a new challenge on Virgin Radio. He encouraged me to write a PFT about the need to move on in life when you're at your peak. Don't wait for the slide to come. Try something new while you still can. It's good advice for broadcasters and for life.

I didn't change my mind about Chris Evans. I didn't need to. Terry told me he would be a delight to work with and he was that and more.

Incidentally, we owe a lot to the late Gerry Ryan. Chris had decided to get out of broadcasting at one point in his life. He was disillusioned with the 'suits' of the broadcasting world. While on holiday in Ireland, he heard Gerry Ryan on air and immediately understood how radio was changing. Gerry's new model was exactly what Chris wanted radio to be. He abandoned his holiday and went straight back home to be part of the new world of instant radio. He always spoke of Gerry with genuine affection.

Early in 2019 I started all over again with another new presenter, Zoe Ball. Zoe is the sixth presenter of the Radio 2 morning show in thirty years with whom I've done PFT. Although I was hesitant about continuing, the producers convinced me I should. They've told me no other religious broadcaster has ever done thirty years on PFT and that when I grow too old to do it, they'll be the first to tell me.

That's how it works at the BBC.

As happens so often in life, getting a job can be about being in the right place at the right time. That's how I got my own show, Sunday with Brian D'Arcy, on BBC Radio Ulster.

One day I was on my way to my aunt's funeral in Kerry when the phone rang in the car. I pulled in to the side and took a call from Dr Bert Tosh, the senior producer of religion in Belfast.

Radio Ulster had a big listenership for their early morning Sunday religious broadcasts. On Sunday morning, the Religion Department is responsible for all programmes on Radio Ulster from 8:30 until 12 noon.

The problem was that the religious service in mid-morning caused quite a few to switch off and by 11 o'clock there was a significant fall in listenership. Back then, if the service came from one of the Protestant churches, Catholics switched off, and the next week the Protestants didn't listen to the Catholic service.

Bert Tosh wondered if I would present a music-driven programme between eleven and twelve on Sunday morning. He felt there was too much talk radio throughout the morning. He and his team were convinced listeners would appreciate a musical break.

It was brave of them to hand over an hour each Sunday to a Catholic priest. This was in 1997. There was some opposition from a small section of the Protestant community at the beginning. But they soon got used to my style and my music and by the end of the year there wasn't a word of opposition.

Sunday with Brian D'Arcy has been running ever since. I love playing the music I think the listeners like. It's not overtly religious and that's the secret. Anyone can listen in. They'll hear familiar music interspersed with a few inspirational thoughts when appropriate. It has turned out to be, like The Sunday World, a magnificent platform from which to break down barriers; it brings a human element to religious broadcasting.

Recently a man approached me in a coffee shop outside Belfast. His opening words were, 'When Barry McGuigan comes here, he signs autographs, what do you do?' I answered jokingly, 'Butter warm scones before they go cold, it appears.'

We spoke in a friendly way for about five minutes. He was a member of the Free Presbyterian Church and he had some weird ideas about what Catholics believe. He listened respectfully as I tried to explain. At the end he told me that I seemed to be the same kind of man in real life as I was on radio. He reached out his hand and said, 'I am going to do two things now I've never done before and will never do again. I am going to shake hands with a Catholic priest, and I am going to call you "Father". I've enjoyed talking with you. Keep up the good work.'

Later I thought it was a brave step for him to take and yet I felt sad. We in Northern Ireland still have a long way to go if a decent man can live his entire life having nothing to do with a Catholic clergyman. However, I take nothing away from him. He made my day. That's an example of how a simple music programme dissolves myths and makes it possible for us to edge across red lines.

Sunday with Brian D'Arcy has been going for over twenty years now. I just love doing it because it gives me the platform to introduce singers and songs and stories to an audience I have come to regard as family.

Naturally, I include a selection of country music. There is a sizeable group of listeners who love good country music but rarely hear it on mainstream radio.

The worldwide governing body for country music recognised the impact the programme was making. The Country Music Association in Nashville was impressed and presented me with the CMA Award for The Country Music Dee Jay of the Year outside the United States – in short, the world. I was tickled pink to think they gave me a real CMA Statuette, with World Dee Jay of the Year inscribed on it, for doing what I love doing and what I've been doing for pleasure for fifty years. I was brought over to London for an official presentation by their representative Bobbi Boyce. It doesn't get any better than that.

The other music programme which I did for years was Sunday Half Hour on BBC Radio 2. One of the longest-running programmes on BBC radio, it's been on air for almost eighty years now. Canon Roger Royle, a good friend, hosted it for years on end. When he decided to move on the head of Radio 2 suggested to the producers I should take it over.

When they approached me I immediately said no. It seemed to me a vicar needed to be in charge of the show because of its format. It was mainly hymns and choirs with short inspirational links based on the liturgical seasons. I didn't feel competent. I wasn't an expert on hymns or choral singing. Most listeners were from traditional Protestant churches for whom it was in reality an Evening Service, so I turned it down.

Next day I had a phone call from Terry Wogan. He was surprised that I had turned down the opportunity to present the most prestigious religious programme on Radio2. At the time it was almost seventy years on air.

I explained my reasons and he understood them but thought I was being unnecessarily reticent. This is where the wisdom of Terry came into play. His voice became that of a concerned parent.

'Brian, let me give you a bit of advice. When the head of Radio2 asks you to do a programme, you don't insult her by turning it down out of hand. She wanted a change of style and considered you to be the perfect man to bring about that change. I understand why you think you're not right for the role but she has listened to your style and she thinks it's the one she wants.

'My advice is to tell her why you are reluctant to do it but that you will try it for six months, and if she decides you're the wrong person, or if you simply can't continue, then both of you can agree on how to bow out gracefully. Don't turn it down. Give it a try. That's the decent way to approach it.'

I don't know who asked Terry to phone me but I learned several lessons that day, principally that Terry was an influential person in the BBC. Secondly, that he was kind enough to take me aside and prevent me from making a total ass of myself.

I did as he suggested. I absolutely loved doing the programme once I got used to the format. It was an honour and a privilege to present it and to host live on air the seventieth anniversary of the show from St Martin's in London.

I quickly learned about hymns and attended live recordings of Sunday Half Hour in the major cathedrals, Anglican and Catholic, all over Britain. I went on to present the programme for five years. It was another beautiful experience, which, in my foolishness, I very nearly missed. After five years I offered my resignation because I knew I had exhausted what I had to say about every liturgical season and I didn't want to recycle old scripts and ideas. I still get letters from listeners who ask for prayers and for consolation. I thank God for the experience.

Now that I am nearing the end of life, I love broadcasting as a way of reaching out in a personal way to so many listeners. However, I see the writing on the wall. Obviously my time is at an end but that's not what I am talking about.

Habits have changed. Because of social media younger people rarely read newspapers. They get all their news in short bursts from phones, laptops and tablets. They rarely buy CDs or watch television. Instead they download music, choose what they view from Netflix and grab news in tweet-sized bites and from Facebook. Newspapers are barely surviving; listeners and viewers both have a high age profile.

This is a serious turn of events. Are we losing the skill of reading at length and deeply? How can we debate and understand current affairs? How do we foster ongoing education? Is anyone interested in spirituality or religion? Who helps the coming generations find spiritual sustenance, ethical guidance or even knowledge of good and evil?

Who influences young adults, children and grandchildren? From whom do they learn values and traditions? How should I attempt to communicate with the churched or unchurched now?

I don't know the answers, but the questions bother me. Whoever takes up where I left off will have to be an expert in a different set of skills and tools than those I used.

Already I feel like 'a relic of aul decency'.

CHAPTER 53

IT'S OKAY TO BE CONFUSED

I thought long and hard before I started this book. I was convinced I had written and spoken enough for one life. I listened to dozens of friends, and almost as many enemies, before one wise woman said, 'You were devastated when the Vatican tried to silence you, why are you silencing yourself now? We depend on you to tell like it is. We need to hear your voice even when we don't agree with everything you say and write.'

I had no answer to that. I don't decide when I get down from the cross. Furthermore, I could die or lose my memory at any time and all would be lost.

An optimist is someone who accepts reality yet recognises there's hope at the end of it. I know I'm not always right but I speak honestly about what's happening to the Church; I'm not living in denial; I'm convinced faith in God will survive despite our worst efforts. That needs to be said.

God has been saving people long before any religion or any church existed and God goes on saving and loving now because that's God.

Life is a journey and though ritual is important it's a small mind that would confine God's power to rituals. For example I now believe that people actually get married years after (or, indeed, years before) the day they exchange vows.

Weddings are beautiful but couples often decide psychologically, to really commit themselves to each other when they've survived a crisis which forced them to choose whether to stay together or fall apart. That becomes their actual marriage. It doesn't neccessarily coincide with the ceremony or sacrament service.

It is the same with priests. I was ordained on 20 December 1969 in St Michael's College, Enniskillen. I was honest and sincere and certain on that winter morning. Yet, years later when the crisis came, I had to decide whether to remain in the priesthood or live more holistically as a layperson. That crisis led me to own my real ordination commitment. There have been other times when I've had to reaffirm that choice to remain a priest.

Life's a journey. As I mature and grow I renew many commitments along the way. I'm not holy in the traditional sense and I'm definitely not pious. Some of the most devious people I've lived with pretended to be the most pious.

I will admit I keep on trying. I am a failed monk, no doubt about that. However, I now understand I am on a journey of searching. At this stage I am faithful to the search, even if I've found few answers. I wouldn't have been happy to say that about myself thirty years ago.

I go for long walks every day if I can. That's where I join the dots. For me sitting down in a chapel mouthing prayers never had an attraction. Mass, yes, I have a great belief in the Eucharist. How anybody can live without that wonderful presence of God as food and drink for the journey, I don't understand.

The faith journey is like a mountain walk. You spend most of your time puffing along looking at your shoes, then you pause, look around and say, 'How did I make that journey?' 'How did I come so far?'

I couldn't live with myself if I dwelt on my mistakes only. The chief mistake I made was silence. I stayed quiet and played the clerical game for too long. I had an inferiority complex, which meant I didn't accept that my own massive doubts about what was happening in the Church were legitimate doubts.

I should have been capable of asking myself honestly: What is the point of this? Why are we always putting people down? Why is the Church so negative about human nature? Why is the headline in the paper always 'Pope Condemns' or 'Bishop Slams'? Why is religion so much about death, sadness and pessimism? Why, to embrace youth, optimism and enjoyment, does one have to leave the Church? Where is God in this almighty mess we have made? Where is the joy?

I should have spoken louder earlier.

Let's be honest here. The Church is in trouble because of our screwed-up attitude to sexuality. Nobody wants to admit that. But surely if we trusted God's promise to be with us, and if we stopped blaming others and recognised that this mess is of our own making, we might then look at how it has come about that people make their own choices, knowing we clergy have little that is helpful to offer them.

The whole clerical system is unhealthy because it is founded on negativity. So much theological reflection admits sexuality is good in theory. In theory sex is good; but in practise it's a sin. We negate the source of human life and human joy! Our theology of human relationships is non-existent.

Compulsory celibacy is unhealthy and yet the Church insists on it to preserve its power structure. We covered up the abuse of innocent children rather than face reality.

I still find it difficult to come to terms with the enormity of the cover-ups which have been unearthed all over the world. It's no accident that the same pattern of abuse and cover-up existed on every continent. It wasn't an Irish thing or an American custom. It happened everywhere, which can only mean it was widely accepted throughout the Roman Catholic Church.

I need to be honest too. I didn't create this situation. Nor did I abuse, cover up, or defend the indefensible. Yet I cannot stand outside the community of priests and claim I am not one of them. That's why it has been so difficult to remain a priest. As long as I remain a priest I have to share the blame for how the Church is seen by the vast majority of Catholics.

The Church to which I belong as one of its priests now scapegoats gays, priests who don't accept what Rome says in every detail, and priests who support married priests or women priests. According to the authorities in Rome we are the cause of the problem. Yet any objective analysis concludes it is the Institution itself that is dysfunctional.

They're putting seminarians back into straitjackets; taking in 'yes' men. They're rowing back on genuine discussion about doctrine and lashing out at gays even though a good percentage of priests are gay!

There is some truth, though, in the widely held opinion that we priests help to maintain the dysfunctional institution by remaining in the priesthood. Only those who have stepped outside the clerical club can claim to have done something about repairing the damage. Those who have walked away from priesthood have a clearer conscience.

So why have I stayed? Because I am convinced God still wants me to be a priest. That is the only honest answer I can give. There are many days, though, when not even I am convinced I'm justified.

That is one of the reasons I wrote this book. I want to admit my faults, not justify them. As a priest I am horrified at the evil that was done in the name of religion, yet feel powerless to articulate meaningfully any other way to be Church in today's world.

My faith tells me to have hope but I struggle to convince myself or others where that hope might lie.

I have lived with doubts for thirty years. Should I stay or leave? How can I abandon the vocation I was gifted with, which is to walk with the suffering, the lost, the lonely and the least; to journey from Passion to compassion?

I am determined to continue saying what needs to be said. Having given fifty years to priesthood I don't need to apologise to anyone! Most guys my age are retired! It's not a question of disloyalty; it is living with integrity and as honestly as possible; to live in well-founded hope and to encourage others to find their loving God wherever they can.

No one can prevent God loving me and no one can tell me how to love God. That's a fundamental truism.

There is room in the Church for those who can't say yes to everything. Loyal opposition is commendable. I have to discern when those in authority are circling the wagons instead of humbly opening our lives to the Holy Spirit. There are still wonderful people continuing to search honestly; we must support one another as 'we take every wrong direction on our lonely way back home'.

It's been a long discernment. I began writing about abuse in 1985. I thought I was being compassionate back then by trying to make excuses for abusers. It was part of the weird thinking of the time not to kick a man when he's down.

It took a couple of years to look into my heart and accept I was being manipulated by the abusers and by the Church authorities. When I placed myself beside the abused enlightenment came. When I realised the full import of abuse I couldn't dream of celebrating my silver jubilee of ordination. I ran off to South Africa for eight months to ensure I wasn't trapped in false triumphalism. Here I am now approaching my golden jubilee and I'm even more frightened. The situation is worse, not better.

The incredible part of the story is that so many people still come to Church for special occasions. There is a thirst for genuine spirituality. Faith is alive despite what we have done to it, to believers and to God. The spirit of goodness and decency is alive and well if we would just step aside and let it blossom.

I now admit joyfully that I have no answers. I was in a hospital ward recently with a woman of thirty-three who won't be here when this book is published. The tears I shed dropped onto her hand and were more effective than my prayers. She has three young children and her husband asked me for a miracle. I'm a believer in miracles but they're not for me to hand out. We chatted and accepted we'd both wait in hope.

Even though I'm realistic enough to be disheartened, I see joy, too, let's not forget that. I love going to concerts and matches and mixing with happy people for that reason – the sensation of enjoyment is enough for me.

I love helping young people to have a memorable wedding. I still cry at weddings. I love to see people in love. I see how they have prepared for their wedding and I try to help them prepare for a marriage. I cannot, like others, say I never had a doubt in my life or that I was never in love.

It annoys the hell out of me when priests start lecturing couples on what music they'll allow or bully them about flowers; don't be a spoilsport; allow couples to celebrate in a way that's meaningful to them. Step aside and let God be God. It's not you who's getting married.

I believe in Providence, the Spirit, and a Lover who never gives up on anyone. My image of God ebbs and flows, as you'll realise if you've tiptoed your way through this book. The God I believe in today could make an atheist of me next week. I've learned not to get hung up on an image of God. That's what I call allowing God to be God. If I put my faith in a God that I created, then God will always be smaller than me. The very essence of God is that even an eternity in God's presence will not be sufficient to comprehend what LOVE is.

Many of the people I meet and chat with can no longer believe in God. After a lifetime of listening without judgement I allow myself now to suspect that maybe they can no longer believe in the concept of the God they once settled for.

Others mistakenly conclude that just because they have decided they no longer believe in some preconceived image of God then God does not exist. I hope I never become so arrogant. For me, God's existence does not depend on what I think or feel or conclude. God exists as long as love exists.

I devoted most of my life to an 'ism' – to what I thought was an ideal. But it was not an ideal. I was so brainwashed by my training that I was not helping to sustain faith; rather I was propping up structures. All that changed when I realised I was living a lie. I really had to think through what my vocation should be.

Today I am floundering. I am confused. Yet I have more peace because I know that God is in the middle of that confusion. What's more, I'm convinced that God is rarely found where there is certainty.

Thomas Merton wrote a consoling prayer, 'Thoughts in Solitude', which I say every day of my life. It keeps me focused on hope in a faithful way. I leave you with these practical words. I hope they help you as much as they've helped me.

My Lord God, I have no idea where I am going,

I do not see the road ahead of me.

I cannot know for certain where it will end.

Nor do I really know myself, and the fact that I think I am

following Your will does not mean that I am actually doing so.

But I believe that the desire to please You does in fact please You.

And I hope that I have that desire in all that I am doing.

I hope that I will never do anything apart from that desire.

And I know that if I do this, You will lead me by the right road,

though I may know nothing about it.

Therefore I will trust You always though

I may seem to be lost and in the shadow of death.

I will not fear, for You are ever with me,

and You will never leave me to face my perils alone.

References:

(1) Dublin: Columba Press, 2015.
(2) London: Orion Books, 2009.
(3) Collegeville, MN: Liturgical Press, 2002.
(4) Marianne Williamson, 'Our Deepest Fear', in A Return to Hope, New York, NY: Harper Collins, 1992.
(5) Learning to Love: Exploring Solitude and Freedom, San Francisco, CA: Harper One, 2010.
(6) 'Celibate Clergy: The Need for Historical Debate', New Blackfriars, Volume 85, Issue 1000, November 2004.